Cognitive Approaches to Early Modern Spanish Literature

COGNITIVE APPROACHES TO EARLY MODERN SPANISH LITERATURE

Edited by Isabel Jaén and Julien Jacques Simon

OXFORD
UNIVERSITY PRESS

OXFORD
UNIVERSITY PRESS

Oxford University Press is a department of the University of Oxford. It furthers
the University's objective of excellence in research, scholarship, and education
by publishing worldwide. Oxford is a registered trade mark of Oxford University
Press in the UK and certain other countries.

Published in the United States of America by Oxford University Press
198 Madison Avenue, New York, NY 10016, United States of America.

© Oxford University Press 2016

First Edition published in 2016

Library of Congress Cataloging-in-Publication Data
Cognitive approaches to early modern Spanish literature / edited by Isabel Jaén
and Julien Jacques Simon.
    p.   cm. — (Cognition and Poetics)
Includes bibliographical references and index.
ISBN 978-0-19-025655-5 (hardcover : alk. paper) — ISBN 978-0-19-025656-2
(ebook) — ISBN 978-0-19-025657-9 (online content) 1. Spanish literature—
History and criticism—Theory, etc. 2. Cognition and culture. 3. Literature and
science. I. Jaén, Isabel, 1970– editor. II. Simon, Julien Jacques, 1974– editor.
  PQ6022.C64 2015
  860.9—dc23
                              2015031646

9 8 7 6 5 4 3 2 1

Printed by Sheridan Books, USA

CONTENTS

ACKNOWLEDGMENTS

Our deepest gratitude goes to all the minds that made this book possible, beginning with our supportive and patient editor, Hallie Stebbins, and our series editors, Alexander Bergs, Margaret H. Freeman, Peter Schneck, and Achim Stephan. Thank you for contributing with your work and vision to the advancement of the field of cognition and poetics and for encouraging its development in relation to Spanish studies. Thank you also to Jamie Chu and everyone who participated in the editing process at Oxford University Press, for your assistance and dedication.

To our contributors: your original ideas and inspired writing are indeed the flesh and blood of this book and we cannot thank you enough for your motivation, for your hard work, and for patiently enduring our obsession to detail.

We are indebted to our reviewers and to the many scholars in diverse fields who read different sections of this manuscript, helping us give it form: Luis Avilés, Donald Beecher, Mary Carruthers, José Cartagena Calderón, William Clamurro, Amy Cook, Terrence Deacon, Craig Epplin, Edward Friedman, Charles Ganelin, Richard Gerrig, Margaret Greer, Meghan Hammond, Suzanne Keen, Paula Leverage, Raymond Mar, Bruce McConachie, Eyda Merediz, Keith Oatley, Daron Olson, DeLys Ostlund, Alan Palmer, Alan Richarson, Marie-Laure Ryan, Felipe Ruan, Robert Sanders, Cynthia Sloan, Teresa Soufas, Gabrielle Starr, Evelyn Tribble, Donald Wehrs, and Amy Williamsen. We also thank George Karnezis and Beth Slattery for their insightful comments.

Finally, we would like to thank our academic institutions, Indiana University East and Portland State University, for their support.

LIST OF CONTRIBUTORS

Bruce R. Burningham is Professor of Hispanic Studies and Theatre at Illinois State University, where he is also Chair of the Department of Languages, Literatures, and Cultures. He is the author of *Tilting Cervantes: Baroque Reflections on Postmodern Culture* and *Radical Theatricality: Jongleuresque Performance on the Early Spanish Stage*. Currently, he is Editor of *Cervantes*, the journal of the Cervantes Society of America. He is also a recipient of an Andrew W. Mellon Postdoctoral Fellowship and a National Endowment for the Humanities grant.

Judith G. Caballero is an Associate Professor of Spanish at Millsaps College in Jackson, Mississippi. Her research focuses on cognitive literary studies, sartorial relevance, and marginalized voices. She is currently working on an anthology of *comedias* with a focus on the figure of the mother. She recently contributed to Gladys Robalino's project *Female Amerindians in Early Modern Spanish Theater* with "The Siren Song and the Enchanted Victim: The Portrayal of the Conquistadors and Tucapela in *Palabras a los reyes y gloria de los Pizarros*."

Catherine Connor-Swietlicki is Professor of Spanish at the University of Vermont. Author of *Spanish Christian Cabala* and numerous essays on early modern Spanish literature, theater, and culture, she has published in *Cervantes, Bulletin of the Comediantes*, and other major journals and books. Since 2001, she has explored the bio-cultural and neuro-scientific processes that make possible our complex personal and social creativity in life and art. Her recent essays investigate how individual embodied minds engage *Don Quixote* and performance arts.

Elizabeth M. Cruz Petersen is a Postdoctoral Fellow with the Center of Mind, Body, and Culture at Florida Atlantic University. Her research is at the crossroads of cognitive studies (specifically somaesthetics) and early modern Spanish theater. She has published articles on theater and translation. Her forthcoming book, *Women's Somatic Training in Early Modern Spanish Theater*, shows how the early modern Spanish woman actor subscribed to various somatic practices in an effort to prepare for a role on stage.

Julia Domínguez is Associate Professor of Spanish at Iowa State University. She has published on Cervantes, the picaresque, and film in the *Bulletin of Comediantes, Hispania, Cervantes*, and *Revista de Estudios Hispánicos*, among others. She is the editor of *Cervantes in Perspective* and the co-editor of *Hispanic Studies in Honor of Robert L. Fiore*. Her present research centers on human cognition as understood during Cervantes' time. She is currently working on a book manuscript tentatively entitled *Cervantes and Memory*.

Isabel Jaén is Associate Professor of Spanish at Portland State University. She is co-founder and co-coordinator of the Literary Theory, Cognition, and the Brain working group at the Whitney Humanities Center in Yale University and former executive member of the Cognitive Approaches to Literature Division of the MLA (chair in 2011). She is co-editor of *Cognitive Literary Studies* and has recently published on Cervantes and human development, cognitive approaches to teaching *Don Quixote*, and empathy and gender activism in Zayas' *Amorous and Exemplary Novels*, among other topics.

Howard Mancing is Professor of Spanish at Purdue University. He is the author of *The Chivalric World of* Don Quijote, *The Cervantes Encyclopedia*, and *Miguel de Cervantes' "Don Quixote": A Reference Guide*. He has co-edited two other books: *Text, Theory, and Performance: Golden Age Comedia Studies* and *Theory of Mind and Literature*. He is the author of some seventy-five articles and essays on Cervantes, the picaresque novel, narrative theory, the teaching of literature, cognitive approaches to the study of literature, and other subjects.

Cory A. Reed is Associate Professor of Spanish at the University of Texas at Austin. His research focuses on early modern performance, the representation of identity in early modern literature, literary responses to the emergence of scientific discourse, and cognitive cultural studies. He has published on Cervantes' drama, the *Novelas ejemplares, Don Quixote*, the drama of Calderón, and opera as a literary/dramatic form. Currently he is completing a book on technological imagery, agency, and aesthetics of instrumentality in *Don Quixote*.

Domingo Ródenas de Moya is Associate Professor of Spanish Literature at Pompeu Fabra University (Barcelona). He is author of *Los espejos del* novelista, *Prosa del 27*, and *Travesías vanguardistas* and co-author with Jordi Gracia of *Ensayo español. Siglo XX*, and *Historia de la literatura española, 7: Derrota y restitución de la modernidad, 1939–2010*. His recent publications include *Guillermo de Torre: De la aventura al orden* and a study on *Don Quixote*'s narrators (*Don Quijote*, Real Academia Española, 2015).

Ryan Schmitz holds a Ph.D. from the University of Texas at Austin and is Associate Professor of Spanish at Texas Christian University. He is the author of numerous articles on selfhood, the body, and courtly conduct in Cervantes' *Novelas ejemplares* and the *Quixote*, as well as early modern transoceanic utopias, which have appeared in *Modern Language Notes, Cervantes: Bulletin of the Cervantes Society of America, Bulletin of Spanish Studies*, and *eHumanista*.

Barbara Simerka is Professor of Spanish and Comparative Literature at Queens College/CUNY. She is author of *Knowing Subjects: Cognitive Cultural Studies and Early Modern Spanish Literature* and *Discourses of Empire*. She co-edited *Cognitive Cervantes*, a special cluster of essays in *Cervantes: Bulletin of the Cervantes Society of America* (Spring 2012). She has published essays on empathy and literature of marginalized groups; prototype theory and literary genres; theory of mind in *privanza* literature; and cognitive theory and science fiction.

Julien J. Simon is Associate Professor of Spanish and French at Indiana University East. He is co-founder of the Literary Theory, Cognition, and the Brain working group at the Whitney Humanities Center in Yale University (2005), former member of the executive committee for the MLA Division on Cognitive Approaches to Literature (chair in 2013), and former steering committee member of the Center for Cognitive Literary Studies at Purdue University. He has recently co-edited *Cognitive Literary Studies* and the special cluster *Cognitive Cervantes* of the *Bulletin of the Cervantes Society of America*.

José Valenzuela is a Doctoral Candidate and Researcher at the Facultat d'Humanitats [Faculty of Humanities] of the Universitat Pompeu Fabra in Barcelona, where he studies the cognitive mechanisms that prompt an emotional response in readers during their transportation to fictional worlds and teaches a course in literature and the cognitive sciences. He is also an electronic engineer and an automatics engineer and holds an M.A. in biomedical engineering and in creative writing. His work experience ranges from nanomaterials physics laboratories to cognitive neuroscience and virtual reality research groups.

Cognitive Approaches to Early Modern
Spanish Literature

Introduction

ISABEL JAÉN AND JULIEN J. SIMON

We are in the midst of an exciting moment in cognitive literary studies, a moment of consolidation and growth. It is also a moment of contemplation, of turning our eyes to our current state and the steps that led us here. We have come a long way since literary critics began in the late 1980s to look for new ways of exploring fiction in relation to the mind. These pioneering cognitive literary scholars[1] paved the way for our current understanding of verbal art as created and received by embodied minds in their physical-social environment. The acknowledgment that literature is as much a biological as a cultural phenomenon led to a willingness to engage with a variety of fields beyond literary criticism, such as psychology, linguistics, neuroscience, philosophy, sociology, and anthropology, among others. In reaching out, cognitive literary scholars found that researchers in some of those disciplines were also beginning to show a strong interest in their work[2] and increasingly understood the importance of storytelling as a resource for their own fields.[3] This was the beginning

1. Groundbreaking studies in cognitive approaches to literature included Mark Turner's *Death Is the Mother of Beauty* (1987) and Norman Holland's *The Brain of Robert Frost* (1988). See also, among others, Reuven Tsur's *Toward a Theory of Cognitive Poetics* (1992), Ellen Spolsky's *Gaps in Nature* (1993), Ellen Esrock's *The Reader's Eye* (1994), and Mark Turner's *The Literary Mind* (1996). Howard Mancing's landmark graduate seminar on Cognition and Literary Theory at Purdue University was created in 1994. The MLA Discussion group on Cognitive Approaches to Literature was founded in 1998 (it reached the status of Division in 2011 with almost 2,000 members).

2. This interest of scholars outside of literary criticism was evidenced at the first major cognitive literary studies conference held at the University of Connecticut, Storrs in 2006.

3. On how literature can inform the cognitive sciences, see Gerrig; Mishara; and Ródenas and Valenzuela (in this volume), among others.

of an integrative and dialogic effort that was not exempt from challenges. Limited by the institutional separation of disciplines within the sciences and the humanities, researchers would often become discouraged at what seemed to be an epistemological tower of Babel. Lost in the translation of diverse methods, philosophies, and ways of knowledge making, they would become frustrated with one another. Scientists would denounce the lack of empirical rigor of humanists, while humanists would lament the inability of scientists to deal with cultural complexity. Permeating these complaints was the unjustified and prevalent assumption that the sciences were a superior entity or some sort of knight-errant, armed with empiricism, coming to the rescue of the humanities in distress. This is a belief that, sadly, still biases the public view of cultural and literary studies, whose role and contribution are often misconstrued and underestimated in this era of STEM hegemony.

Although there are certainly significant differences in how the humanities and the sciences think about the world, these differences can and should be maintained, negotiated, and incorporated into an inclusive convergent approach to human biology and culture, a consilience approach. The notion of consilience has often borne the stigma of science dominance.[4] However, striving for consilience in cognitive literary studies does not imply—and should not be understood and practiced in this manner—the subjugation of the humanities to the sciences and its "exact and infallible" empirical methods. In fact, the cognitive approach does not depend on importing ideas and methodologies in a unidirectional fashion but on sharing and co-constructing knowledge; it is a multidirectional endeavor.[5] Thus, a consilience, integrative, or convergent approach (whichever term one prefers to name these efforts towards inclusiveness), as it should be viewed and practiced, is premised on multidisciplinary dialogue and collaboration among researchers. Regardless of the particular discipline in which we are rooted, we all have much to gain from exchanging ideas and methods as we contribute to widening our understanding of the relationship between literature and cognition. As we have written elsewhere, in the multidisciplinary environment promoted and inhabited by cognitive literary studies, consilience "implies cooperation among disciplines. Rather than conceiving our particular fields as isolated tiles that constitute a local pattern, we

4. For a recent discussion on the relationship between the sciences and the humanities and the way in which the notion of consilience has been associated with science dominance, see Zunshine.

5. On how cognitive literary studies engage other disciplines, see Jaén and Simon; Bernaerts et al.; Herman; Shaughnessy; Bruhn; Danta and Groth; Johnson, Sutton, and Tribble; and Zunshine, among others.

must consider their role in the whole epistemological mosaic" (Jaén and Simon 3). It is important to note that a mosaic is not a puzzle; it is not a problem that needs to be solved, nor a static pattern whose pieces must fit neatly together to eventually show us the face of human nature. Rather, this mosaic resembles a heterogeneous and dynamic landscape, a system, or even an organism—to focus on a sense of the term that is relevant for us here—formed by a community of disciplines, in which both centrifugal and centripetal forces operate. It is decentralized by its diversity and held together by the common interests among the many fields that integrate it, interests that gravitate around a central objective: making sense of our human selves and our environments. The diversity of perspectives and ideas that emerge during this quest generates in turn new themes and paths of inquiry. Indeed, "cognitive approaches today flourish at unexpected intersections" (Zunshine 2–3), which include fruitful emerging areas such as cognitive disability studies, cognitive queer theory, or cognitive postcolonial studies, among others.

Another connotation often ascribed to the consilience, convergent, or integrative approach is that it aims at creating a comprehensive theory of everything, a "unified theory of knowledge."[6] Apropos of this belief, it is important to remain aware of the fact that, in the same manner that we cannot think of cognitive literary studies as an all-encompassing "theory" to explain mind and fiction, we cannot subscribe to the myth of unified knowledge, for it, despite its quality of attractive utopia, remains precisely that: a myth. However, the fact that unified knowledge is realistically unattainable does not and should not stop us from looking for new connections and wider perspectives to contemplate the biological and cultural complexity of our species. Aiming to establish those new connections entails traveling outside of our disciplinary lands into unfamiliar territory. Thus, the cognitive literary scholar must behave like the goat-like wits described by sixteenth-century mind theorist Juan Huarte de San Juan: always looking for new pastures and delivering "contemplaciones, nunca oídas, en que ejercitarse. Porque de esta manera van creciendo las artes, y los hombres saben más cada día" (346) ["contemplations not heard of wherein they may exercise themselves, for after this manner, arts take increase and men daily know more and more" (132)].[7]

This book represents a milestone in the consolidation and diversification of cognitive literary studies. It is the child of our current understanding of

6. On the myth of unified knowledge, see Zunshine 1–2, Crane 14.
7. All citations from Huarte's *Examen de ingenios* are from the recent edition by Rocío Sumillera of the early modern translation by Richard Carew.

cognitive approaches to literature as a heterogeneous, dynamic, inclusive interface whose strength resides in integrating or blending diverse perspectives and methodologies—without surrendering to disciplinary prejudices and resulting hierarchies—as well as in considering the biological-universal aspects of human nature and human cognition in relation to cultural-specific contexts.[8]

By bringing together and exploring early modern representations of consciousness articulated through a diversity of genres (e.g., novels, plays, medical treatises, psychological treatises, philosophical works, testimonies, manuals of conduct), this volume seeks to exemplify the permeability that existed in early modernity between different epistemological realms that we today tend to separate and label as "scientific" or "literary."[9] When exploring the relationship between fiction and the mind in the context of the Spanish Renaissance, it is tempting to talk about the "influence" of science on literature—for instance, that of the medical-psychological theories of Huarte on Cervantes' work—an approach that reinforces the superior status that science enjoys over literary creation today and can easily fall into anachronistic interpretations, but yet is useful in certain ways to frame our discussions.[10] What we find in early modern Spain is a multiplicity of discourses and ideas about human consciousness and human nature that form a colorful epistemological pattern. These ideas are not imported from a particular domain and imposed on another in a top-down fashion; rather, they are parallel and dynamically co-constructed by all the embodied minds that participate in early modern culture. In this sense, we may think of the early modern mind as "a dynamic interplay between embodied intelligent agents and their broader environments for action and interaction" (Herman 47), or as a collective mind[11] that both inhabits and shapes its environment.

In its emphasis on the discursive diversity and permeability as well as the enactive aspects (dynamic interaction of agents with their environment) that relate to the study of mind and literature in early modern

8. On the importance of considering literature in relation to its historical, social, and cultural contexts and the idea of historicizing the study of mind and literature, see Spolsky, "Cognitive"; Richardson, chapter 1 ("Introduction: Cognitive Historicism"); and Bruhn, among others.

9. See Simon (in this volume).

10. In the words of Mary Thomas Crane, "Of course, as many scholars have argued, early modern philosophical, religious, and even literary discourse cannot be definitively separated from something anachronistically called 'science,' and the disciplines into which knowledge was divided were not as discrete as they are today. Still certain kinds of discrimination can and should be made" (14).

11. See Palmer.

Spain, this volume also contributes a novel perspective to the field of early modern studies. Especially useful to scholars outside the Spanish literary tradition will be the discussion of ideas by early modern Spanish thinkers who, in many respects, can be considered pioneers of the so-called cognitive revolution in Europe and who are precursors to René Descartes and Francis Bacon, among other important figures.[12]

Two major orientations converge in this book: how early modern thinkers and writers understood the mind in early modernity and how we understand it today. These two orientations are blended into a methodology that we could denominate contemporaneous-contemporary. This methodology constitutes a powerful tool to examine how early modern subjects viewed and portrayed consciousness as well as to address some wider-scope questions that are relevant to the study of early modern culture and are explored throughout the book from a variety of angles: How did early modern subjects engage in fictional worlds? How can the cross-examination of early modern discourses from different epistemological realms provide us with a clearer picture of the early modern mind? How can a cognitive approach that blends contemporaneous and contemporary cognitive theories facilitate our understanding of the relationship between the mind and the arts in this period? How does the historicist component of such an approach help us trace the Iberian contribution to models of mind that circulate in early modern and modern Europe? Finally, and more broadly, how can cognitive literary studies shed light on how humans create and engage with fiction and on how the study of fiction and the arts is fundamental to explore and understand human cognition?

The book is divided into five sections. Section I offers an overview of the field of cognitive approaches to early modern Spanish literature by Julien Simon.[13] This chapter acts as a grand organizer, introducing readers to the history of the field and its main themes and directions. The essays in Section II focus on Cervantes' *Don Quixote* to trace the creation of self in the context of the novel. Howard Mancing demonstrates how autopoiesis (a notion introduced by Chilean scientists Humberto Maturana and Francisco Varela to discuss how a living organism generates itself within its physical, historical, social, and linguistic context) can shed light not only on Cervantes' metafictional novel of self-creation but also on how fiction mirrors the biological and cultural process of

12. See Bullón y Fernández; Martín-Araguz and Bustamante-Martínez; and Watson, among others.
13. See Simon's previous overviews of the field, "Introduction" and "Intersection."

inventing ourselves in the act of living. Both autopoiesis and the related concept of structural coupling (the dynamical interaction of body and context) are important notions from biology that can help literary scholars explore literary representations of consciousness. Following up on the concept of autopoiesis in relation to *Don Quixote*, Catherine Connor discusses how, from a microcosmic, cellular level each human genetically and biologically self-organizes and remembers herself in the process of becoming her own complex macrocosmic systems. She proposes that Cervantes' self-conscious chapters on arms, letters, and Morisco relations elucidate his autopoietic development, while challenging readers to mirror and develop greater awareness of self and others. In this way, *Don Quixote* teaches individual biocultural awareness and the complementarity of science and art. Finally, Julia Domínguez discusses how Cervantes portrays, through the character of Don Quixote, the process of self-creation as based on the faculties of memory and imagination. She argues that Cervantes understood how memory is not separate from present or future creative processes and thus represented Don Quixote's problem as embedded in imagination and its relation to memories that are rooted in the past but available for future recall. For Domínguez, Don Quixote embodies the characteristics of the Janus face, a visual representation of one who looks at the past and the future simultaneously, thereby intertwining seemingly dissimilar timeframes into a continuum. Sections III and IV deal with how early modern Spanish subjects perceive and react to their physical and social environment. In Section III, Bruce Burningham and Elizabeth Cruz Petersen show how the concept of embodiment is especially pertinent to delve into the mechanics of the interaction between actors and audience both in the jongleuresque (Burningham) and the *comedia* (Cruz Petersen) traditions. Burningham reminds us that, as performers have always known, theater begins and ends in the imagination and that, ultimately, the work of actors is to make audiences see precisely that which does not exist. Through an analysis of the work of two contemporary performers (Pedro Elis and Benjamin Bagby) he discusses the genesis of early modern drama as unembellished performance rooted in the jongleuresque tradition, as opposed to in play scripts. By doing so, he reevaluates the contribution of the performative aspects of theater, *vis-à-vis* the textual/literary in the historiography of the Renaissance Spanish drama, while shedding new light on the origins of the early modern stage. In her essay, Cruz Petersen contends that a somaesthetics approach (which stresses the role of the body as a living, feeling, and intentional entity) is particularly useful to explore the dynamic interactions that occur among the embodied minds in the physical and social environment of the *corral* (the Spanish theatrical space), as well as how individuals of certain social groups push, as audience members, the limits of prescribed behavior. She argues that, motivated by a need to move freely from "object" to "subject" to establish their subjectivity, many women and men of seventeenth-century Madrid interpreted their role in society not by mirroring the reflection presented to them in literature or books of manners or by Church or government authorities, but instead in relation to their own theatrical experience. In Section IV, Judith Caballero discusses how cognitive theories of perception can shed light on cross-dressing and gender identification in the Spanish *comedia*. Other characters' acceptance of the cross-dresser as a member of the opposite sex is typically dismissed as a mere theatrical device to advance the storyline. Yet, in the mindset of early modern Spanish people, sexual distinction was not solely defined on a biological basis; it was defined by personality traits, behaviors, and sartorial conventions. To distinguish between male and female in everyday life, people relied heavily on socially contrived signifiers, such as clothing, gender roles, and engendered spaces. Caballero argues that in Ángela de Azevedo's *El muerto disimulado* [The Feign Death] the characters' inability to determine correctly the sex of the cross-dresser is a manifestation of an attentional set that assigns sex according to gendered behaviors. In this same section, Domingo Ródenas and José Valenzuela focus on the Maese Pedro's puppet show episode in *Don Quixote* in connection to the metaphor of transportation to fictional worlds. They show how the episode illustrates and also enriches this metaphor by directing our attention to discursive and behavioral aspects of the transportation phenomenon. In doing so, they propose an alternative view of Don Quixote's inability to distinguish reality from fiction. Don Quixote, who is *not* a madman but a transported reader unable to construct disbelief, represents both the power and effect of fiction over the human mind. These first two essays, which illustrate how misperception is often related to our inability to understand social situations, pave the way for the third and last essay of the section, centered on the human ability to understand others. In his essay, Ryan Schmitz analyzes the key concepts of early modern courtly conduct manuals, such as dissimulation, discretion, prudence, and impression management. By bringing together mind models of the period and modern-day notions of intentionality, he shows how an integrated contemporaneous-contemporary approach sheds light on the astute physiological and psychological insights that court writers made in the sixteenth and seventeenth centuries. He focuses on Damasio de Frías' *Diálogo de la discreción* [Dialogue of Discretion] and Baltasar Gracián's *Oráculo manual y arte de prudencia* [The Art of Worldly Wisdom], works that advise their readers on how to prosper at court, including the themes of self-observation, control of emotions, and obfuscation of one's interior and exterior, as well as the ability to perceive and understand a rival's interior (thoughts, intentions, and emotions). Perceiving and understanding others leads us to the notion of empathy or feeling with others. In Section V, Cory Reed demonstrates how cognitive approaches to live performance may allow us to approximate the emotional and intellectual dimensions of audience–performer interactions in the shared space of the theatrical *corrales*. He shows how Cervantes' early play, *El trato de Argel* [The Trade of Algiers], which may have been part of a campaign to raise public awareness of the plight of enslaved Spaniards in Algerian prisons, lends itself to a cognitive analysis of the role of empathy in creating audience sympathy that might ultimately lead to an early modern form of proto-activism. Finally, Barbara Simerka looks at how cognitive theories of empathy can help us to assess the original impact and subsequent legacy of activist Dominican friar Bartolomé de las Casas, who wrote *Brevísima relación de la destrucción de las Indias* [A Short Account of the Destruction of the Indies] and was known as "the protector of the Indians" during the Spanish colonization of America. She suggests that an alternative perspective on the role of emotion and empathy in the literature classroom can inform new approaches to presenting the Las Casas corpus in human rights and postcolonial contexts. Simerka's pedagogical discussion takes us to the last essay in the volume, the afterword, in which Isabel Jaén, drawing on her experience teaching with a cognitive focus,[14] offers strategies to design a course on mind and literature in early modernity.

Cognitive Approaches to Early Modern Spanish Literature is the first anthology exploring human cognition and literature in the context of early modern Spanish culture. It represents the culmination of the cognitive literary studies research that has been taking place over the last fifteen years within early modern Spanish studies and includes the leading voices in the field, along with the main themes and directions that this important area of study has been producing. We are confident that it will be an invaluable resource for early modern scholars both inside and outside of Spanish studies. Regardless of their theoretical orientation, they will find in this book new and original perspectives as well as paths for innovative research. Indeed, as Zunshine reminds us, "at this point, cognitive literary studies have something to offer to a scholar of any theoretical persuasion; the entry point into the field can be as individualized as one wishes" (4).

14. See Jaén.

The contributors to this volume are providing readers with their own indi-vidualized points of entry to explore the early modern mind and its cul-tural offspring. With this compass, they hope to guide them on a journey of discovery, as they in turn beget new ideas and avenues for future scholarship.

WORKS CITED

Bernaerts, Lars, Dirk De Geest, Luc Herman, and Bart Vervaeck. "Introduction: Cognitive Narrative Studies: Themes and Variations." *Stories and Minds: Cognitive Approaches to Literary Narrative*. Ed. Lars Bernaerts, Dirk De Geest, Luc Herman, and Bart Vervaeck. Lincoln: U of Nebraska P, 2013, 1–20.

Bruhn, Mark J. "Introduction: Integrating the Study of Cognition, Literature, and History." *Cognition, Literature, and History*. Ed. Mark J. Bruhn and Donald R. Wehrs. New York: Routledge, 2014, 1–14.

Bullón y Fernández, Eloy. *Los precursores españoles de Bacon y Descartes*. Salamanca: Imprenta de Calatrava, 1905. *Archive.org*. Web. June 30, 2015.

Crane, Mary Thomas. *Losing Touch with Nature: Literature and the New Science in Sixteenth-Century England*. Baltimore: Johns Hopkins UP, 2014.

Danta, Chris, and Helen Groth. "Introduction: Between Minds." *Mindful Aesthetics: Literature and the Science of Mind*. Ed. Chris Danta and Helen Groth. New York: Bloomsbury, 2014, 1–14.

Esrock, Ellen J. *The Reader's Eye: Visual Imaging as Reader Response*. Baltimore: Johns Hopkins UP, 1994.

Gerrig, Richard J. "Why Literature Is Necessary, and Not Just Nice." *Cognitive Literary Studies: Current Themes and New Directions*. Ed. Isabel Jaén and Julien Jacques Simon. Austin: U of Texas P, 2012, 35–52.

Herman, David. *Storytelling and the Sciences of Mind*. Cambridge: MIT P, 2013.

Holland, Norman N. *The Brain of Robert Frost: A Cognitive Approach to Literature*. New York: Routledge, 1988.

Huarte de San Juan, Juan. *Examen de ingenios para las ciencias*. Ed. Guillermo Serés. Madrid: Cátedra, 1989.

Huarte de San Juan, Juan. *The Examination of Men's Wits*. Trans. Richard Carew. Ed. Rocío G. Sumillera. London: Modern Humanities Research Association, 2014.

Jaén, Isabel. "Teaching Cervantes' *Don Quixote* from a Cognitive Historicist Perspective." *Cognition in the Classroom*. Ed. Nancy Easterlin. Spec. issue of *Interdisciplinary Literary Studies* 16.1 (2014): 110–26.

Jaén, Isabel, and Julien Jacques Simon. Introduction. *Cognitive Literary Studies: Current Themes and New Directions*. Ed. Isabel Jaén and Julien Jacques Simon. Austin: U of Texas P, 2012, 1–9.

Johnson, Laurie, John Sutton, and Evelyn Tribble. "Introduction: Re-cognising the Body-Mind in Shakespeare's Theatre." *Embodied Cognition and Shakespeare's Theatre: The Early Modern Body-Mind*. Ed. Laurie Johnson, John Sutton, and Evelyn Tribble. New York: Routledge, 2014, 1–11.

Martín-Araguz, A., and C. Bustamante-Martínez. "*Examen de ingenios*, de Juan Huarte de San Juan, y los albores de la Neurobiología de la inteligencia en el Renacimiento español." *Revista de Neurología* 38.12 (2004): 1176–85.

Mishara, Aaron L. "The Literary Neuroscience of Kafka's Hypnagogic Hallucinations: How Literature Informs the Neuroscientific Study of Self and Its Disorders." *Cognitive Literary Studies: Current Themes and New Directions*. Ed. Isabel Jaén and Julien Jacques Simon. Austin: U of Texas P, 2012, 105–23.

Palmer, Alan. *Social Minds in the Novel*. Columbus: Ohio State UP, 2010.

Richardson, Alan. *The Neural Sublime: Cognitive Theories and Romantic Texts*. Baltimore: Johns Hopkins UP, 2010.

Shaughnessy, Nicola. "General Introduction: Operating in Science Theatres." *Affective Performance and Cognitive Science: Body, Brain, and Being*. Ed. Nicola Shaughnessy. London: Bloomsbury, 2013, 1–24.

Simon, Julien Jacques. "The Intersection of Mind and *Don Quixote*: Overview and Prospects." *Don Quixote: Interdisciplinary Connections*. Ed. Matthew D. Warshawsky and James A. Parr. Newark: Juan de la Cuesta, 2013, 19–34.

Simon, Julien Jacques. "Introduction to 'Cognitive Cervantes': Integrating Mind and Cervantes' Texts." *Cognitive Cervantes*. Ed. Julien J. Simon, Barbara Simerka, and Howard Mancing. Spec. cluster of essays of *Cervantes: Bulletin of the Cervantes Society of America* 32.1 (2012): 11–23.

Spolsky, Ellen. "Cognitive Literary Historicism: A Response to Adler and Gross." *Poetics Today* 24.2 (Summer 2003): 161–83.

Spolsky, Ellen. *Gaps in Nature: Literary Interpretation and the Modular Mind*. Albany: SU of New York P, 1993.

Tsur, Reuven. *Toward a Theory of Cognitive Poetics*. Amsterdam: North-Holland, 1992.

Turner, Mark. *Death Is the Mother of Beauty: Mind, Metaphor, Criticism*. Chicago: U of Chicago P, 1987.

Turner, Mark. *The Literary Mind*. New York: Oxford UP, 1996.

Watson, Foster. "The Father of Modern Psychology." *Psychological Review* 22.5 (1915): 333–56.

Zunshine, Lisa. "Introduction to Cognitive Literary Studies." *The Oxford Handbook of Cognitive Literary Studies*. Ed. Lisa Zunshine. New York: Oxford UP, 2015, 1–9.

SECTION I

*An Overview of Cognitive
Approaches to Early Modern
Spanish Literature*

CHAPTER 1

Contextualizing Cognitive Approaches to Early Modern Spanish Literature

JULIEN J. SIMON

INTRODUCTION

In 2012 the field of cognitive approaches to early modern Spanish literature was mapped for the first time in relation to Cervantes' prose. Two
main lines of inquiry could be identified then, namely "Embodiment" and
"Theory of Mind" (Simon, "Introduction" 13).[1] A few years later and looking at a larger body of texts (e.g., other prose fiction texts, plays [including
Cervantes'], poetry, courtly manuals, and so forth), we see that these lines
of inquiry remain active and have branched out while newer ones have
formed. In this essay I offer a brief introduction to the recent developments at the intersection of early modern literature and cognition, pointing to the most relevant themes and their contexts and identifying
established as well as emerging paths of research.

The essay is organized around four main areas. "Embodiment and
Beyond" focuses on the concept that is at the root of the cognitive literary
studies project and has provided the theoretical substrate, the impetus,
and the tools to shift the focus of *comedia* studies (early modern Spanish
theater studies) from discourse-based analysis to performative aspects and
spectatorship. Additionally, some of the early scientific theories promoting

---

1. For further discussion of the current state and prospects of cognitive approaches to early modern Spanish literature, see Simerka, "Afterword," and Simon,
"Intersection."

a more embodied view of human cognition also initiated a reflection on the notion of literary genres. "Theory of Mind and Development" explores the interplay of minds in literature in connection to the cultural and sociopolitical context of early modern Spain. The increasingly complex portrayal of intentionality in Renaissance Spanish narratives points to the importance that early modern culture placed on the capacity to understand other minds, imperative to thrive in courtly circles, to climb up the social ladder, or simply to survive in a society ever more urban and exhibiting great inequities. This ability to understand others is closely related to human development as represented by early modern fictional characters. "Empathy, Ethics, and Multiculturalism" delves into a group of studies that, weaving the sociopolitical with the emotional-cognitive, shed light on the strategies that some early modern Spanish authors (namely Cervantes and Bartolomé de las Casas) employed to manipulate the emotions of readers and spectators of this era. Finally, the last section, "Mind Science and Culture," examines the interrelation of literary texts and the ideas about the mind of the time. It highlights the permeability among different discourses (e.g., philosophical, medical, artistic), explores the coordinates of the cultural *matière* of mind, and discusses the relation between contemporaneous and contemporary "sciences."

EMBODIMENT AND BEYOND

Embodiment: Definition and Relevance to Cognitive Literary Studies

Embodiment, or embodied cognition,[2] is the notion that brain, body, and the environment are interconnected, that human cognition is shaped by aspects of the body and its interaction with the physical and social world.[3] The initial findings on the embodied nature of human cognition sparked a conversation about the relation between human subjectivity and culture.[4] The postmodern "subject" was increasingly seen as having more "agency" than many of the schools of thought in literary criticism purported. In light of this new knowledge of the mind, the extreme form

2. There are related terms/concepts that either overlap with or are synonymous with the idea of embodied cognition. These include, among others, grounded cognition (e.g., Barsalou), enactive cognition (e.g., Varela, Thompson, and Rosch), and extended cognition (e.g., Clark and Chalmers).

3. For a brief overview and chronology of the studies that ushered in embodied cognition, see Barsalou, sec. 2, "The past 30 years," pp. 717–8.

4. For an overview of the influence of embodied cognition on literary studies, see Mancing, "Embodied."

of relativism, or social constructivism, of certain literary theories was being challenged.[5]

The theoretical reflection on the nature of the relationship between culture and biology constitutes an important (and the initial) line of inquiry in early modern Spanish studies. It was an attempt to re-biologize our critical approaches to literature, and it led to conclusions such as the following: fact and fiction should not be dichotomized, since our ability to understand fictional characters relies on our cognitive abilities to understand people (Mancing, "Against"),[6] the author is a human being of flesh and blood that permeates her or his work (Mancing, "Cervantes as Narrator" and this volume), and the mind is not a disembodied entity on which the body has no bearing (Mancing, "Against"). This important path of research in literary studies continues to be strong, as evidenced by the essays in this volume by Howard Mancing and Catherine Connor around the notion of autopoiesis.

It must be noted that although this theoretical reflection—as well as the whole cognitive literary studies project—relies on research that emphasizes the body-mind as a biological entity, this does not mean that the human subject is reduced to a set of universal cognitive principles. In fact, by stressing the key role of the environment, an embodied view of the brain safeguards the notion of cultural complexity and individuality, sacrosanct in the humanities. Indeed, as Connor reminds us:

> A particular embodied mind is also rich in the abundant differences produced by the uniqueness of an individual's personal experience—unique in the distinctive details of one's cellular development "memory," or "knowledge" as well as in the idiosyncrasies of one's processes of perception and interactive conceptualization of life as lived by that individual. ("Bridging" 13)

In view of the fact that the uniqueness of the human individual in a particular cultural context is preserved with a cognitive approach, there is room for a dialogue with poststructuralist critical theories. Many cognitive scholars have indeed argued that in spite of some theoretical

5. For an overview of the impact of cognitive and cognitive-evolutionary research on literary criticism and of the various positions (among cognitive literary scholars) at the science–literature interface, see Hart, "Epistemology." See also Katherine Hayles' notion of "constrained constructivism," which points at the complex interplay (or tug-of-war) between human perception and reality (Hayles, "Constrained Constructivism").

6. Howard Mancing's 1999 article "Against Dualisms" can be considered the inaugural work at the convergence of mind and literature in early modern Spanish studies.

differences negotiating the biology–culture interface with traditional schools of thought, such dialogue can be productive and a rapprochement is (and has been) feasible.[7]

Interpreting the Body and Senses in Literature

The concept of embodiment has also been influential at the interpretive level, initiating a discussion on the body and the senses in literature from a novel perspective. In his essay for this volume, Mancing explains that one not only needs a Theory of Mind (an ability to follow the minds of fictional characters) to read *Don Quixote* but also a "Theory of Body," for the body occupies a prominent place in the novel. Regarding the senses, Elena Carrera shows in "Embodied Cognition and Empathy in Miguel de Cervantes' *El celoso extremeño*" how the restricted sensory information that the literary characters have access to in this *novela ejemplar* [exemplary novel] affects their interpretation of what unfolds, thus allowing the reader to step back and reflect on these effects. For his part, Steven Wagschal, in a recent essay entitled "The Smellscape of *Don Quixote*: A Cognitive Approach," explores the representation of the characters' olfactory experience in Cervantes' novel. In all these studies, an embodied cognitive approach is crucial to fully understand how these themes play out in the texts under scrutiny.

Embodiment and Performance Studies

Embodiment also constitutes the bedrock of a shift in the study of *comedias* (early modern Spanish theater)—spearheaded by Catherine Connor[8]—from textual discourse-based analyses to a focus on the interactive nature of theatrical performances. Spanish theater was a thriving art form in the early modern period, one over which Lope de Vega, the "Prodigy of Nature" (because of the approximately 1,800 plays that he is said to have written), reigned supreme. *Comedia* performances were lively spectacles on and off stage, attended by virtually all sectors of Spanish

7. See, among others, Connor, "Bridging" and "Why"; Hart, "Epistemology"; Jaén and Simon, "Introduction" and this volume; Simerka, *Knowing* 4; Zunshine, "Introduction" 2. In this volume, see the essays by Caballero, Cruz Petersen, and Simerka.

8. See especially her 2003 essay "Bridging the Performance Gap: The Body, Cognitive Theory, and *Comedia* Studies" as well as "Why," "Scientific," "Creative," and "Embodying."

society. As cognitive *comedia* scholars have shown (in this volume and in other fora), theories of human perception, memory, affect, and concepts such as empathy, simulation, and so forth are useful in examining the dynamic interaction between actors and audiences, as well as among audiences and the actors themselves.

Two orientations can be discerned in the research at the confluence of cognition and *comedia* studies: one exploring the relationship between text, spectators, and performance and another one focusing on the nature of spectating.[9] The latter, under the premise that the human brain has not evolved significantly over the four or so centuries that separate us from the theatergoers who saw these *comedias*,[10] has tended to discuss audience response when *comedias* were first staged.[11]

Embodiment and Genres

The work of Eleanor Rosch on categories has also had an enormous impact on the understanding of conceptual knowledge and the interconnectedness of environment, body, and cognition.[12] What her work showed was that categories (such as color, animal, bird, furniture) should not be seen as disembodied entities governed by pure logic (by objective observation of the world—that is, by a set of necessary and sufficient criteria) and as having clear boundaries, neatly differentiating members from nonmembers of a category.[13] Instead, categories should be viewed as contextualized graded concepts (with a radial structure) that form around a clear case or "prototype."

With literary genres being another kind of category, this research has naturally drawn the interest of literary scholars. In early modern Spanish studies, it has illuminated the debate on a series of generic conundrums, such as the classification of Cervantes' *Novelas ejemplares* (Mancing, "Prototypes"), of early modern Spanish tragedies (Simerka,

---

9. On the relationship between text, spectators, and performance, see Burningham, this volume; Connor, "Bridging" and "Why"; and Mancing, "See the Play." Studies on the nature of spectating include Connor, "Scientific," "Creative," and "Embodying"; Caballero, this volume; Cruz Petersen, "Designed" and this volume; Greer; and Reed, this volume.

10. For a recent discussion on the extent to which there is a stability of human brain structures across centuries, see Phillips, especially pp. 66–69.

11. See for instance the essays by Cruz Petersen, Caballero, and Reed in this volume as well as Cruz Petersen, "Designed."

12. See especially Rosch.

13. What she calls "The Classical View"; see Gabora, Rosch, and Aerts 87–88.

"Cognitive Theories"), and of the *género celestinesco* [*Celestina* genre] (Simon, "Schema").[14] These studies emphasize how context-dependent, mutable, and ultimately personal our generic knowledge is and show how an embodied cognitive approach that can really account for the biocultural nature of genres helps us better understand the relationship between embodied minds and a literary corpus, enriching without replacing the careful examination of texts and their characteristics.

THEORY OF MIND AND DEVELOPMENT

The concept of Theory of Mind (ToM; the human ability to understand what other people think, feel, and want) has historically influenced (and continues to influence) the research at the crossroads of cognition and early modern Spanish literature.[15] This notion has been associated with the emergence of mind in literature (Hart, "Reading" 120–5; Mancing, "Sancho" 127–9; Simon, "Celestina") as well as with the psychological development of characters (Jaén, "Literary"), and it is particularly useful to examine the relationship between literary representations of consciousness and early modern Spanish culture. Below I discuss briefly some of the socio-historical circumstances that help us contextualize intersubjectivity and the emergence of the social mind as portrayed in early modern Spanish narratives.

Understanding others' states of mind in order to survive in society is a literary motif that permeated the fabric of many genres of the epoch and

14. For other research on Prototype Theory and literary genres from outside Spanish studies, see Swales; Steen; and Sinding, "After Definitions." On conceptual blending and literary genres, see Sinding, "A Sermon" and "Blending."

15. The concept of ToM originated in the field of primatology with the work of Premack and Woodruff, who wondered if chimpanzees could recognize the intentions of a human being. Representative studies in the area include Gopnik and Meltzoff, Gordon, Dennett, Goldman, Gallagher, and Gallagher and Hutto, among others. Other related notions that have been employed to discuss our ability to understand the mental states of others are mindreading, intentionality, intersubjectivity, and the umbrella term folk psychology. ToM is also related to the concepts of social intelligence (see Humphrey), Machiavellian intelligence (see Byrne and Whiten), and deception (see LaFrenière). In the field of cognitive literary studies, the human ability to "read" mental states, understand the thoughts, beliefs, feelings, desires, and intentions of others, and to engage socially with them has also been discussed in terms of sociocognitive complexity (Zunshine, "Sociocognitive"), nested mental states (Zunshine, "Approaching"), deep intersubjectivity (Butte), and intermental thought (Palmer), among others. For further discussion of the notion of ToM in relation to literature, see Leverage et al.; Mancing, "James."

is perhaps more patent in the picaresque novel.[16] Indeed, the picaro, the hero of the genre, must live by his own wits to survive in a Spanish society in which vast social inequalities exist, in spite of the enormous fortune plundered from its American possessions. Throughout the story of his survival, the protagonist will rely on his own ability to read others' mental states and manipulate them. The resulting complexity of the interplay of minds, between the picaro and the other characters (picaros or otherwise) who are all trying to outsmart each other, is a central feature of this genre. In sum, as need breeds ruse and craftiness, the social-economic disparities of early modern Spain are an essential component of the genre and serve as an important contextual factor in the rise of the literary representation of intentionality.

Furthermore, the religious unification and centralization of the Peninsula—under one monarchy, one religion—started by the Catholic monarchs in 1469 constituted the officialization of a process that would splinter the society. For almost eight centuries the Iberian Peninsula had been a multiconfessional society with Muslims, Jews, and Christians living side by side, prior to 1492, when the last Muslim kingdom fell (that of Granada) and when the Jews who had not converted to Catholicism were expelled. Following this last event, the unification process was in full force and led to fear and paranoia regarding who was a "New Christian" (i.e., a Jew or Muslim who had converted to the Christian faith), a true convert, or an "Old Christian" (i.e., a Christian with an "unadulterated" bloodline, with no trace of Jewish or Muslim heritage, who was "*limpio*" [clean] and could demonstrate *limpieza de sangre* [purity of blood]). These are some of the questions that remained at the back of people's minds in the era—even more so if they were converts, or descendants of the many converts who lived in Spain. The most telling literary rendering of this obsession with the purity of blood is perhaps Cervantes' *entremés* [interlude] *El retablo de las maravillas* [The Marvelous Puppet Show]. Published over a century later in 1615 and based on the medieval story that also inspired Andersen's "The Emperor's New Clothes," it features two picaros who deceive a small town by putting on a play that only people who are not illegitimate or who are of Old Christian blood can see.[17] The ideas of the Reformation that started to spread in the sixteenth century did not ease this situation and soon became an added layer of complexity in the

16. For an analysis of the interplay of minds in *Lazarillo de Tormes*, considered the first picaresque novel, see Mancing, "The Mind."

17. For a full summary of this play, see Mancing, *The Cervantes Encyclopedia*, 610–1.

minefield of Spain's society, the Spanish "¿Qué dirán?" (literally: "What will they say?"), or the sense that one's behavior was being scrutinized by others constantly and that one needed to watch what she or he did or said at all time.[18]

Social intelligence was key to surviving not only the turbulent times of the early modern era but also in the courtier culture, a corollary of the development of urban culture. The sixteenth-century vogue of the book of manners coming out of Italy, among which one of the most influential was Baltasar de Castiglione's *Il libro del cortegiano* [The Book of the Courtier] (1528), soon reached Spain too. The fact that these books were quickly translated into Spanish shows that the sharpening of one's social skills was believed to be of the utmost importance in this environment (see Schmitz in this volume).[19]

The ability to "read" (and manipulate) another person's mind in society was portrayed in fiction with an increasing complexity during the early modern period. Several texts—Fernando de Rojas' *Celestina* (1499), the anonymous picaresque novel *La vida de Lazarillo de Tormes* [The Life of Lazarillo de Tormes] (1554), and *Don Quixote (Part I & II)* (1605, 1615)—have been shown to feature multiple levels of intentionality and characters with well-defined psychologies who not only show a human-like ability to read their literary counterparts' mind but also develop through interaction with their social environment.[20] Thus, a cognitive approach to early modern Spanish literature that focuses on Theory of Mind and development is particularly useful to trace the early modern origins of deep intersubjectivity in literature.[21]

---

18. The *Diccionario de la lengua española* [Dictionary of the Spanish Language] defines "el qué dirán" as "La opinión pública reflejada en murmuraciones que cohíben los actos" ["The public opinion reflected in gossip that inhibits behavior"].

19. Interestingly, one of the representatives of this genre, Niccolò Machiavelli, whose *The Prince* (1513) is an atypical example of the book of manners, became the inspiration for the psychological concept of Machiavellian intelligence (concomitant with Theory of Mind), which was coined by Byrne and Whiten in 1988. Both Theory of Mind and Machiavellian intelligence are banner terms that refer to the ability to understand somebody else's states of mind, beliefs, and desires. However, while the former is more neutral and refers to the cognitive ability itself, the latter refers to its social implications and to how one can rely on Theory of Mind to survive and climb in a particular social setting.

20. Studies include Simon, "Celestina"; Mancing, "The Mind" on *Lazarillo*; Jaén, "Literary"; Mancing, "Sancho"; and Reed on *Don Quixote*. See also Barroso Castro in relation to Cervantes' *El casamiento engañoso*.

21. Deep intersubjectivity has been previously discussed by English scholars in connection to eighteenth- and nineteenth-century literature (mainly the work of Jane Austen). See for example Butte; Zunshine, *Why* and "Why Jane."

Empathy (feeling with others),[22] a much-studied concept in both the sciences and the humanities, has recently drawn more interest on the part of early modern Spanish scholars. One of the characteristics of this emerging line of inquiry is that the scholars involved are historicizing to various degrees their studies on empathy and literature. Below I discuss the main themes addressed and the historical backdrop of these studies, further highlighting the importance that cognitive literary studies place on context.

Empathetic Cervantes

Cervantes' empathetic portrayal of the Morisco (Muslim *converso*) minority[23] has received much attention from cognitive literary scholars working on this area of research. Connor, in a 2012 essay entitled "Beyond Cognition: Don Quijote and Other Embodied Minds," highlights the central role that Cervantes' five-year captivity in Algiers, along with his travels in Spain and the Mediterranean, may have played in the composition of his writings. Recalling the Ricote episode in Chapter 54 of *Don Quixote (Part II)*, Connor links the humanity and empathy with which Cervantes writes about the impact of the 1609 edict of expulsion of the Moriscos to the deep knowledge of Islamic-Christian relations he acquired in Spain

22. Several definitions exist for empathy or the ability to feel with others. The origin of this concept is generally associated with the idea of *Einfühlung* (feeling into) disseminated by Robert Visher and Theodor Lipps (see Hammond and Kim 5), although it can be traced back to the early modern notion of *misericordia* as described by Juan Luis Vives in his treatise of emotions included in *De anima et vita* (Jaén, "Empathy"). Empathy and Theory of Mind are related concepts. Empathy is sometimes divided up into "affective empathy" (the ability to share the emotional states of others), a notion akin to emotional contagion, and "cognitive empathy" (the ability to understand the emotional states of others). The latter is at times used interchangeably with Theory of Mind. For a survey of the different uses of the term "empathy" in scientific research, see Batson. On cognitive vs. affective empathy, see Shamay-Tsoory and Strayer. A definition of empathy that also includes the aspect of prosocial behavior is "the natural capacity to share, understand, and respond with care to the affective states of others" (Decety vii).

23. The Moriscos were more than a minority group, since their presence and influence in the Iberian peninsula was by the 1600s almost 900 years old (711 is considered the beginning of the Muslim presence in Iberia). Circa 1500, the Iberian Muslims were forced to convert to Christianity; however, they were not forced to leave the Peninsula until the edict of 1609 and they were allowed to speak their language for half a century, until Phillip II's edict banning the use of Arabic in 1566.

and the Mediterranean. Cervantes' ability to empathize with the plight of this group was also, Connor claims, due to his first-hand experience with the Islamic cultures. Indeed, soon after the 1571 Battle of Lepanto (in which Spanish ships led the Holy League forces against the Ottoman Empire and in which Cervantes took part and lost the use of his left arm) he was held hostage by privateers and taken to the Turks-controlled city of Algiers. There, Cervantes was surprised by the vibrancy[24] of a bustling city and the peaceful coexistence of a variety of racial and religious communities, light-years from the Spanish context.[25] These five years in captivity in Algiers—along with the time he spent prior to that as a Spanish soldier stationed in several Italian cities (then part of the Spanish crown)—broadened Cervantes' horizons. His experience in Algiers, as reflected in his fictional works, conferred upon him a cultural sensitivity that is not seen in many of his contemporaries and that many scholars have discussed. Donald Wehrs, for his part, argues that it is precisely the ethical reflection elicited by the way in which Cervantes walks the fine line existing at the time between the sociocultural rhetoric of the epoch and the human reality of the exile of the Moriscos that is at the core of his literary genius.[26] Less attention has been paid, however, to the narrative and theatrical strategies employed by Cervantes to lead his contemporary audience to empathize with his characters. In this volume, for instance, Cory Reed examines how Cervantes' play *El trato de Argel* [The Trade of Algiers], in the socio-historical context of the sixteenth century's

24. "When he [Cervantes] expected to find nothing but a nest of pirates, he discovers a city of 15,000 inhabitants, more populous than Palermo or Rome, whose bustling streets remind him of Naples" (Canavaggio 77).

25. "What he uncovers for us—with a light touch, never descending to didactic exposition or mere depiction of quaint customs—is the functioning of an extremely open society . . . in which the distinctions appear based less on occupation and wealth than on religious or racial alliances. At the top of the pyramid, the Turks . . . [and] with them the corsairs, natives from all around the Mediterranean basin and representing almost 'all the Christian nations.' At the bottom of the ladder, the mass of captives . . . [and] black slaves. Between these two poles, a series of communities, in which a Jewish colony is highly conspicuous amid the dubious motley world of Morisco artisans, and Kabyle day laborers. These colonies maintained complex relationships among themselves, and Cervantine fictions present to us, behind the play of conventions, a vision of them without Manicheanism" (Canavaggio 81).

26. This posture echoes the philological work carried out recently in Morisco historiography, which strives to reassess the role of the Morisco minority in sixteenth- and seventeenth-century Spain. See Childers' article "Cervantes in Moriscolandia": "The new Morisco historiography paints a more varied and dynamic picture, giving greater attention to class differentiation and above all to the growing numbers who successfully integrated and improved their status within the host society" (287). On Cervantes' literary genius and embodiment, see Connor, "Seeing."

fin-de-siècle described above, may lead the audience to engage in pro-social action—defined in this case as the act of paying ransoms that would free the Christian captives held by the Turks.[27] Overall, rather than focusing on the trauma that Cervantes' captivity could have caused him,[28] these scholars (Connor, Wehrs, and Reed) emphasize its positive outcomes—that is, the humanity of the characters portrayed in his works, the empathy-inducing strategies employed by the author, his ethical reflection on the cultural context, and so forth.

The Spanish Colonization of America

The encounter with the indigenous civilizations of the Americas led in the sixteenth century to an ethical-philosophical discussion on what constituted humankind, illustrated for instance by the Valladolid debate (1550–1), the activism of Bartolomé de las Casas, and the resulting *Leyes Nuevas* [News Laws] (1542) to fight the abuses against the indigenous peoples under the encomienda system. Las Casas' testimonial writing illustrates how early modern narratives could act as a political tool and thus adds to the current interest and debate about whether minds can be changed through narratives. Barbara Simerka (this volume) explores how the concept of empathy is vital to examine the narrative strategies employed by Las Casas. She also shows how an empathy approach to his work is a powerful pedagogical tool to reflect on the ways that teachers avoid an emotion-centered discussion of literature in favor of an "objective" perspective.

MIND AND CULTURE IN EARLY MODERNITY

This section deals with a series of studies that could be lumped together under the banner of "cognitive historicism," defined in the Spanish realm as the interrelation of literary texts and ideas about the mind that existed in the sociocultural context in which they were produced.[29]

27. In cognitive studies, the contours of the topic of whether or how empathy can lead to pro-social behavior are still hotly debated. Part of this line of research relates to whether narrative empathy can also lead to pro-social behavior (on this controversy, see Keen). In early modern Spanish studies, see Simerka, "Mirror" and this volume; Williamsen.

28. See María Antonia Garcés' book, *Cervantes in Algiers*.

29. For other descriptions of cognitive historicism as understood and practiced in British literature, see Richardson and Spolsky.

Science and Literature: Permeable Discourses

One of the characteristics of this area of research is that literary and "scientific" texts are viewed as permeable discourses that both reflect and shape the culture of the time. In the early modern period, the notion of science is somewhat problematic in that our current view of literature and science as separate and easily distinguishable entities is not applicable to an era in which science, as we view it today, does not yet exist.[30] Indeed, as Javier Puerto states in his book *La fuerza de Fierabrás: Medicina, ciencia y terapéutica en tiempos del* Quijote, literature and science in the early modern period should not be seen as separate realms. Natural philosophers looked into literature for examples and literary authors drew material from "scientific" treatises. He adds: "No había tanta distancia, entre otras cosas, porque todavía el lenguaje era común. De esa manera se puede hacer un tratado con las ideas científicas de Lope de Vega, de Quevedo o de la *Celestina*" (35–36) ["There was not as much distance, since the language was still shared. Hence, one can create a treatise with the scientific thought of Lope de Vega, Quevedo, or *Celestina*"].[31] The dichotomy between science and literature is a post–early modern creation and science per se would only come about in the Enlightenment (35). For Isabel Jaén, a cognitive historicist scholar, "both Renaissance medical philosophers such as [Juan Luis] Vives and [Juan] Huarte [de San Juan] and fiction writers such as Cervantes shared an empirical agenda whose purpose was to understand and illuminate the workings of the human soul, the mind" ("Cervantes and the Cognitive" 72). In sum, an early modern cognitive historicist approach to literature is based on recuperating the view that literature and "science" share the common goal of understanding human nature (i.e., the essence of Renaissance thinking) and thus helps us study early modern Hispanic culture without artificially separating epistemological realms.

The *Matière* of the Exploration of Mind

In the Renaissance, when the body and the brain become important objects of study, what is not perceptible to the eye, what is not directly observable, increasingly draws interest. The understanding of human nature is turning inward; the inside of the cultural *matière* constitutes the next

---

30. See also the introduction to this volume.
31. All translations are mine.

frontier of knowledge (as illustrated by the work of physician and anatomist Andreas Vesalius). As Mary Thomas Crane reminds us in *Losing Touch With Nature* (2014), it is a transition period in which the intuitive connection with nature and the Aristotelian legacy were slowly fading.

The notion of mind was developing during this period, as reflected also in the language: in Spanish in early modernity, *celebro* (or *cerebro*) referred to the organ, the brain, inside the *casco* [skull] or *cabeça* [head].[32] While cerebro/celebro were commonly used terms in the first part of the early modern period, the noun *mente* [mind] was starting to appear,[33] although not fully in its modern acceptation. Rather, in its early usage, *mente* was sometimes used in a religious sense, as in *mente divina* (i.e., synonymous with *alma divina* [divine soul]). Later on, in the seventeenth century, its meaning would shed its religious connotation and move closer to its modern acceptation, being equated with the capacity of judgment.[34]

To capture this notion of mind in constant flux in the early modern era, cognitive historicism seeks to explore the ideas about the mind as reflected in a variety of discourses (e.g., treatises, manuals, prose fiction, and poetry) as well as any "secondhand" accounts of behaviors and performances revealing expressions of mind (e.g., testimonies, chronicles). Indeed, the exploration of the intangibles in the culture under investigation cannot be dismissed on the grounds that there is no tangible, physical trace or "proof" that could have "enshrined" thought. Thought, for cognitive historicist scholars, is manifested through any cultural expression: artifacts, performances, as well as behaviors, and thus their goal is to look for zones of convergence in the cultural masse where shared visions of the mind arise. These loci of convergence are of course transient and historically contingent (i.e., situated within an environment, a place, a community of people, a socio-political dynamic, and so forth). "Historical" dimensions will also alter, filter, or taint the exploration of mind and thus represent as so many coordinates. In many ways, the cognitive historicist can be compared to a cultural archeologist of the mind who needs to gather as many perspectives as she or he can (literary, scientific, philosophical, historical, political, testimonial, and so forth) to make sense of early modern culture, to penetrate its conception of mind.

32. See Covarrubias' *Tesoro de lengua castellana o española* [Treasure of the Castilian (or Spanish) Language] (1611), pp. 208v (for "casco") and 269 (for "celebro").
33. Based on a search in *Corpus del Nuevo Diccionario Histórico del Español* (s.XII-1975) [Corpus of the New Spanish Dictionary (12c-1975)].
34. See, for example, "mente" in *Diccionario de Autoridades—Tomo IV* [Dictionary of Authorities] (1734).

Defining the Relationship Between Contemporaneous and Contemporary Science

The cognitive historicist approach in its *sensu stricto* strand relies mainly on *contemporaneous* science[35]—that is, the focus is primarily on the ideas about the mind as reflected in literary texts, treatises, and so forth of the era in question. Modern cognitive scientific paradigms can help define the scope and orientation of the research: new ways to think about the mind can inspire novel ways to explore the interface between mind and literature in early modernity. They can also help the scholar discuss and appraise the *contemporaneous* science (e.g., when studying how early modern subjects imagined brain functioning, knowing about the current science on brain anatomy helps the scholar explain and evaluate early modern views). In the cognitive historicist approach modern science may or may not be explicitly apparent; when not included in a study, however, it will often constitute the background knowledge that will guide the cognitive literary scholar in her or his exploration.

It is important to specify that cognitive historicism as described above is a slight departure from how other scholars have viewed it.[36] Although their conception is not antonymic to the one proposed here—nor are they mutually exclusive—the difference lies in the place reserved to the cognitive ideas about the mind that circulated in the era being studied. "Historicizing," within the frame presented here, means making sure that the cognitive conceptions of the epoch are always part of the study. In the field of cognitive approaches to early modern Spanish literature, this position is increasingly being integrated and holds much promise as we attempt to delve into the interrelation of mind, body, society, and culture.[37]

EPILOGUE: COGNITIVE APPROACHES IN THE EARLY MODERN CLASSROOM

Finally, I would like to highlight how research in cognitive and neurocognitive science is inspiring a group of early modern Spanish scholars to take

35. Studies in this line of inquiry include in early modern Spanish studies Jaén, "Cervantes and the Cognitive" and "Cervantes on Human"; Schmitz. From outside the field of cognitive literary studies per se, other scholars have (or are) engaged in related research projects. These include Soufas and Folger. See also, from a history-of-science perspective, López-Muñoz, Álamo, and García-García; from a medical humanities perspective, Bravo Vega; Carrera, "Lovesickness" and "*Pasión*"; Wagschal, "Medicine."
36. See Richardson (Chapter 1); Spolsky; Zunshine, *Introduction* 61–63.
37. See Carrera, "Embodied," as well as Domínguez, Cruz Petersen, Caballero, and Schmitz in this volume.

the pedagogy of early modern literature in new directions. For instance, Catherine Connor explores, in this volume, how experimental techniques used by scientists in labs to measure empathy (such as the Davis Interpersonal Reactivity Index) can help students assess their own empathic levels and compare them to those of their peers. This, in turn, permits them to realize how it can affect their own interpretation of artistic and literary works such as *Don Quixote*. In Connor's view, engaging with literary texts provides students with an opportunity to challenge their own biocultural boundaries and grow as persons. This perspective is framed in the wider debate about the extent to which literature can elicit empathy and lead to pro-social action, led, among other scholars, by Suzanne Keen and Frank Hakemulder.[38] One of the latest manifestations of this line of research has been the widely publicized study "Reading Literary Fiction Improves Theory of Mind" by David Comer Kidd and Emanuele Castano.

Also on the topic of empathy and literature, Barbara Simerka (in the study included in this volume and mentioned earlier in this essay) questions and ultimately rejects the "standard" pedagogical praxis that advocates for a nonemotional (read "rational") discussion of Bartolomé de las Casas' texts. She claims that "interrupting" students' emotional responses can significantly affect a literature professor's ability to foment empathy and ultimately reduce prejudice toward the other.

Finally, at the intersection of the cognitive historicist approach and pedagogy, Jaén shows how we can teach Cervantes' account of cognition in the *Quixote* in parallel with early modern medical philosophical treatises by articulating a course around the themes of "(1) psychiatry (the senses, perception and delusion, emotional imbalance), (2) differential psychology (typology of wits, humoral theory, gender difference), and (3) human development (from animal to rational, the cognitive faculties)" ("Teaching" 110).

FINAL REMARKS

It is important to consider the literary and "scientific" production in the early modern period as a transnational phenomenon. As Lucien Febvre and Henri Jean Martin note: "Literature and learning were still international in the 16th century despite the decline of Latin. The books published in the various national languages could expect to be translated into many languages, as we have seen, if they were worthy of interest. But

---

38. See Keen's *Empathy and the Novel* and Hakemulder's *The Moral Laboratory*.

little by little the fragmentation of the world of letters began to take effect" (332). In this sense, cognitive literary studies, being an endeavor that includes scholars working in a variety of literary traditions, can become instrumental in today's academic world not only in promoting multidisciplinarity (and diversity of perspectives within disciplines) but also communication and exchange among the scholars from those different traditions, such as Spanish or English, that are heavily invested in early modern studies.

WORKS CITED

Barroso Castro, José. "Theory of Mind and the Conscience of *El casamiento enga-ñoso.*" *Theory of Mind and Literature.* Ed. Paula Leverage, Howard Mancing, Richard Schweickert, and Jennifer Marston William. West Lafayette: Purdue UP, 2011, 289–303.

Barsalou, Lawrence W. "Grounded Cognition: Past, Present, and Future." *Topics in Cognitive Science* 2 (2010): 716–24.

Batson, Daniel C. "These Things Called Empathy: Eight Related but Distinct Phenomena." *The Social Neuroscience of Empathy.* Ed. Jean Decety and William Ickes. Cambridge: MIT P, 2009, 3–15.

Bravo Vega, Julián. "El *Quijote* médico." *Anales Cervantinos* 41 (2009): 105–15.

Butte, George. *I Know that You Know that I Know: Narrating Subjects from* Moll Flanders *to* Marnie. Columbus: Ohio State UP, 2004.

Byrne, Richard W., and Andrew Whiten, eds. *Machiavellian Intelligence: Social Expertise and the Evolution of Intellect in Monkeys, Apes, and Humans.* Oxford: Clarendon P, 1988.

Canavaggio, Jean. *Cervantes.* Trans. from the French by J. R. Jones. New York: Norton, 1990.

Carrera, Elena. "Embodied Cognition and Empathy in Miguel de Cervantes' *El celoso extremeño.*" *Hispania* 97.1 (March 2014): 113–24.

Carrera, Elena. "Lovesickness and the Therapy of Desire: Aquinas, *cancionero* Poetry, and Teresa of Avila's 'Muero porque no muero.'" *Bulletin of Hispanic Studies* 86.6 (2009): 729–42.

Carrera, Elena. "*Pasión* and *afección* in Teresa de Avila and Francisco de Osuna." *Bulletin of Spanish Studies* 84.2 (2007): 175–91.

Childers, William. "Cervantes in Moriscolandia." *Cervantes: Bulletin of the Cervantes Society of America* 32.1 (2012): 277–90.

Clark, Andy, and David J. Chalmers. "The Extended Mind." *Analysis* 58.1 (January 1998): 7–19.

Connor (Connor-Swietlicki), Catherine. "Beyond Cognition: Don Quijote and Other Embodied Minds." *Cognitive Cervantes.* Ed. Julien Simon, Barbara Simerka, and Howard Mancing. Spec. cluster of essays of *Cervantes: Bulletin of the Cervantes Society of America* 32.1 (2012): 231–61.

Connor (Connor-Swietlicki), Catherine. "Bridging the Performance Gap: The Body, Cognitive Theory, and *Comedia* Studies." *Bulletin of the Comediantes* 55.2 (2003 [2004]): 11–53.

Connor (Connor-Swietlicki), Catherine. "Creative Cognition for Staging." *Comedia Performance: Journal of the Association for Hispanic Classical Theater* 4.1 (2007): 67–96.

Connor (Connor-Swietlicki), Catherine. "Embodying Rape and Violence: Your Mirror Neurons and 2RC Teatro's *Alcalde de Zalamea*." *Comedia Performance: Journal of the Association for Hispanic Classical Theater* 7.1 (Spring 2010): 9–52.

Connor (Connor-Swietlicki), Catherine. "The Scientific Arts of Theater: The Bio-Social World-Theater with Examples from Lope, Calderón, and Others." *Bulletin of the Comediantes* 58.2 (2006): 457–67.

Connor (Connor-Swietlicki), Catherine. "Seeing Like Sancho: Embodiment, Cognition and Cervantine Creativity." *Cervantes y su mundo III*. Ed. A. Robert Lauer and Kurt Reichenberger. Kassel, Germany: Reichenberger, 2005, 61–79.

Connor (Connor-Swietlicki), Catherine. "Why We Don't Get No Respect and What We Are Doing about It; Or, the Rapprochement of Body and Mind and the Return of *Comedia* Studies." *Bulletin of the Comediantes* 56.1 (2004): 153–61.

Corpus del Nuevo Diccionario Histórico del Español (version 3.0). *Real Academia de la Lengua*. Web. June 15, 2015. <http://web.frl.es/CNDHE/>.

Covarrubias Horozco, Sebastián de. *Tesoro de la lengua castellana o española*. Madrid, 1611. *Fondo Antiguo*. Web. June 15, 2015. <http://fondosdigitales.us.es/fondos/>.

Crane, Mary Thomas. *Losing Touch with Nature: Literature and the New Science in Sixteenth-Century England*. Baltimore: Johns Hopkins UP, 2014.

Cruz Petersen, Elizabeth M. "Designed for an Experience: The Natural Architecture of *Corrales*." *Comedia Performance* 7.1 (2010): 170–99.

Decety, Jean. "Why is Empathy so Important?" Introduction. *Empathy: From Bench to Bedside*. Ed. Jean Decety. Cambridge: MIT P, 2012, vii-ix.

Dennett, Daniel C. "The Intentional Stance in Theory and Practice." *Machiavellian Intelligence: Social Expertise and the Evolution of Intellect in Monkeys, Apes, and Humans*. Ed. Richard W. Byrne and Andrew Whiten. Oxford: Clarendon P, 1988, 180–210.

"El qué dirán." *Diccionario de la lengua española*. 23rd ed. 2014. *Real Academia Española*. Web. June 15, 2015. <http://http://lema.rae.es/drae/>.

Febvre, Lucien, and Henri-Jean Martin. *The Coming of the Book: The Impact of Printing 1450–1800*. Trans. David Gerard. New York: Verso, 1997.

Folger, Robert. *Images in Mind: Lovesickness, Spanish Sentimental Fiction and Don Quixote*. Chapel Hill: U of North Carolina, 2002.

Gabora, Liane, Eleanor Rosch, and Diederik Aerts. "Toward an Ecological Theory of Concepts." *Ecological Psychology* 20.1 (2008): 84–116.

Gallagher, Shaun. "The Practice of Mind: Theory, Simulation, or Primary Interaction?" *Journal of Consciousness Studies* 8.5–7 (2001): 83–108.

Gallagher, Shaun, and Daniel D. Hutto. "Understanding Others through Primary Interaction and Narrative Practice." *The Shared Mind: Perspectives on Intersubjectivity*. Ed. Jordan Zlatev. Amsterdam: John Benjamins, 2008, 17–38.

Garcés, María Antonia. *Cervantes in Algiers: A Captive's Tale*. Nashville: Vanderbilt UP, 2002.

Goldman, Alvin I. "Interpretation Psychologized." *Mind and Language* 4.3 (1989): 161–85.

Gopnik, Alison, and Andrew N. Meltzoff. *Words, Thoughts, and Theories*. Cambridge: MIT P, 1997.

Gordon, Robert M. "Folk Psychology as Simulation." *Mind and Language* 1.2 (1986): 158–71.

Greer, Margaret R. "Mirror Neurons, Theatrical Mirrors and the Honor Code." *Anuario Calderoniano: Acal* 5 (2012): 85–100.

Hakemulder, Jèmeljan (Frank). *The Moral Laboratory: Experiments Examining the Effects of Reading Literature on Social Perception and Moral Self-Conce*pt. Amsterdam: John Benjamins, 2000.

Hammond, Meghan M., and Sue J. Kim. Introduction. *Rethinking Empathy through Literature*. Ed. Meghan M. Hammond and Sue J. Kim. New York: Routledge, 2014, 1–18.

Hart, F. Elizabeth. "The Epistemology of Cognitive Literary Studies." *Philosophy and Literature* 25.2 (2001): 314–34.

Hart, F. Elizabeth. "1500–1620: Reading, Consciousness, and Romance in the Sixteenth Century." *The Emergence of Mind: Representations of Consciousness in Narrative Discourse in English*. Ed. David Herman. Lincoln: U of Nebraska P, 2011, 103–31.

Hayles, Katharine N. "Constrained Constructivism: Locating Scientific Inquiry in the Theater of Representation." *Realism and Representation: Essays on the Problem of Realism in Relation to Science, Literature, and Culture*. Ed. George Levine. Madison: U of Wisconsin P, 1993, 27–43.

Humphrey, Nicholas K. "The Social Function of Intellect." *Growing Points in Ethology*. Ed. Patrick P. G. Bateson and Robert A. Hinde. Cambridge: Cambridge UP, 1976, 303–17.

Jaén, Isabel. "Cervantes and the Cognitive Ideas of his Time: Mind and Development in *Don Quixote*." *Cognitive Cervantes*. Ed. Julien Simon, Barbara Simerka, and Howard Mancing. Spec. cluster of essays of *Cervantes: Bulletin of the Cervantes Society of America* 32.1 (2012): 71–98.

Jaén, Isabel. "Cervantes on Human Development: *Don Quixote* and Renaissance Cognitive Psychology." *Don Quixote: Interdisciplinary Connections*. Ed. Matthew D. Warshawsky and James A. Parr. Newark: Juan de la Cuesta, 2013, 35–57.

Jaén, Isabel. "Empathy and Gender Activism in Early Modern Spain: María de Zayas' *Amorous and Exemplary Novels*." *Rethinking Empathy through Literature*. Ed. Meghan M. Hammond and Sue J. Kim. New York: Routledge, 2014, 189–201.

Jaén (Jaén-Portillo), Isabel. "Literary Consciousness: Fictional Minds, *Real* Implications." *Selected Papers from The 22nd International Literature and Psychology Conference, June 29—July 4, 2005*. Ed. Norman Holland. IPSA. Web. June 15, 2015. <http://www.clas.ufl.edu/ipsa/2005/proc/portillo.pdf>.

Jaén, Isabel. "Teaching Cervantes' *Don Quixote* from a Cognitive Historicist Perspective." *Interdisciplinary Literary Studies* 16.1 (2014): 110–26.

Jaén, Isabel, and Julien Jacques Simon. Introduction. *Cognitive Literary Studies: Current Themes and New Directions*. Ed. Isabel Jaén and Julien Jacques Simon. Austin: U of Texas P, 2012. 1–9.

Keen, Suzanne. *Empathy and the Novel*. New York: Oxford UP, 2007.

Kidd, David Comer, and Emanuele Castano. "Reading Literary Fiction Improves Theory of Mind." *Science* 342 (Oct. 18, 2013): 377–80.

LaFrenière, Peter J. "The Ontogeny of Tactical Deception in Humans." *Machiavellian Intelligence: Social Expertise and the Evolution of Intellect in Monkeys, Apes, and Humans*. Ed. Richard W. Byrne and Andrew Whiten. Oxford: Clarendon P, 1988, 238–52.

Leverage, Paula, Howard Mancing, Richard Schweickert, and Jennifer Marston William. Introduction. *Theory of Mind and Literature*. Ed. Paula Leverage, Howard Mancing, Richard Schweickert, and Jennifer Marston William. West Lafayette: Purdue UP, 2011, 1–11.

López-Muñoz, Francisco, Cecilio Álamo, and Pilar García-García. "Locos y dementes en la literatura cervantina: A propósito de las fuentes médicas de Cervantes en materia neuropsiquiátrica." *Revista de Neurología* 46.8 (2008): 489–501.

Mancing, Howard. "Against Dualisms: A Response to Henry Sullivan." *Cervantes: Bulletin of the Cervantes Society of America* 19.1 (1999): 158–76.

Mancing, Howard. "Cervantes as Narrator of *Don Quijote*." *Cervantes: Bulletin of the Cervantes Society of America* 23.1 (2003): 117–40.

Mancing, Howard. *The Cervantes Encyclopedia*. Vol. 2. Westport: Greenwood P, 2004.

Mancing, Howard. "Embodied Cognitive Science and the Study of Literature." *Cognitive Cervantes*. Ed. Julien J. Simon, Barbara Simerka, and Howard Mancing. Spec. cluster of essays of *Cervantes: Bulletin of the Cervantes Society of America* 32.1 (2012): 25–69.

Mancing, Howard. "James Parr's Theory of Mind." *Critical Reflections on Golden Age Spanish Literature in Honor of James A. Parr*. Ed. Barbara Simerka and Amy R. Williamsen. Lewisburg: Bucknell UP, 2006, 125–43.

Mancing, Howard. "The Mind of a Pícaro: Lázaro de Tormes." *Cognition, Literature, and History*. Ed. Mark J. Bruhn and Donald R. Wehrs. New York: Routledge, 2014, 174–89.

Mancing, Howard. "Prototypes of Genre in Cervantes' *Novelas ejemplares*." *Cervantes: Bulletin of the Cervantes Society of America* 20.2 (2000): 127–50.

Mancing, Howard. "Sancho Panza's Theory of Mind." *Theory of Mind and Literature*. Ed. Paula Leverage, Howard Mancing, Richard Schweickert, and Jennifer Marston William. West Lafayette: Purdue UP, 2011, 123–32.

Mancing, Howard. "See the Play, Read the Book." *Performance and Cognition: Theatre Studies and the Cognitive Turn*. Ed. Bruce McConachie and F. Elizabeth Hart. New York: Routledge, 2006, 189–206.

"Mente." Entry 1. *Diccionario de Autoridades—Tomo IV (1726–39). Real Academia de la Lengua*. Web. June 15, 2015. <http://web.frl.es/DA.html/>.

Palmer, Alan. *Social Minds in the Novel*. Columbus: Ohio State UP, 2010.

Phillips, Natalie M. "Literary Neuroscience and History of Mind: An Interdisciplinary fMRI Study of Attention and Jane Austen." *The Oxford Handbook of Cognitive Literary Studies*. Ed. Lisa Zunshine. Oxford: Oxford UP, 2015, 55–81.

Premack, David, and Guy Woodruff. "Does the Chimpanzee Have a Theory of Mind?" *Behavioral and Brain Sciences* 1.4 (1978): 515–26.

Puerto, Javier. *La fuerza de Fierabrás: Medicina, ciencia y terapéutica en tiempos del Quijote*. N.p.: Editorial Just in Time, 2005.

Reed, Cory. "'¿Qué rumor es ése?': Embodied Agency and Representational Hunger in *Don Quijote* I.20." *Cognitive Cervantes*. Ed. Julien Simon, Barbara Simerka, and Howard Mancing. Spec. cluster of essays of *Cervantes: Bulletin of the Cervantes Society of America* 32.1 (2012): 99–124.

Richardson, Alan. *The Neural Sublime: Cognitive Theories and Romantic Texts*. Baltimore: Johns Hopkins UP, 2010.

Rosch, Eleanor. "Principles of Categorization." *Cognition and Categorization*. Ed. Eleanor Rosch and Barbara B. Lloyd. Hillsdale: Erlbaum, 1978, 27–48.

Schmitz, Ryan. "Cervantes' Language of the Heart in the *Novelas ejemplares* and *Don Quijote*." *Cervantes: Bulletin of the Cervantes Society of America* 32.2 (Fall 2012): 171–95.

Shamay-Tsoory, Simone G. "Empathic Processing: Its Cognitive and Affective Dimensions and Neuroanatomical Basis." *The Social Neuroscience of Empathy*. Ed. Jean Decety and William Ickes. Cambridge: MIT P, 2009, 215–32.

Simerka, Barbara. "Afterword: The Future of Cognitive Literary Studies." *Cognitive Cervantes*. Ed. Julien J. Simon, Barbara Simerka, and Howard Mancing. Spec. cluster of essays of *Cervantes: Bulletin of the Cervantes Society of America* 32.1 (2012): 263–75.

Simerka, Barbara. "Cognitive Theories of Genre: The Prototype Effect and Early Modern Spanish Tragedy." *Bulletin of the Comediantes* 64.2 (2012): 153–70.

Simerka, Barbara. *Knowing Subjects: Cognitive Cultural Theory and Early Modern Spanish Literature*. West Lafayette: Purdue UP, 2013.

Simerka, Barbara. "Mirror Neurons, Subjectivity, and Social Cognition in *Don Quixote*." *Don Quixote: Interdisciplinary Connections*. Ed. Matthew D. Warshawsky and James A. Parr. Newark: Juan de la Cuesta, 2013, 59–82.

Simon, Julien J. "Celestina, Heteroglossia, and Theory of Mind: The Rise of the Early-Modern Discourse." *Proceedings of the 2008 International Conference in Literature and Psychology*. Lisbon: Instituto Superior de Psicologia Aplicada, 2009, 119–26.

Simon, Julien J. "The Intersection of Mind and *Don Quixote*: Overview and Prospects." *Don Quixote: Interdisciplinary Connections*. Ed. Matthew D. Warshawsky and James A. Parr. Newark: Juan de la Cuesta, 2013, 19–34.

Simon, Julien J. "Introduction to 'Cognitive Cervantes': Integrating Mind and Cervantes' Texts." *Cognitive Cervantes*. Ed. Julien J. Simon, Barbara Simerka, and Howard Mancing. Spec. cluster of essays of *Cervantes: Bulletin of the Cervantes Society of America* 32.1 (2012): 11–23.

Simon, Julien J. "Schema Theory, Prototype Theory, and the *Novela Dialogada*: Toward a Perspectivist and Dynamic View of Literary Genres." *Laberinto: An Electronic Journal of Early Modern Hispanic Literatures and Culture* 7 (2014): 64–90. Web. June 15, 2015.

Sinding, Michael. "After Definitions: Genre, Categories and Cognitive Science." *Genre* 35.2 (2002): 181–220.

Sinding, Michael. "Blending in a *baciyelmo*: *Don Quixote*'s Genre Blending and the Invention of the Novel." *Blending and the Study of Narrative: Approaches and Applications*. Ed. Ralf Schneider and Marcus Hartner. Berlin: De Gruyter, 2012, 147–71.

Sinding, Michael. "'A Sermon in the Midst of a Smutty Tale:' Blending in Genres of Speech, Writing, and Literature." *Cognitive Literary Studies: Current Themes and New Directions*. Ed. Isabel Jaén and Julien Jacques Simon. Austin: U of Texas P, 2012, 145–61.

Soufas, Teresa S. *Melancholy and the Secular Mind in Spanish Golden Age Literature*. Columbia: U of Missouri P, 1990.

Spolsky, Ellen. "Cognitive Literary Historicism: A Response to Adler and Gross." *Poetics Today* 24.2 (Summer 2003): 161–83.

Steen, Gerard. "Genres of Discourse and the Definition of Literature." *Discourse Processes* 28.2 (1999): 109–20.

Strayer, Janet. "Affective and Cognitive Perspectives on Empathy." *Empathy and Its Development*. Ed. Nancy Eisenberg and Janet Strayer. Cambridge: Cambridge UP, 1987, 218–44.

Swales, John M. *Genre Analysis: English in Academic and Research Settings*. Cambridge: Cambridge UP, 1990.

Varela, Francisco J., Evan Thompson, and Eleanor Rosch. *The Embodied Mind: Cognitive Science and Human Experience*. Cambridge: MIT P, 1991.

Wagschal, Steven. "Medicine, Morality, Madness: Competing Models of Insanity in Calderón's *El mayor monstruo del mundo*." *Revista Canadiense de Estudios Hispánicos* 32.2 (Winter 2008): 227–45.

Wagschal, Steven. "The Smellscape of *Don Quixote*: A Cognitive Approach." *Cognitive Cervantes*. Ed. Julien Simon, Barbara Simerka, and Howard Mancing. Spec. cluster of essays of *Cervantes: Bulletin of the Cervantes Society of America* 32.1 (2012): 125–62.

Wehrs, Donald R. "Affective Dissonance and Literary Mediation: Emotion Processing, Ethical Signification, and Aesthetic Autonomy in Cervantes' Art of the Novel." *Cognitive Cervantes*. Ed. Julien Simon, Barbara Simerka, and Howard Mancing. Spec. cluster of essays of *Cervantes: Bulletin of the Cervantes Society of America* 32 1. (2012): 201–30.

Williamsen, Amy R. "Quantum Quixote: Embodying Empathy in the Borderlands." *Cervantes: Bulletin of the Cervantes Society of America* 31.1 (2011): 171–87.

Zunshine, Lisa. "Approaching Cao Xueqin's *The Story of the Stone* (*Honglou meng* 紅樓夢) from a Cognitive Perspective." *The Oxford Handbook of Cognitive Literary Studies*. Ed. Lisa Zunshine. Oxford: Oxford UP, 2015, 176–96.

Zunshine, Lisa, ed. *Introduction to Cognitive Cultural Studies*. Baltimore: Johns Hopkins UP, 2010.

Zunshine, Lisa. "Introduction: What Is Cognitive Cultural Studies?" *Introduction to Cognitive Cultural Studies*. Ed. Lisa Zunshine. Baltimore: Johns Hopkins UP, 2010, 1–33.

Zunshine, Lisa. "Sociocognitive Complexity." *NOVEL: A Forum on Fiction* 45.1 (2012): 13–18.

Zunshine, Lisa. "Why Jane Austen Was Different and Why We May Need Cognitive Science to See It." *Style* 41.3 (2007): 275–99.

Zunshine, Lisa. *Why We Read Fiction: Theory of Mind and the Novel*. Columbus: Ohio State UP, 2006.

SECTION II

The Creation of Self

CHAPTER 2

Embodied Cognition and Autopoiesis in *Don Quixote*

HOWARD MANCING

EMBODIED COGNITION

In his book *Embodiment and Cognitive Science* (2006), psychologist Raymond Gibbs defines what he calls the "embodiment premise":

> People's subjective, felt experiences of their bodies in action provide part of the fundamental grounding for language and thought. Cognition is what occurs when the body engages the physical, cultural world and must be studied in terms of the dynamical interactions between people and the environment. Human language and thought emerge from recurring patterns of embodied activity that constrain ongoing intelligent behavior. We must not assume cognition to be purely internal, symbolic, computational, and disembodied, but seek out the gross and detailed ways that language and thought are inextricably shaped by embodied action. (9)

This sort of definition of cognition as embodied was impossible as little as a quarter of a century ago when, at least in the humanities and many of the social sciences, we talked and wrote of socially constructed subject positions. But one of the great contributions of the cognitive sciences has been to remind us that we are evolved animals, with an imaginative mind-brain that enables us to be unique, individual, contextualized agents who use language as a tool in our complex social relationships.

But what does that have to do with *Don Quixote*? Quite simply, one of the tenets of all cognitive approaches to literature is that we deal with literary characters as if they were real human beings. Marisa Bortolussi and Peter Dixon, for example, write that "literary characters are processed as if they were real people, and real people are processed in terms analogous to the categories brought to bear on the interpretation of literary characters" (140). Leading theorists and critics like Alan Palmer, Lisa Zunshine, and Suzanne Keen make the same argument.

Let me be clear: no one is saying that literary characters *are* real human beings; no one is that naïve. What is being said is that we have to think of and talk and write of characters *as if* they were real. That is, we have to ascribe to literary characters a Theory of Mind (ToM), so that we can talk about what they are doing, feeling, and thinking.[1] In the field of cognitive literary studies, we have in the last decade or so taken advantage of the concept of ToM when dealing with literary characters in order explicitly to discuss characters' thoughts and feelings. Here is Sanjida O'Connell's definition of ToM:

> the mechanism we use to understand what is going on in other people's heads. How we react to one another socially is the most important aspect of our lives. Without an understanding of what people think, what they want and what they believe about the world, it is impossible to operate in any society. Theory of Mind is the name given to this understanding of others. It is the basic necessity of humanity and is understood the same way the world over. (2)

But a ToM necessarily implies what we might call a "Theory of Body" (ToB). If we treat literary characters as if they had minds and thoughts we must necessarily also treat them as if they had physical bodies, for there is no thought without embodiment. Philosopher Michelle Maiese makes it explicit that the mind and the body are inseparable: "Building on the claim that the mind is essentially embodied and enactive, I will argue that processes of so-called 'mind-reading' and 'body-reading' are inherently intertwined and that understanding other people's minds and behavior relies necessarily on the desire-based emotive, essentially embodied interaction process itself" (151).

---

1. O'Connell's *Mindreading* (1997) is perhaps the best single introduction to Theory of Mind, but *Mindblindness* (1995) by Baron-Cohen is also fundamental. For the importance of Theory of Mind to the study of literature, see Zunshine's *Why We Read Fiction* (2006) and *Theory of Mind and Literature* (2011) edited by Leverage et al. See also *Literature and the Brain* (2009) by Holland and *Why Do We Care about Literary Characters?* (2010) by Vermeule.

So when we read Cervantes' novel, we have to think of Don Quixote as if he were embodied, and the same goes for all the other characters. But that is not very hard to do. After all, in the very first chapter there is a brief and partial description of the protagonist: "de complexión recia, seco de carnes, enjuto de rostro" (I.1.114) ["his complexion was weathered, his flesh scrawny, his face gaunt" (19)].[2] That may not provide many details, but I think that all readers of the novel already begin to form a mental image of Don Quixote; that is, a mental image of his body. Throughout the novel the importance of Don Quixote's embodied cognition is abundantly evident. Let me discuss but a single classic example that plays out over a series of chapters in the novel: Part I, ch. 8–11.

After routing the friars of San Benito, Don Quixote talks with the woman riding in a coach, offering her his services. The woman's Basque squire interrupts the conversation and insults Don Quixote, which leads to a scene of singular combat between them, the sort of scene that Don Quixote remembers so well from his romances of chivalry. As the fight gets under way the Basque strikes first: "dio el vizcaíno una gran cuchillada a don Quijote encima de un hombro, por encima de la rodela, que, a dársela sin defensa la abriera hasta la cintura" (I.8.174) ["struck a great blow with his sword to his shoulder, and if it had not been protected by armor, he would have opened it to the waist" (64)]. The hyperbolic description of the blow reproduces exactly the exaggeration common in the romances of chivalry, where almost every blow is potentially mortal. But it does have its effect: Don Quixote feels "la pesadumbre de aquel desaforado golpe" (I.8.174) ["the pain of that enormous blow" (64)]. Don Quixote invokes his beloved Dulcinea, and then both men raise their swords and are about to strike what are intended to be fatal blows—when the manuscript comes to an end and the author has to search for another account of the story.

The next chapter begins with the great scene—again a perfect parody of the pseudo-history romances of chivalry—where the narrator locates in Toledo the manuscript written by Cide Hamete Benengeli, which will be the historical source for the remainder of the novel. The first thing noted is a page on which the figures of Don Quixote, the Basque, Rocinante, and Sancho Panza are all drawn, again reminding the reader that these characters have bodies and that the reader is to imagine seeing them. This new manuscript seems to begin exactly where the previous source left off with

2. All citations from *Don Quixote* are from the edition by Allen and refer to part, chapter, and page. The translations are from Grossman, citing page only.

the two combatants raising their swords with anger. The first to strike is the Basque:

> Puestas y levantadas en alto las cortadoras espadas de los dos valerosos combatientes, no parecía sino que estaban amenazando al cielo, a la tierra y al abismo: tal era el denuedo y continente que tenían. Y el primero que fue a descargar el golpe fue el colérico vizcaíno, el cual fue dado con tanta fuerza y tanta furia, que, a no volvérsele la espada en el camino, aquel solo golpe fuera bastante para dar fin a su rigurosa contienda y a todas las aventuras de nuestro caballero; mas la buena suerte, que para mayores cosas le tenía guardado, torció la espada de su contrario, de modo que, aunque le acertó en el hombro izquierdo, no le hizo otro daño que desarmarle todo aquel lado, llevándole, de camino, gran parte de la celada, con la mitad de la oreja; que todo ello con espantosa ruina vino al suelo, dejándole muy maltrecho. (I.9.182–83)

> With the sharp-edged swords of the two valiant and enraged combatants held and raised on high, they seemed to threaten heaven, earth, and the abyss: such was their boldness and bearing. The first to strike a blow was the choleric Basque, and he delivered it with so much force and fury that if his sword had not turned on its way down, that single blow would have been enough to end this fierce combat and all the adventures of our knight; but good fortune, which had greater things in store for Don Quixote, twisted the sword of his adversary, so that although it struck his left shoulder, it did no more than tear through the armor along that side, taking with it as it passed a good part of his helmet and half an ear, both of which, in fearful ruin, fell to the ground, leaving him in a very sad state. (69)

Note that the hyperbolic and grandiose chivalric rhetoric of the passage is undercut by the ironic brief mention of the one serious effect of the Basque's blow—the severing of half of Don Quixote's ear—at the end of the long sentence. Don Quixote of course strikes back and is about to kill his opponent, but others intervene to prevent that outcome. After the matter is settled Quixote and Sancho ride off, discussing the event, with the knight boasting of his prowess.

And here we must recall what Don Quixote had said a short while earlier in the previous chapter, after the encounter with the windmill-giants: "y si no me quejo del dolor es porque no es dado a los caballeros andantes quejarse de herida alguna, aunque se le salgan las tripas por ella" (I.8.169) ["and if I do not complain about the pain, it is because it is not the custom of knights errant to complain about any wound, even if their innards are spilling out because of it" (60)]. At that point, of course, Sancho observes that, as long as the rules of chivalry do not also apply to him, he will indeed complain of pain: "De mí sé decir que me he de quejar del más pequeño dolor que tenga" (I.8.169) ["As for me, I can say that I'll complain about the smallest pain I have" (60)]. Sancho keeps his word and complains repeatedly in scenes like that of the beating he receives from the Galician drovers (I.15), the brawl in the inn of Juan Palomeque and the balm of Fierabrás (I.16), his blanketing as they try to leave the inn (I.17), and many others.

But, to return to the aftermath of the battle between Don Quixote and the Basque squire, Sancho worries about Don Quixote's loss of blood: "Lo que le ruego a vuestra merced es que se cure; que le va mucha sangre de esa oreja" (I.10.187) ["What I beg of your grace is that we treat your wounds; a lot of blood is coming out of that ear" (71)]. Don Quixote does not respond directly as he talks about the magic balm of Fierabrás, but very shortly he does indeed begin to complain about the pain of the injured ear: "y por agora, curémonos, que la oreja me duele más de lo que yo quisiera" (I.10.188) ["for now, let us treat these wounds, for my ear hurts more than I should like" (72)]. Note that for the first time reality—the reality of bodily pain—trumps theory. Don Quixote does not want his ear to hurt so badly; it is not supposed to hurt this way. Amadís de Gaula or Belianís de Grecia never complain about pain; pain is not much of a problem in the romance world of chivalry. Don Quixote is beginning to recognize, at least implicitly, that he is not living in the same kind of world as his literary heroes. And then he goes on to complain twice more about the pain of his ear: "porque yo te voto a Dios que me va doliendo mucho la oreja" (I.10.189) ["because I swear before God that my ear is hurting a good deal" (74)]; "sería bien, Sancho, que me vuelvas a curar esta oreja, que me va doliendo más de lo que es menester" (I.11.200) ["Even so, Sancho, it would be good if you tended this ear again, for it is hurting more than is necessary" (80)].

In effect, Don Quixote is saying that the ear hurts a lot; it shouldn't do that—but help me, because it really hurts. Well, the ear is then cured—not by a magic balm or ointment as in the romances of chivalry (where, by the way, the cure is very frequently carried out by a *doncella*, or maiden, as the knight recuperates in a luxurious bed in a castle)—but by a goatherd with a simple folk recipe of herbs, saliva, and salt: "y aplicándoselas a la oreja, se la vendó muy bien, asegurándole que no había menester otra medicina, y así fue la verdad" (I.11.200) ["and applied them to Don Quixote's ear and bandaged it carefully, assuring him that no other medicine was needed, which was the truth" (81)]. Don Quixote never complains about the ear again.

This scene, it seems to me, is of crucial importance in the novel. Don Quixote proclaims that he will never complain of pain because his literary model does not permit that. But mere pages later he complains repeatedly about the pain, which is implicitly an admission that in real life—in his life—things are different from what they are in fiction. It is the first step in his long and slow accommodation with reality and recognition that his dream of chivalry was impossible. The process ends on his deathbed when he says:

> Dadme albricias, buenos señores, de que ya yo no soy don Quijote de la Mancha, sino Alonso Quijano, a quien mis costumbres me dieron renombre de *Bueno*. Ya soy enemigo de Amadís de Gaula y de toda la infinita caterva de su linaje; ya me son odiosas todas las historias profanas del andante caballería; ya conozco mi necedad y el peligro en que me pusieron haberlas leído; ya, por misericordia de Dios, escarmentando en cabeza propia, las abomino. (II.74.634)

> Good news, Señores! I am no longer Don Quixote of La Mancha but Alonso Quixano, once called the Good because of my virtuous life. Now I am the enemy of Amadís of Gaul and all the infinite horde of his lineage; now all the profane histories of knight errantry are hateful to me; now I recognize my foolishness and the danger I was in because I read them; now, by God's mercy, I have learned from my experience and I despise them. (935)

"Truth comes in blows," observes Leo Henderson, protagonist of Saul Bellow's quixotic novel *Henderson the Rain King* (1959), a phrase picked up by Theodore Solotaroff, who used it as the title of his memoir (1998). Brute physical reality and bodily pain can lead to self-understanding and the truth. That certainly is the case for Don Quixote; it is a major factor in our understanding of the novel. You cannot read *Don Quixote* or any other work by Cervantes—or any other work of fiction—if you do not recognize the embodied reality of the characters. Literary characters are not simply word masses, mere language or discourse, subject positions, or debiologized subjects. Literary characters are virtual human beings with virtual bodies and minds, and we must use our ToM and our ToB in order to understand them.

But, on a more fundamental level, we may ask: What does it mean to have (to be) a body? What, in the most literal sense, is embodiment? What is the difference between, say, a body and a machine?

AUTOPOIESIS

"Autopoiesis" is not a word known to many humanist scholars, but it is a key concept in today's understanding of embodied cognition. The concept comes from the revolutionary work done in biology by two Chilean neuro-biologists some four decades ago. Autopoiesis importantly modifies Darwin's theory of evolution and the "new synthesis" of that theory that was worked out in the first half of the twentieth century. It is also a concept that has much to offer the literary scholar. It is a concept that, as we will see, can be illustrated perfectly by *Don Quixote*. It also has some important implications for literary theory in general.

Humberto Maturana, professor of biology at the University of Santiago de Chile in the mid-twentieth century, had already begun to formulate the ideas that were going to result in the theory of autopoiesis when he began his collaboration with his ex-student Francisco Varela. The two of them collaborated on their important book *Autopoiesis and Cognition: The Realization of the Living* (1972; in Spanish: *De máquinas y seres vivos: Autopoiesis: La organización de lo vivo* [1973]). Their collaboration culminated in the publication of the work that was above all to define the idea of autopoiesis: *The Tree of Knowledge: The Biological Roots of Human Understanding* (1992; original title *El árbol del conocimiento: Las bases biológicas del entendimiento humano* [1984]).

The etymology of the word makes clear its meaning: *auto*, "one's self," and *poiesis*, "creation." The idea captures the essence of the fact that a living organism generates itself within its context, its physical, historical, social, linguistic context. Maturana and Varela began to develop the concept as they worked with individual cells and realized that every cell of every living being generates, remakes, reforms itself during the process of living, and that is what it means to be alive; that continual self-making is the very definition of life. Further, the self-formation of each cell depends crucially upon its context, on what surrounds it, both within the living being and outside it.

Maturana has explained the way in which he hit upon the idea of autopoiesis:

> Así, un día que yo visitaba a un amigo, José María Bulnes, filósofo, mientras él me hablaba del dilema del caballero Quejana (después Quijote de la Mancha) en la duda de si seguir el camino de las armas, esto es el camino de la *praxis*, o el camino de las letras, esto es el camino de la *poiesis*, me percaté de que la palabra que necesitaba era *autopoiesis* si lo que quería era una expresión que captase plenamente lo que yo connotaba cuando hablaba de la organización circular de lo vivo. (17)

> It was in these circumstances that one day, while talking with a friend (José Bulnes) about an essay of his on Don Quixote de la Mancha, in which he

analyzed Don Quixote's dilemma of whether to follow the path of arms (*praxis*, action) or the path of letters (*poiesis*, creation, production), and his eventual choice of the path of *praxis* deferring any attempt at *poiesis*, I understood for the first time the power of the word "poiesis" and invented the word that we needed: *autopoiesis*. This was a word without a history, a word that could directly mean what takes place in the dynamics of the autonomy proper to living systems. (Translation mine)

It is, I believe, not coincidental that Don Quixote was present at the moment of birth of the term; that is one reason why it is appropriate to write about autopoiesis in *Don Quixote*. But before turning specifically to the role of autopoiesis in Cervantes' novel, I would like to explore a little more the implications of the idea.

A living being is not a machine. A machine is something made by human beings to be used in a certain way. If it breaks or if part of it fails to function properly, it has to be repaired or it is useless. A machine (or any material product or artifact made by humans) depends on this sort of intervention—or it is nothing at all. A living being is radically different: it constantly remakes itself. A living being, according to Maturana and Varela, is, unlike a machine, an "autopoietic system" in the sense that "it pulls itself up by its own bootstraps and becomes distinct from its environment through its own dynamics, in such a way that both things are inseparable" (*The Tree* 46–47). All living beings, all dynamic systems, are continually creating themselves—producing, inventing, modifying, renovating themselves. They need no external intervention in order to continue to exist. Of course, in the case of human beings, there can be intervention by a physician or surgeon (e.g., a heart transplant), but that is not the issue here. Rather, a living being *lives*, and does not merely *exist*, like a machine. What matters are the ongoing interrelationships that exist among mind, brain, body, and context, the way we create our cognitive worlds, the way in which we make our pragmatic knowledge in relationship with external reality, our social as well as our physical external reality.

Take, for example, a machine like a computer. It is the same thing in the Amazon rainforest as it is in the frozen regions of the Arctic. But a living being, an animal, is not; an animal adapts itself to the context in which it lives. It adapts physically, emotionally, and socially to its context. It adapts throughout its entire life in order to continue living; it adapts in everything it does. And this is another key aspect to the work of Maturana and Varela: all cognition is self-defining action: "*All doing is knowing, and all knowing is doing*" (*The Tree* 26; emphasis in the original). What we know and what we do are not only features of our cognitive being, they are equally part of our physical being. All biological or evolutionary adaptations are part of our knowledge of the world. We are what we do, what we know; to live is to know, to know is to do.

In his book *Darwin Machines and the Nature of Knowledge* (1993), British psychologist Henry Plotkin makes essentially the same argument when he sets forth the following thesis: "To know something is to incorporate the thing known into ourselves" (ix). The evolutionary process of natural selection by adaptation is, in and of itself, a process of acquiring knowledge that makes possible the existence of living things in the world. To know something is to know how to do it, and to do something, we must have the body and the mind-brain that make it possible. Everything we do, we do as a result of the evolutionary adaptations of our species. The inevitable conclusion, then, is that all knowledge is, at its heart, biological. But at the same time it is a universally recognized and fundamental fact that all knowledge is only possible within social contexts. Thus all knowledge is, at the same time, fully social and fully biological: 100% social and 100% biological. Knowing something consists of the relationship between the person who knows and what is known; it is an act that takes place within a context.

This organism–environment inseparability comes about by means of a process Maturana and Varela call "structural coupling," the result of "recurrent interactions leading to the structural congruence between two (or more) systems" (*The Tree* 75). For human beings, everything we do is part of "a world brought forth in coexistence with other people" (239). Recall Gibbs' definition of cognition cited at the beginning of this essay: "Cognition is what occurs when the body engages the physical, cultural world and must be studied in terms of the dynamical interactions between people and the environment." Structural coupling, the dynamical interaction of body and context, is what life is all about; it is the definition of life.

Maturana and Varela insist—completely obviating the validity of any subject–object, mind–body, self–other, or nature–nurture dualism—that knowledge is "enactive," that "human cognition as effective action pertains to the biological domain, but it is always lived in a cultural tradition . . . for cognition is effective action; and as we know how we know, we bring forth ourselves" (244). The authors conclude, again erasing the line between the biological and the social, as follows: "Whatever we do in every domain, whether concrete (walking) or abstract (philosophical reflection), involves us totally in the body, for it takes place through our structural dynamics and through our structural interactions. Everything we do is a structural dance in the choreography of coexistence" (248).[3]

I would like to look specifically at the beginning of the novel, with the passage that Humberto Maturana's friend, philosopher José Bulnes, was contemplating: the moment in the first chapter when the *hidalgo* from La Mancha is vacillating between a career in arms and one in letters. The narrator says that the protagonist was thinking about a certain romance of chivalry (specifically *Belianis of Greece*) and that he was strongly tempted to write a sequel: "muchas veces le vino deseo de tomar la pluma y dalle fin al pie de la letra, como allí se promete" (I.1.116) ["he often felt the desire to take up his pen and give it the conclusion promised there" (20)]. But our hero rejects the idea of a writing career and opts for the path of arms, deciding to *become* a knight-errant. So it is that the novel begins with an act of self-creation, an autopoietic act within a specific context.

Once this decision is made, the hidalgo begins to create his new life:

- He baptizes his horse—Rocinante;
- He chooses a new name for himself—Don Quijote de la Mancha;
- He dresses for the role—preparing his helmet and cleaning his great-grandfather's armor;
- He invents a history for himself—being in love with a peerless princess named Dulcinea del Toboso; and
- He imagines his future exploits—defeating in singular combat the fearful giant Caraculiambro, lord of the island Malandrania.

All of this can be understood as a series of acts of structural coupling with the world he envisions.

What is most important here is the last fact: his structural coupling is not with the world as it really is but as he imagines it, based on his vision from the many romances of chivalry he has read. For his role as knight-errant to be possible, there has to be a world in which there are knights, ladies, giants, castles, and adventures. And what is surprising, when he sallies forth for the first time, is that it appears to him that the world *is* exactly as he had envisioned it. When he arrives at the first inn, he is

---

3. Shortly after his work with Maturana, Varela teamed with philosopher Evan Thompson and psychologist Eleanor Rosch to write *The Embodied Mind* (1993), which combines the contemplative tradition of Buddhism with embodied cognitive science. It is a fundamental work in the understanding of embodiment.

received (he believes) exactly as a knight-errant should be received with honor when he arrives at a castle. There is a dwarf who announces his arrival with a trumpet (a pig farmer who blows his horn); the lord of the castle (the innkeeper) and two damsels (prostitutes) help him dismount and remove his armor, and serve him a sumptuous meal of fine trout (cheap codfish). That very night he stands guard over his arms in the courtyard, since the lord of the castle tells him that the chapel is under repair and cannot be used for that purpose. After he punishes two evildoers (simple mule drivers) who dare to touch the arms of a soon-to-be-knighted warrior, the lord of the castle dubs him a knight (in a parody of that solemn process), and the two princesses strap on his belt and spurs. In other words, the world, such as he perceives it, has received and treated him in exactly the way a knight-errant should be received and treated; that is to say, he has coupled structurally very well with his environment: his self-creation has been a success.

In the few chapters remaining of his first sally, this process of structural coupling continues uninterruptedly as he invokes the love of his peerless lady and imagines the wise enchanter/historian who will write his glorious history. The first thing that happens after he leaves the castle is that he rescues an innocent young boy (a shepherd who has apparently stolen some sheep) who is being lashed by his evil master (an innocent, if cruel, farmer), making the man promise to stop his lashes and pay the youth's salary. (After Don Quixote departs, the man reties the boy and whips him all the harder.) Next, our proud adventurer encounters some traveling knights (merchants) who refuse (without seeing her) his command to admit that Dulcinea del Toboso is the most beautiful woman in the world (a challenge frequent in the romances of chivalry). He berates them and charges, but, just as he is about to gain an important victory, his horse stumbles and falls (as sometimes happens in the romances of chivalry).

Although the reader might think at this moment that Don Quixote's structural coupling has failed, such is not the case, because as he lies on the ground unable to move "se tenía por dichoso, pareciéndole que aquélla era propia desgracia de caballeros andantes" (I.4.143) ["And still he considered himself fortunate, for it seemed to him that this was the kind of mishap that befell knights errant" (41)]. A neighbor who passes by chance helps Don Quixote return home, where he is received with honor, as his housekeeper and niece take him to his bed and promise to call on the wise enchantress Urganda la Desconocida to come and cure his wounds. Thus, everything that happens to him on this first sally seems to conform with the chivalric world with which Don Quixote has tried to couple structurally. In his eyes, his autopoietic acts have been a complete success.

At least, that is what our Manchegan hidalgo believes. And he believes it because he believes that others also believe what he believes. He believes it because he interprets the words and deeds of others as if they were in agreement with the world with which he has structurally coupled, as if they were full participants in his cognitive environment. And so we see that biosocial structural coupling also necessarily involves a ToM and a ToB. Again, we need to remember explicitly that literary characters are not living beings; they have no body, brain, or mind; they do not exist in the real world. But we must speak of fictional characters *as if* they were real and *as if* they had minds that are constantly thinking about what other characters are thinking. If we do not talk about Don Quixote and his squire Sancho Panza *as if* they were living human beings, we cannot talk of them at all.

Don Quixote knows that others treat him as if he were a knight-errant because for him (according to his ToM) that is exactly what he is. The most important confirmation of his reality is when the housekeeper and his niece, together with his best friends, the local priest and barber, seem to recognize that he is a knight-errant. And the most important thing of all: these friends and family inform him that an evil enchanter, envious of his success and scheming to harm him, has been at work by making his library disappear (they have taken and/or burned all his books). This enchanter is absolutely fundamental in the confirmation that he has successfully coupled structurally with the world. From this point on (at least for some while) Don Quixote will know that he is a great knight-errant, the hero of a sweeping epic tale of chivalry, with a wicked enemy constantly working against him, but in full knowledge that he will emerge victorious and that a second enchanter, this one wise and an ally of his, will write the history of his life and adventures.

There is not enough space in this essay to trace the way in which Don Quixote comes to admit that the world in which he lives is not the fantastic world of chivalry that he has imagined. But, as noted earlier, the loss of part of his ear and a good deal of blood begins to undermine his ability to maintain the sort of structural coupling with which he began his chivalric career. Throughout the rest of the novel Don Quixote slowly but inexorably comes to recognize his cognitive error and reach an accommodation with reality. It took Cervantes hundreds of pages to write about the long, slow process by which Don Quixote comes to recognize this fact, and this psychological process cannot be summarized here.[4] Let us accept, however, that the protagonist of the novel slowly evolves and that by the work's end, he admits that the chivalric world with which he believed he has coupled structurally so successfully does not in fact exist.

But there are two other important autopoietic processes that take place in the novel. First is the fact that the character who is most successful in the novel is Sancho Panza. Unlike his master, Sancho does not enter the scene with an already complete theory of what the world is like. He does not have to transform reality in order to function successfully; he simply acts pragmatically in such a way that he successfully adapts (structurally couples) with actual conditions. He learns all about chivalric adventures, islands (*ínsulas*), peerless ladies, enchanters and enchantments, ducal palaces, and much more—and he succeeds in dealing brilliantly with all of them.[5] Like his master, Sancho creates himself in the act of living; unlike his master, Sancho responds well to the thoughts and deeds of others and learns to live and function within the world as it actually is.

And if we can consider Don Quixote and Sancho as prototypes of literary characters who invent themselves in the act of living, prototypes of autopoiesis in literature, we must also recognize that all the other characters in the novel also create themselves autopoietically throughout their lives. And just like these literary characters, all of us who live in the real world are constantly creating ourselves throughout our lives. Autopoiesis is a constant and universal process both in reality and in fiction.

Finally, we can extend metaphorically the concept of autopoiesis to literature itself, and we can consider that *Don Quixote* is the prototype of the novel that invents itself: think of the search for and discovery of the manuscript of Cide Hamete Benengeli, supposed (fictional) Arabic historian and author of the original historical work translated and edited for us the readers; of the self-consciousness of Don Quixote and Sancho as literary characters in Part II when they learn that they are the heroes of a

4. I have previously attempted—with a certain degree of success, I believe—to trace this process in *The Chivalric World* (1982). The great majority of Cervantes scholars recognize that this psychological process does indeed take place over the course of the novel. But there has always been a small group that steadfastly denies it, insisting that Quixote and Sancho never change, never evolve. The most recent has been José Manuel Martín Morán in essays from the 1990s incorporated into his book *Cervantes y el "Quijote"* (2009).

5. I have traced this process in Sancho, with emphasis on his "enchantment" of Dulcinea, in "Sancho Panza's Theory of Mind." See also Jaén, "Literary" and "Cervantes and the Cognitive."

published book; of the criticism and parody of the false sequel to Part I written by another author; and much more. All metafiction is by definition autopoietic, and Don Quixote illustrates—embodies—this perfectly.

IMPLICATIONS

It is important to put embodiment and autopoiesis in perspective. I certainly am not the first person to have noted that Don Quixote literally creates his identity. Recall, for example, Juan Bautista Avalle-Arce's classic essay on Don Quixote's "acto gratuito" of self-creation in his book *Don Quijote como forma de vida* (1976). Everyone who reads the novel understands that the characters shape themselves, act, and live in the world they perceive. And this is exactly what we living human beings also do. Life itself is an autopoietic act. All living beings are embodied autopoietic systems.

The aim of this essay has been to remind the reader that the complete understanding of a work of literature involves a recognition of the biological reality of life. Human beings are living beings, animals. (And, remember, all fictional characters are understood *as if* they were living beings.) This means that we have physical bodies and an evolutionary and personal history that makes us what we are. To deny the importance of the biological, the embodiedness, of the human animal is equivalent to denying that the world is round or that stars exist billions of miles away from our earth.

When we read *Don Quixote*, or any other work of literature, it is important to remember that we are animals with bodies, living beings, dynamic systems, and not simple (and simplistic) linguistic subjects. And we should remember also that the very act of living is an autopoietic act, and that we are all constantly creating ourselves in everything we do, whether it be reading a novel or sallying forth in search of adventures.

WORKS CITED

Avalle-Arce, Juan Bautista. *Don Quijote como forma de vida*. Madrid: Fundación Juan March/Castalia, 1976.

Baron-Cohen, Simon. *Mindblindness: An Essay on Autism and Theory of Mind*. Cambridge: MIT P, 1995.

Bellow, Henderson. *Henderson the Rain King*. New York: Viking P, 1959.

Bortolussi, Marisa, and Peter Dixon. *Psychonarratology: Foundations for the Empirical Study of Literary Response*. Cambridge: Cambridge UP, 2003.

Cervantes, Miguel de. *Don Quixote*. Trans. Edith Grossman. New York: Ecco-HarperCollins, 2004.

Cervantes, Miguel de. *El Ingenioso Hidalgo Don Quijote de la Mancha*. Ed. John J. Allen. 25th ed. Madrid: Cátedra, 2005 [1977].

Gibbs, Raymond W., Jr. *Embodiment and Cognitive Science*. Cambridge: Cambridge UP, 2006.

Holland, Norman N. *Literature and the Brain*. Gainesville, FL: The PsyArt Foundation, 2009.

Jaén, Isabel. "Cervantes and the Cognitive Ideas of His Time: Mind and Development in *Don Quixote*." *Cognitive Cervantes*. Ed. Julien Simon, Barbara Simerka, and Howard Mancing. Spec. cluster of essays of *Cervantes: Bulletin of the Cervantes Society of America* 32.1 (2012): 71–98.

Jaén (Jaén-Portillo), Isabel. "Literary Consciousness: Fictional Minds, Real *Implications*." *Selected Papers from the 22nd International Literature and Psychology Conference, June 29–July 4, 2005*. Ed. Norman Holland. IPSA, n.d. Web. May 25, 2014.

Keen, Suzanne. *Empathy and the Novel*. Oxford: Oxford UP, 2007.

Leverage, Paula, Howard Mancing, Richard Schweickert, and Jennifer Marston William, eds. *Theory of Mind and Literature*. West Lafayette: Purdue UP, 2011.

Maiese, Michelle. *Embodiment, Emotion, and Cognition*. London: Palgrave Macmillan, 2011.

Mancing, Howard. *The Chivalric World of* Don Quijote: *Style, Structure, and Narrative Technique*. Columbia: U of Missouri P, 1982.

Mancing, Howard. "Sancho Panza's Theory of Mind." *Theory of Mind and Literature*. Ed. Paula Leverage, Howard Mancing, Richard Schweickert, and Jennifer Marston William. West Lafayette: Purdue UP, 2011, 123–32.

Martín Morán, José Manuel. *Cervantes y el "Quijote" hacia la novela moderna*. Alcalá de Henares: Centro de Estudios Cervantinos, 2009.

Maturana Romesín, Humberto. "Veinte años después." Preface. *De máquinas y seres vivos: Autopoiesis: La organización de lo vivo*. By Humberto Maturana Romesín and Francisco J. Varela. 6th ed. Buenos Aires: Lumen, 2004 [1973], 9–33.

Maturana Romesín, Humberto, and Francisco J. Varela. *Autopoiesis and Cognition: The Realization of the Living*. Dordrecht: Reidel, 1972.

Maturana Romesín, Humberto, and Francisco J. Varela. *De máquinas y seres vivos: Autopoiesis: La organización de lo vivo*. 6th ed. Buenos Aires: Lumen, 2004 [1973].

Maturana Romesín, Humberto, and Francisco J. Varela. *El árbol del conocimiento: Las bases biológicas del conocimiento humano*. Madrid: Editorial Debate, 1990 [1984].

Maturana Romesín, Humberto, and Francisco J. Varela. *The Tree of Knowledge: The Biological Roots of Human Understanding*. Trans. Robert Paolucci. Rev. ed. Foreword by J. Z. Young. Boston: Shambhala, 1992 [1984].

O'Connell, Sanjida. *Mindreading: An Investigation into How We Learn to Love and Lie*. New York: Doubleday, 1997.

Palmer, Alan. *Fictional Minds*. Lincoln: U of Nebraska P, 2004.

Plotkin, Henry. *Darwin Machines and the Nature of Knowledge*. Cambridge: Harvard UP, 1993.

Solotaroff, Theodore. *Truth Comes in Blows: A Memoir*. New York: W. W. Norton, 1998.

Varela, Francisco J., Evan Thompson, and Eleanor Rosch. *The Embodied Mind: Cognitive Science and Human Experience*. Cambridge: MIT P, 1993.

Vermeule, Blakey. *Why Do We Care about Literary Characters*? Baltimore: Johns Hopkins UP, 2010.

Zunshine, Lisa. *Why We Read Fiction: Theory of Mind and the Novel*. Columbus: Ohio State UP, 2006.

CHAPTER 3

Why Autopoiesis and Memory Matter to Cervantes, *Don Quixote*, and the Humanities

CATHERINE CONNOR-SWIETLICKI

In memory of M. Lynn Rupe, artist and scientist (December 5, 1951—December 20, 2014)

OVERVIEW: AUTOPOIESIS AND *DON QUIXOTE*

For most literary scholars, autopoiesis may be the most consequential yet least familiar concept relevant to the future of the humanities today. Autopoiesis is a term invented in the early 1970s to account for how all living organisms co-emerge simultaneously with and within their surroundings. Autopoiesis thus explains how any individual mind is truly embodied. Inspired by Cervantes' initial chapter of *Don Quixote,* the neurobiologist Humberto Maturana invented the term autopoiesis, encapsulating how we living beings necessarily co-create our internal biology and external sociocultural ecosystems. With his collaborator Francisco Varela, the pair explained these complex systems and dynamic, autopoietic processes by which an individual continually self-realizes at every living moment.[1] In short, autopoiesis is a neurobiological model for how every living being operates as a complex, organic society of self. This autopoietic model accounts for all living organisms—as simple as a single cell or as complex as

---

1. See Maturana and Varela, *Árbol; Autopoiesis and Cognition; De máquinas;* and *The Tree.*

a human body-brain or even an entire ecological and social-cultural system. Thus, each individual's patterns of development and neurological architecture start at a microcosmic level and become increasingly more complex macrocosmic systems of autopoiesis.

This autopoietic or neurobiological model of being elucidates cognitive science notions of the mind's embodiment. Autopoiesis has become increasingly significant in all fields of scholarly endeavor from the arts, humanities, and social-cultural fields to physics, chemistry, medicine, biology, and especially neuroscience. In this volume, Howard Mancing calls attention to how *Don Quixote* inspired the term autopoiesis and then indicates how autopoietic principles affect Cervantes' masterpiece. With broad strokes he outlines how autopoiesis demonstrates the need to restore interactive biological and environmental notions to literary scholarship.

However, in the forty years since Maturana and Varela invented the term autopoiesis, their heirs in neuroscience, biochemistry, anthropology, philosophy, literature, and other areas of arts and sciences have expanded research on the authors' complex neurobiological model for living systems. In the present study I discuss the current state of autopoietic research, its neuroscience updates, and its humanistic impact, particularly with respect to Cervantes' *Don Quixote*. I explore three interrelated ways that Cervantes' work illustrates the progressive processes of autopoiesis in life and art:

1. Cervantes creates his characters as individual and bioculturally complex in their autopoiesis or self-realization. They co-emerge within their individual biological and sociocultural ecosystems.
2. These portrayals arise from Cervantes' lifetime of experiences and growing self-realization. He redevelops his own autopoiesis in *Don Quixote* by creating characters who self-realize according to the biocultural processes he sets in motion for each.
3. In the final level of autopoietic engagement, readers integrate with *Don Quixote*, each according to her individual processes of self-realization and to what Cervantes' characters afford each reader.

ESSENTIAL TERMS OF AUTOPOIESIS

Since publishing their joint work, Maturana and Varela's autopoietic explanations have resonated powerfully in complex-systems research. When we literary scholars demonstrate the biocultural complexity of Cervantes and his art, we too are participating in the study of our own complex living systems. This is the sense of autopoiesis that has continued to grow from Varela's later work with Evan Thompson and/or Eleanor Rosch and their contributions to the humanities.[2] In *The Systems View of Life* (2014), Fritjof Capra and Pier Luigi Luisi have recently updated the impact of Maturana and Varela's "Santiago school" for complexity studies in human biological and sociocultural systems. Although trained as a physicist, Capra specializes in ecoliteracy (i.e., the social and philosophical implications of natural complex systems). Luisi is a biochemist focusing on the philosophical origins of life and self-organization of complex living systems. Like Varela and his heir Thompson, both explore the intersection of self-awareness or mindfulness practices and neuroscience. My discussion below applies their clear explanations of autopoiesis and supports it with neurological terms and evidence developed cooperatively by humanists and neuroscientists. With this renovated autopoietic vocabulary humanists gain greater self-awareness of how their brains and bodies always operate together bioculturally in art and life. Thus, my discussion of Cervantes' treatment of autopoiesis indicates how these new developments strengthen and expand Maturana and Varela's initial autopoietic connections with *Don Quixote* for all readers.

The interrelated terms discussed below are a vocabulary of autopoietic processes. These overlapping synonyms explain how autopoiesis occurs inside oneself and, by extension, in each individual's co-emerging sociocultural and ecological relations—such as reading. Even reading is a process of self-realization, a constant reorganizing of self. Each process must begin at an individual's microcosmic level of neural–chemical exchanges occurring inside and outside a single cell. Interconnected groupings of cells then continue these exchanges at macrocosmic levels. This is how someone like Cervantes co-emerges within ever more complex body-brain levels to become the Cervantes we know as a wounded soldier, a captive, a reader, and a writer. As his biocultural experiences of life constantly reorganize, he simultaneously self-realizes in creating his fictional characters and plots. Then, as readers engage with Cervantes' self-realized creations, each individual reader necessarily reorganizes her own internal-to-external macrocosm, recycling what she can of Cervantes' *Don Quixote*. As in life, readers realize their individual macrocosms of complex brain processes but always according to their own abilities and experiences. Such individual autopoietics of body and brain are, like artistic practices and reading, continually mirroring and imitating but also co-developing, recreating,

2. See Varela, Thompson, and Rosch; and Thompson.

recycling, reworking, reorganizing, remembering, relearning, reconnecting, looping, reemerging, and, eventually, co-evolving among humans in their societies and cultures. All these aspects of autopoiesis currently resonate in scholarship and research on mind-brain operations in the arts and life. Three current terms significant to the humanities—*mindfulness*, *self-awareness*, and *algorithms*—are treated below in discussing autopoiesis in scholarship and teaching today.

Autopoietic terminologies account for the dynamic "working together" of multiple brain areas and the new vocabularies we need as scholar-teachers to explore literature and the arts in conjunction with neuroscience. This overarching sense of autopoiesis makes visible the complex interdependence of scholarship and research based on the recreative processes in life, literature, and all the arts. A key example is neuroscientist Stanislas Dehaene's *Reading in the Brain* (2009). Although he does not use the term autopoiesis, his research employs the self-realizing, biocultural principles of Maturana and Varela. Dehaene traces how an individual's neuronal recycling must link together multiple brain areas in order to build memory and neuronal circuits. These constitute what I have referred to as the *macrocosmic* level of biocultural self-realization and which Dehaene establishes as the basis for the reading self. These include the multiple motor-sensory and sociocultural contributions we need for creating meanings and feelings associated with poetry, visual and performance arts, and fiction and nonfiction.[3] Dehaene has strongly influenced Paul B. Armstrong's brain-focused reconsideration of the hermeneutic *circle of aesthetics*.[4] The latter discusses how imitation, emotion, and empathy contribute neurologically in the creation and recycling of memory in the arts. While Suzanne Keen's *Empathy and the Novel* (2007) does not draw significantly on neuroscience terminology, her sociocultural examples suggest how readers develop autopoietic complexity as they process empathy and emotion of different types and levels.[5] Emotional diversity among writers, artists, and their audiences is one of the great discoveries of neurobiology that literary scholars are beginning to explore more boldly. Neuroscientists unabashedly rely on the arts and the humanities to research

---

3. Although Dehaene refers to these genres in general ways, he provides significant evidence for tracing their profound evolutionary and biocultural foundations in cave arts and perhaps earlier. In reading Dehaene's revelations together with autopoietic principles, scholars in all the arts can help us realize how we recreate and reorganize ourselves as we participate in cultural artifacts.

4. See Armstrong, *How Literature*.

5. While Keen indicates that neural imaging and intersubjective evaluating systems are significant to her analysis, mirror neurons are the most discussed feature of her work on empathy and the novel.

individuals' differing emotions and levels of empathy. This is readily seen in titles and works such as Semir Zeki's *Splendors and Miseries of the Brain: Love, Creativity and the Quest for Human Happiness* (2009) and Antonio Damasio's *The Feeling of What Happens* (1999) or his subtitle *Joy, Sorrow and the Feeling Brain* on Spinoza (2003). Even Gerald Edelman's title *Bright Air, Brilliant Fire* (1992) expresses his frequent references to poetry, art, and music. Although these works do not refer directly to the term autopoiesis, they demonstrate its principles of self-realization and all the co-emergent neurochemical processes that make human life and artifacts possible.

In her extraordinary book *Feeling Beauty: The Neuroscience of Aesthetic Experience* (2013), literary scholar and neuroscience researcher G. Gabrielle Starr describes cultural and neurobiological evidence for how individuals integrate emotional, empathic, multisensory, motor (movement), and memory components of their brain architecture in experiencing art. With neuroaesthetic data, she shows how each one self-realizes art "with networked interactions in which large swaths of interconnected neurons work together to perform a number of complex functions" (146). Her examples based on body-brain operations in literature, music, painting, and other visual arts rely on an interactive approach to self-realization. The depth of Starr's work enables her to transcend leading neuroscientists' descriptions of brain processes in the arts (Kandel, *The Age*; Ramachandran). Because she examines individualized, detailed neural circuitry of memory and emotions in artistic experience, her scholarship surpasses the neuroscientists' references to the general effects of "overlapping tissue and analogous functions" (146).

Just as significantly, she provides a balanced evaluation of the possible contributions of mirror neurons to learning and empathy.[6] Because Starr can demonstrate how mirroring systems integrate with aesthetics and memory operations, her work surpasses the limitations of anti–mirror-neuron criticism based mainly on motor systems (199n37, 199–200n38). In these ways, she strengthens and advances the conclusions about mirror neurons in the arts as discussed by neuroscientists Marco Iacoboni (*Mirroring*), Giacomo Rizzolatti and Corrado Sinigaglia (*Mirrors*), Damasio (*Self*), Christian Keysers (*The Empathic*), V. S. Ramachandran (*The Tell-Tale*), and Eric Kandel (*The Age*). In addition, Starr's authoritative discussion on the interactive role of mirror neurons highlights the autopoietic

6. Starr's research on mirror neurons in literature and art should help Armstrong reconsider his conclusions on them (2013). Starr's work also supports Keen's evaluation of empathy and mirror neurons in reading (see note 3).

work of her research on individual levels of empathy. Similarly, Thompson, with whom Varela elaborated autopoiesis, discusses mirror neurons and neuronal self-realization.[7] Both authors' analyses help readers self-evaluate their capacities to imitate, to mirror, and thus to empathize, learn, and conceptualize their own encounters with the arts. Mirror neuron discoveries also connect well with the growing body of neuroaesthetic research such as Rodrigo Quian Quiroga's discovery of "Jennifer Aniston neurons"—groups of neurons responding to one-person identification (*Borges and Memory*). Like Starr's work, his analyses of how these neurons contribute to memory and conceptualizing can help scholar-teachers understand their individual biocultural development in literature. In sum, Starr's neuroaesthetics strengthen my discussion of how multiple brain operations work together in Cervantes' *Don Quixote* as well as in the performance arts of his time (Connor-Swietlicki, "Bridging," "Embodying," "Beyond"). Her conclusions corroborate this essay's study of autopoietics at micro- and macrocosmic levels of biocultural realization in Cervantes' *Don Quixote*. Along with Dehaene and other scientists referred to herein, Starr informs much of the discussion below.

AUTOPOIESIS OF MEMORY: CELLS TO SOCIETIES

Memory is much more than what we ordinarily refer to as "memory." Kandel, neuroscientist of memory and art, demonstrates how cellular memory and learning make possible all forms of life. As his chapter "One Cell at a Time" and all his works indicate, Kandel explains how an individual's cellular memory activities establish a neurobiological architecture for how all larger brain-body areas learn to work together (*In Search*). That is, memory is microcosmic before it becomes a macrocosmic process. It is significant that his accounts are very autobiographical and autopoietic. Kandel frequently explains memory with examples from the arts, history, and his own life (*In Search* and *The Age*). He calls attention to the role art plays for neuroscientists, especially for Santiago Ramón y Cajal, "arguably the most important brain scientist who ever lived" (*In Search* 61). First trained as an artist, Ramón y Cajal observed and made visible the neuronal structures that his contemporaries in neuroscience had not been able to imagine.

Memory is an autopoietic, neurobiological organizer of art and life. From cell to self in society, memory is a key synonym for biocultural

7. See Thompson, *Mind*.

self-realization in art and life. Cellular-level operations form the basis for all the artistic and literary realizations of self that I have been discussing. Cells summarize and illustrate the processes of brain architecture described by Starr, Dehaene, and the others referred to herein. In Figure 3.1, an updated drawing of Maturana's early sketch,[8] we can see how a human cell's flexible form is always incorporating and recreating "outside cultural" influences according to its abilities. It is, in effect, a microcosmic illustration of the macrocosmic, biocultural autopoiesis that Cervantes demonstrates in *Don Quixote*. Each cellular component and process reorganizes inside–outside exchanges in parallel with the macrocosmic brain areas and connections discussed by Starr, Dehaene and the others.[9] In sum, individual cells illustrate "the mystery of memory and learning" (Kandel, *In Search* 6) in the autopoiesis of biochemical fusion between internal (genetic) and external (environmental/cultural) components.

It is probable that Maturana and Varela were not familiar with the neurological work on memory accomplished after they developed their theory of autopoiesis in the 1970s. That would explain why they referred to *cognition* and *learning* to describe many of the processes of self-realization we now study as memory. As in Figure 3.1, cellular memory and learning begin when receptors straddling the cellular membrane allow nutrients like oxygen to enter as they let CO_2 escape. These transmembrane receptors thus allow external "cultural" factors to become part of an individual at the cellular level. Together these biocultural factors learn and create a cellular "society of self" that we easily observe in our individual macrocosmic relations of one's body-brain-environment on an everyday basis or in the arts (Varela, Thompson, and Rosch). The biocultural interactions of these macrocosmic body-brain societies have been described by Dehaene, Starr, and the others cited herein. These biocultural processes are how our brains remember and learn each time they transform messages across interconnected brain areas. They are macrocontributors of one's individual

---

8. Maturana's simple drawing of a plant cell as first formulated in the 1970s for autopoiesis (see Maturana and Varela, Autopoiesis) does not reflect current knowledge of human cell complexity. With medical science illustrator Gary Carlson, I designed Figure 3.1 depicting the dynamic architecture of human cells. Our drawing has since been confirmed by Capra and Luisi's new illustrations of autopoiesis (*The Systems*).

9. This brief descriptive summary is based on my extensive and intensive reading of key neuroscientists whose discussions roughly coincide in explaining cellular-to-brain processes of self. In addition to Maturana and Varela, these include the work of the following authors: Capra and Luisi, Edelman, Damasio, Dehaene, Iacoboni, Kandel, Ramachandran, and Starr. See "Works Cited" at the end of the chapter.

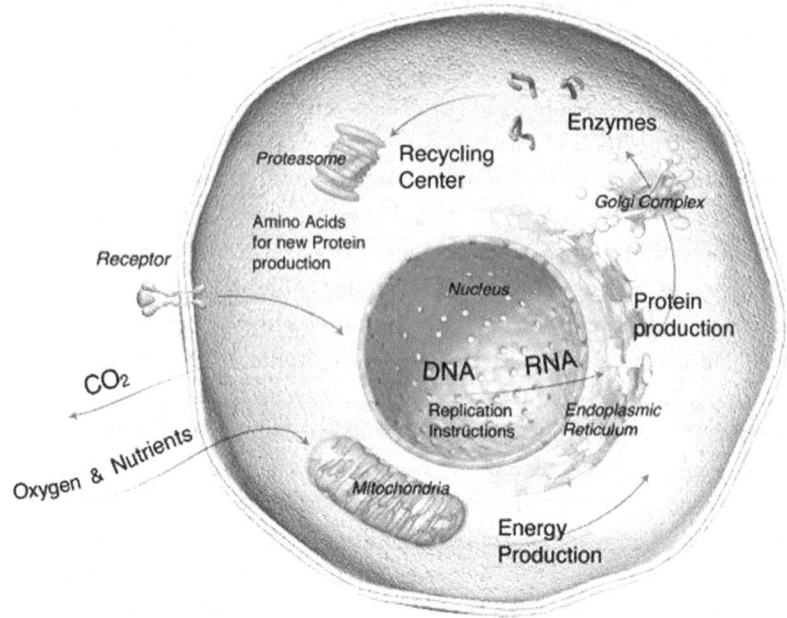

Figure 3.1: Autopoiesis and memory at the microcosmic level.

The self-realizing cell continually adapts its algorithmic patterns and memory to its experiences and surroundings. A cell self-organizes incoming eco-cultural material, processing it biochemically and recycling
for growth and change. This cellular-level process is paralleled at the macrocosmic level, where an individual's entire network of body-brain systems cooperate to self-organize input from one's sociocultural-
ecological systems. (Drawing by Gary Carlson)

autopoiesis of memory and self, differing according to the biocultural exchanges that started at the microcosmic, cellular level. It is literature and
all the arts, as I argue herein, that afford us concentrated opportunities to
increase self-awareness of each individual's biocultural realization. When
we read and discuss literature or interact with plastic and performance
arts we necessarily remember, reorganize, recreate, and bioculturally realize ourselves through them.

Forms of memory are, in effect, prime examples of biocultural autopoiesis in life and art. These cognitive learning processes depend on retracing and reorganizing our previously realized societies of self as we try
to interactively remember a memory. In adapting a memory, an individual necessarily accommodates her existing internal biocultural constitu-
ents of self in terms of new biocultural input from her surroundings.
These are, in effect, individual neurobiological algorithmic processes that
one's internal society of self develops before contributing to external

social algorithms.[10] Such internal-to-external algorithmic relations of an individual in her surroundings can thus be very useful in explaining how readers of *Don Quixote* necessarily develop their own emotional and empathic levels of processing his art. This is how Cervantes' masterpiece can coax us to read in so many ways.

Thus memory, as many aspects of *Don Quixote* demonstrate, is a distributed and continually changing biocultural organizer of life, whether for a cell, a self, or society.[11] Neurobiology and artistic examples, as in *Don Quixote*, are profoundly updating how we imagine memory. It is literally a neurobiological "membering again" before it takes shape in conscious thought. As I have discussed earlier, Starr demonstrates how an individual's reorganization of memory strongly contributes to how that person experiences art. She highlights the way that memory's default mode network influences how one perceives new experiences. Similarly, I have discussed how Don Quixote's visual perception defaults to his memory system, weakening his ability to recognize sheep that are not armies, the basin that is not a helmet, and so forth (Connor-Swietlicki, "Beyond Cognition").

This sense of memory as a biocultural interaction of cell to self and society is highly applicable to Cervantes' *Don Quixote*. His autopoietic artistry and content point to his experiences, intuition, and likely familiarity with the medical and mind sciences of his time.[12] Cervantes did not have, in the current sense, a two-hundred-plus-volume library of medical, scientific, or literary works to which he referred in the process of writing. Cultural histories, biographies, and histories of medicine and science can elucidate our knowledge of what circulated among the societies and cultural groupings in which he moved and was continually observing,

10. Algorithms are biologically occurring natural processes of autopoiesis in life as Thompson, Varela's intellectual heir, discusses (211–3). Complex-systems biologist Kauffman explains that algorithms are a natural organizing principle of evolution. More recently autopoietic algorithms figure prominently in Capra and Luisi's explanations of autopoiesis and complex life systems (*The Systems*). Significantly, Damasio (*Self*) refers to individual algorithms in explaining emotions and self-awareness. Although Edelman disassociates his work from computer analogies (*The Remembered* and *Bright Air*), his account of how consciousness arises overlaps with the descriptions of the looping and circulatory brain processes that Damasio's works treat and that Thompson, Capra, and Luisi refer to as "algorithmic."

11. The early twentieth-century psychologist Frederic Bartlett foresaw the personal, social, and cultural variables in how memories change. Without modern knowledge of neurological anatomy, he imagined memory as a schema of connections (Kandel and Squire, *Memory* 6).

12. On Cervantes and the medical and mind sciences of his time, see, among others, Martín-Araguz and Bustamante-Martínez; López-Muñoz, Álamo, and García-García; Palma and Palma; and Domínguez, this volume.

learning, and incorporating from his personal and intellectual development into his writing. His familial circles and wide variety of well-read acquaintances were certainly factors in how he was able to adapt medical and scientific knowledge to the individualized characters and real-life situations he portrays in more culturally connected and broadly autopoietic ways. In this regard Cervantes is a significant example of how literary and cultural studies need to claim the cognitive field as their own by showing the relationships of neuroscience and medicine to personal and cultural development—within academe and certainly in more popular and easily accessible media.

Autopoiesis and its synonym memory account for how Cervantes could artistically self-realize his biocultural experiences in *Don Quixote*. The evidence supports the remarkable accuracy of Cervantes' changing characterization of the old hidalgo's body-brain conditions. Cervantes doesn't just insert preexisting medical or neurological descriptions into his masterpiece; his treatment of Quixote's body-brain alterations stimulates readers to recreate the sensations with their own experiences. A prime example is Cervantes' explanation of how sleep-deprived reading of chivalric novels drastically alters his memory: "y así, del poco dormir y del mucho leer, se le secó el celebro" (I.1.23) ["with too little sleep and too much reading his brains dried up, causing him to lose his mind" (21)].[13] Current neurological research on sleep loss, even at the cellular level, demonstrates the accuracy of Cervantes' account. Especially among the aging, sleep deprivation drastically alters anyone's mind because it disrupts each cell's biocultural exchanges. Sleeplessness cuts off the steady stream of nutrients required for continuous self-realization (Naidoo et al.). Without requisite sleep the microcosmic recycling or recreative processes of memory and cognition are blocked. The long-term effects of such problems of sleeplessness and memory loss of the sort Quixote experienced are played out in Cervantes' entire novel, as Quixote responds to his changing environments.

Another key autopoietic process Cervantes employs in structuring *Don Quixote* and in transforming his characters can be summarized in a metaphor from Francisco Varela. "Laying down a path walking" is the phrase he applied to express how individuals develop autonomously yet bioculturally and socially in life and art (Varela, Thompson, and Rosch 237). This is not a conventional metaphor for life as a path. Rather, Varela's "laying down a path in walking" emphasizes that each individual's life/path is

---

13. All citations from *Don Quixote* are from the edition by Lathrop and refer to part, chapter, and page. The translations are from Grossman, citing page only.

truly self-realized and continually reorganized. Each one's path/life comes into being in her act of creating and living it neurobiologically and socio-culturally. Cervantes calls our attention to the internal–external inter-changes of self and society when the old hidalgo interacts with others and his Manchegan environment. Other characters, in turn, lay down their individual paths as they encounter Don Quixote and necessarily recreate themselves. Over the course of the novel, the indeterminate nature of the knight's memory is constantly reworking knight-errantry as "laying down his path." His self-realization of a path is always subject to the biocultural moment—as in Rocinante's whims. Then, with each new encounter—especially with other readers, like the priest, barber, students, innkeepers, and dukes, Cervantes exposes them all to other reworked memory sys-tems of others laying down their paths.

AUTOPOIESIS OF ARMS AND LETTERS AND CAPTIVITY: DON QUIXOTE I.37–38, 39

The following section focuses on Cervantes' autopoietic treatment of the arms-versus-letters topic in *Don Quixote*, illustrating how autopoiesis op-erates therein and in readers' personal and scholarly abilities to self-realize as they engage his masterpiece. Autopoiesis and Cervantes teach us that the old hidalgo's initial choice between arms and letters did not result from pure logic or from absolute free will. Rather, what we call rea-soning will necessarily develop according to how intensely an individual reorganizes biocultural exchanges of self at every stage of life. Readers necessarily regenerate and realize their own algorithmic "decisions" as they rework Cervantes' text along the way. In fact, the whole notion of a dilemma about arms and letters points to how autopoiesis encourages critics to widen and deepen their approaches to and debates about *Don Quixote*. Pre-autopoietic literary criticism trains scholars to focus on topics like arms and letters along with genres, plots, and other tradi-tional cognitive categories. Autopoiesis' biosocial core is appropriately in tune with how individuals self-realize in reading and with how Cervantes realizes the inseparability of praxis and poiesis to resolve Quixote's dilemmas.

In Chapters 37 and 38 of *Don Quixote (Part I)*, when Cervantes has the old knight directly discuss the relative values of arms and letters, it is late and nearing the final chapters of the first part of *Don Quixote*. By that point, questions of memory, self, and society have already become much more complex and even contradictory. Cervantes has already created a surprising range of complicated relationships with his characters, contexts, and readers. In effect, by Chapters 37 and 38, individual readers necessarily develop their diverse autopoietic interactions with the text. For all these reasons, the questions of arms and letters that Cervantes has his old knight discuss in these chapters need scholarly, autopoietic, and neurobiological updating. In the author's hands, the usual arguments on the relative merits of arms and letters also intertwine with close-up emotive-cognitive body-brain recreations. Here Cervantes displays his own reorganized memories as he enriches the old knight's delivery of his highly affective oration on the suffering soldier. Nothing Cervantes shows readers about Quixote's life experiences prior to this moment in Chapters 37 and 38 can account for the intensity of emotive experiences and lived suffering that Cervantes expresses in discussing the trauma of warfare and the pursuit of peace that the soldier experiences.

Readers need to bring their own emotive and empathic self-awareness to these chapters. By this point, their individual engagements with all aspects of *Don Quixote* should have been adapting along the way. This is where Starr's and Dehaene's discussions of recreated or recycled connections among brain areas account for how individual readers will necessarily realize their own levels of emotive, empathic, and other biocultural experience in reading Chapters 37 and 38. This includes retracing brain-based linguistic factors, as per Dehaene, to their own multisensory and motor abilities for "feeling beauty" as Starr has so carefully analyzed. This autopoietic method of mindful reading should help readers realize more profoundly personal meanings of Quixote's oration. In these chapters Cervantes offers opportunities for readers to feel/think how hunger and suffering of all kinds relate to biocultural longing for peace. Readers need to bring attention to their varying levels of self-awareness to the analysis below. Italics will emphasize passages relevant to their potential aesthetic, emotive, and empathic interaction with the text.

In the old knight's discourse, arms and letters are contrasted by comparing "the student" and "the soldier" (I.37–38). What of the hypothetical Cervantes-the-student who might have brought memories of suffering to bear on Quixote's arms-and-letters discussion in Chapters 37 and 38? If Cervantes did indeed receive some formal education—a matter yet to be proved beyond doubt—the author does not bring emotionally or intellectually convincing evidence to bear in this context. If Cervantes did indeed experience the comparatively lighter level of suffering he describes for the hypothetical student, he went to extraordinary measures to express it matter-of-factly in comparison with the intense description he paints of the soldier's anguished suffering and, above all, in comparison with the significance that the soldier's sacrifices represent for the peace achieved for others.

Indeed, Cervantes seems to relish contrasting the happy self-realization of students who have earned their academic titles in law, theology, or classical studies "*como llevados en vuelo* de la favorable fortuna" (I.37.312; my emphasis) ["*as if carried on the wings* of good fortune" (330)] and who come to "*mandar y gobernar el mundo desde una silla,* trocada su *hambre en hartura,* su *frío en refrigerio,* su *desnudez en galas* y su dormir en una estera en reposar en holandas y damascos" (I.37.312; my emphasis) ["*command and govern the world from a chair,* their *hunger* turned into a *full belly,* their *cold into comfort,* their *nakedness to finery,* and their straw mat into linen and damask sheets" (330)]. And if perhaps Cervantes was recreating some faded memory of having suffered like students in his era, he does not have Don Quixote describe them in this context. Rather, Cervantes' mouthpiece concludes that the students "*contrapuestos y comparados sus trabajos con los del mílite guerrero, se quedan muy atrás en todo*" (I.37.312; my emphasis) ["hardships, measured against and compared to those of a *soldier and warrior, fall far behind*" (330)]. More importantly, this incident, like so much of the entire novel, ironically underscores the long-term advantages of Cervantes' largely autodidactic formation, his poverty and "education in life" in the company of humanistic-scientific acquaintances, in soldiering and participating in the battle of Lepanto, in captivity and in itinerant government service in the Spanish region of La Mancha.[14] All such biosocial experiences enrich more profoundly his memory and creativity. Had he received more formal schooling and/or some higher education, let alone a degree, he would not have become "wealthy" in terms of a self-realizing individual whose freedom from academia, life of action, and multiplicity of experiences and creative viewpoints are expressed in *Don Quixote*.

In the arms-and-letters oration discussion, Cervantes affords readers opportunities for their individual empathic and biocultural self-realization as they mirror and rework Cervantes' own recreation of his experiences self-realizing in his characters. Cervantes-the-soldier and Cervantes-the-captive can be detected in the profoundly embodied values the author includes, particularly as expressed in Chapters 37 and 38. An autopoietic approach allows us to recreate within ourselves the "remembered self" that Cervantes renders in Quixote's descriptions of the soldier. It should be apparent to Cervantes scholars that autopoiesis deepens what

---

14. Connor-Swietlicki indicates the scholarly potential for neurobiological and autopoietic approaches to Cervantes' traumatic experiences and his paralyzed arm with relation to his art ("Beyond Cognition").

their investigations can gain beyond documented, historical influences on Cervantes' treatment of arms, warfare, peace, and/or the soldier's fate. Indeed, rather than relying on direct influences alone, Cervantes' treatment of the topics is highly "digested" in how he recycles and biologically reacculturates his memories.[15] Moreover, when the autobiographical material of Chapters 37 and 38 flows into Chapter 39, he presents sly, bioculturally recycled "memories" with notable repercussions for current scholarship focusing on genetic and ethnic evidence. With clever references to Spain's remembered present in 1605, Cervantes reorganizes his memories of Spain's Moorish and Morisco past, his battle wounds and Algerian captivity, and his knowledge of Manchegan Moriscos. His autopoietic treatment of those experiences in *Don Quixote* I.37–39 provides his readers with opportunities to realize and to recreate their own biocultural memories of ethnic residues. Readers' attention to these chapters should provoke their individualized levels of cognitive-emotive engagement with the text.[16]

In the autobiographical framework of Chapters 37 and 38, Quixote's discourse on arms begins just after the Moor Zoraida has insisted she be called María—like a Christian—and sits down with Luscinda. Simultaneously her companion the captive sits with Fernando and Cardenio to dine as they all marvel at the old knight's oration (328). The peaceful scene and the irenic longing for peace will resonate in the captive's autobiographical account right after Quixote has spoken (I.39–42: 334–74). Moreover, the Captive's action-oriented and mirroring narrative will detail the suffering that Cervantes, the wounded soldier and captive, expressed in Quixote's brief, intensely embodied and poetic discourse in Chapters 37 and 38.

First Cervantes has his spokesman detail the emotional experiences of the stressed soldier as he silently anticipates the enemy attack. The soldier is "*quieto, temiendo y esperando cuándo improvisamente ha de subir a las nubes sin alas y bajar al profundo sin su voluntad*" (I.38.314; my emphasis) ["*quiet, fearing and waiting* for the moment when he will suddenly *fly up* to the clouds without wings or *plunge down* to the abyss against his will" (332)]. Then Cervantes focuses on more personal details of how it feels to "steal" because of *hunger and to suffer cold* in his doublet's doubly "*slashed and torn*" shreds of protection. But Cervantes' voice is most affective and autobiographical when he focuses on deeply embodied and dreadful descriptions

15. In this regard, readers should recall how Dehaene indicates that reading brain areas recycle literature.

16. These are the very sorts of neural processes Armstrong, Dehaene, and Starr have referred to regarding how literature can stimulate diverse brain areas to connect as we recreate them.

of "the soldier's" trauma.[17] The soldier's only "*borla en la cabeza, hecha de hilas, para curarle algún balazo que quizá le habrá pasado las sienes, o le dejará estropeado de brazo o pierna*" (I.38.313; my emphasis) ["tasseled academic cap [is] made of bandages to *heal a bullet wound*, perhaps one that has passed through his temples or will leave him with a *ruined arm* or leg" (331)], so similar to what Cervantes' contemporaries knew about his three chest-area war wounds and especially the paralytic arm for which he gained the epithet "*manco* [one-armed man] of Lepanto." His trauma culminates amid "*la espantable furia de aquestos endemoniados instrumentos de la artillería*" (I.38.315; my emphasis) ["the *horrifying fury of the diabolical instruments of artillery*" (332)] where the soldier is caught between two ships:

> viendo que tiene delante de sí tantos *ministros de la muerte* que le amenazan cuantos cañones de artillería se asestan de la parte contraria, que no distan de su cuerpo una lanza, y viendo que al primer *descuido de los pies* iría a visitar los *profundos senos* de Neptuno, y con todo esto, con intrépido corazón llevado de la *honra que le incita*, se pone a ser *blanco* de tanta arcabucería y procura pasar por tan estrecho paso al bajel contrario. (I.38.314; my emphasis)

> seeing that he has in front of him as many *ministers of death* as there are artillery cannons aimed at him from the other side, only a lance's throw away, and seeing that at the first *misstep* he will visit the *deep bosom* of Neptune, despite this with an *intrepid heart*, carried by the *honor that urges* him on, he makes himself the *target* of all their volleys and attempts to cross that narrow passage to the enemy vessel. (332; my emphasis)

Emphasized areas of the passage illustrate the sorts of "feeling" that readers should self-realize as per Starr's account of how emotive, empathic, and conceptual brain areas work together as we experience art. These passages offer literary scholars and critics a more profound sense of how Cervantes' artistry affects individual readers and their lives than do matter-of-fact scholarly summations stating merely that "this passage is autobiographical."

In effect, Cervantes-the-soldier and Cervantes-the-captive interweave lived feelings of what happens across Chapters 37 and 38. Cervantes transitions readers from Quixote's discourse on arms and letters into the next speaker's life story—that of the captive and former soldier Viedma (I.39–42.334–74). It is significant that recent Cervantes scholarship on Morisco

---

17. In "Beyond Cognition," I argue that Cervantes' trauma in battle and elsewhere profoundly affected his experience and artistry.

and Moorish matters in *Don Quixote* is reinforced by the biocultural, auto-poietic evidence I have been discussing in Cervantes' recreated memories of soldiering and his Algerian captivity and the peaceful presence of Viedma with the Morisca Zoraida-María. What we have in Don Quixote's emotional and moral-social focus on peace resembles the ironic and irenic longing Cervantes came to know over five long years of Algerian captivity better than any other major writer of his time. That experience allowed him a lived recreation of recollections he might have retained about the rich heritage of *Andalusí*[18] or tricultural cooperation in Spain prior to Castilian dominance. Jean Canavaggio cogently describes how Algiers altered Cervantes' memory when he was "free to come and go across the city, rubbing elbows with a world of people whose practices and customs he was unaware of until then" (80). Most significantly to writing and publishing *Don Quixote* with its complex perspectives, Canavaggio concludes that Cervantes in Algiers absorbed "what Inquisitorial Spain knew nothing about: the *peaceful coexistence of these communities*" (81; my emphasis). Canavaggio is describing the Andalusian cultural residues in Cervantes' ironically nuanced treatment of Moorish and Morisco questions throughout *Don Quixote*.

The bio-cultural and autopoietic Quixote that I have been discussing in this essay sheds new light on the ethnically complex Cervantes being rediscovered, most recently by Robert S. Stone and his scholarly predecessors, on the Morisco-focused aspects of *Don Quixote*. Cervantes subtly refers to the lost eras of *Andalusí* cultural cooperation and its residues among Moriscos and conversos, especially in Toledo, gateway to La Mancha. There the all-important lost manuscript of Cide Hamete Benengeli, *Don Quixote*'s Arab author, is recovered (I.10). But just as significantly for Cervantes scholarship are the miserable, biosocial residues of *Andalusí*-style peace that Cervantes ironically connects in *Don Quixote (Part I)*. When Quixote honors the prostitute la Tolosa with the title of *doña* [lady], the narrator indicates that she is the "hija del un remendón natural de Toledo . . . a las tendillas de Sancho Bienaya" (I.3.37) ["daughter of a Toledo cobbler [or clothing mender?] . . . [from] the old Sancho Bienaya market" (34], the old ethnic quarters of Toledo. Cervantes points out similarly ironic ethnic references, although with even more bite, when the narrator describes how Maritornes, the self-proclaimed, pure-blooded

18. The terms refer to the biocultural cooperation and achievements in *al-Andalus*, the areas long occupied under Muslim rule. Their nostalgic residues in science and the arts are sensitively summarized in Menocal's *The Ornament of the World: How Muslims, Jews and Christians Created a Culture of Tolerance in Medieval Spain*.

Christian *hidalga* working as a servant-girl at Palomeque's inn, tries to sleep with her Morisco lover. Here we have Cervantes cleverly satirizing the peaceful biocultural mingling so debated by his contemporaries. Cide Hamete's narration describes that lover as a wealthy muleteer from Arévalo[19] and a relative of the Arab author himself. Cervantes thus makes visible his keen observations about miscegenation in early modern Spain for those who want to see and enjoy his surreptitious play. Amid such multiple perspectives of interest in the same chapter, Cervantes slyly comments on what "he knew" as a great observer of the link between biology and culture. In these ways autopoiesis makes visible more details than ever about Cervantes' life experience in relation to his artistry in *Don Quixote*. Rather than replace cognitive or more traditional literary criticism, readers should be able to see how these discoveries verify and strengthen multiple readings of *Don Quixote*, as long as they do not attempt to deny the biocultural-emotional validity Cervantes so astutely incorporates throughout the text.

IN CONCLUSION: AUTOPOIESIS AND REINVENTING THE HUMANITIES

The autopoietic approach is potentially more thorough than any single psychological, philosophical, neurological, sociological, or historical methodology. Because autopoiesis is necessarily all-inclusive, it explains, substantiates, and reinforces all other approaches. It recognizes individual complexity, whether neurobiological, cultural, social, "natural," and so forth, and affords each of us greater self-awareness of how we are always becoming ourselves in anything we do—whether in reading, working, sleeping, or dreaming. In sum, in reading *Don Quixote* with updates to Maturana and Varela's autopoiesis, we enhance our own development. According to each one's self-realization, we enrich our individual biocultural relationships with other readers and their societies, arts, and cultures. Autopoiesis thus heightens each one's unique complexity as creator, reader, spectator, or listener and simultaneously advances humanistic and scientific scholarship.

19. Arévalo, a town of Old Castile near Valladolid, was particularly known for its large Morisco population. Many were active as muleteers in a "Morisco network" smuggling Moriscos in and out of Spain, carrying them along with legitimate mercantile goods along a route from the north, passing through La Mancha and Albacete to Murcia or Valencia. The frequency of their movement and their "normal" mercantile cargo provided camouflage for their more discreet operations. See De Tapia.

As we incorporate and adapt autopoietic principles to our research and teaching, we are demonstrating the essential and profound values the humanities offer all human endeavors. In the brief discussion below I outline key ways in which scholar-teachers can realize the benefits of autopoiesis. I draw on my experiences teaching Spanish literature to undergraduates and leading an honors college sophomore seminar, "Humanities and Neuroscience." Materials for the latter can be adapted for literature and humanities classes, depending on the artifacts selected and the mix of students and their interests in self-realization.

Starting with *embodiment, memory,* and *mindfulness*—familiar terms from popular media or their classrooms—students learn to identify how their individual body-brains self-realize in daily activities, especially as they perceive others, listen to music, observe plastic or performance arts, and read fiction or poetry. Versus conventional methods, they study the interconnected processes of their mind-brains in tandem with autopoietic engagement of the artifacts we discuss. The point is to know one's embodied algorithms, one's society of mind, and how each individual reworks memory while interacting with the artwork. Readings from Maturana and Varela, *Árbol*; Ramachandran; Kandel, *The Age*; Dehaene; and others illustrate the micro- and macrocosmic brain areas corresponding to individual involvement with life/art and help each student understand how and why she realizes such "universal" experiences in her own way. In discussing neuroscience research on the literary and other artworks we study, students develop greater awareness of how their self-realization compares to others'. Autopoietic self-assessment is always part of the discussion on the artifacts. Students apply personal evaluative tools and consider their individual abilities to "read" bodily/facial expressions and to identify their empathic "mirroring" of characters or contexts. Many students are familiar with evaluative tools, given the rising number of individuals using them to self-identify across the Asperger's spectrum or who claim learning and behavior difficulties. In self-assessment, students use the Davis Interpersonal Reactivity Index in Keysers' study of mirroring, empathizing, and social connectivity (2011). Instead of the expensive brain scans that Starr was able to use, students learn to compare with each other their algorithms of empathy and aesthetic self-realization of the artifacts we consider. In addition, they learn about mindfulness techniques for increasing memory and awareness of one's algorithms. Varela and his heirs found similarities among meditative practices and the processes of mind-brain reorganization and self-awareness in autopoiesis (Varela, Thompson, and Rosch; Thompson; Capra and Luisi). Today's students are learning greater self-realization through mindfulness practices developed by neuroscientists and experienced Buddhists, as seen in Davidson's work with the Dalai Lama and school systems currently teaching meditation.

Music is the artistic genre that most students readily engaged with when we learned how body-brains self-realize in listening, singing, dancing, or playing instruments. In the seminar of fourteen students, only one—who self-identified as "on the Asperger's spectrum and not particularly empathic"—reported his lack of interest in any kind of music. The same student identified closely with "Funes the Memorious," Borges' fictional savant studied by neuroscientist Quian Quiroga to illustrate abnormal memory. Like Funes, my student could memorize material, but he could not easily reorganize memories in new contexts. However, most students in the seminar and in my *Quixote* class gained insight from understanding how the old knight's default system of memory strongly colored his ability to perceive new objects and experiences.[20] This helped them realize how much individual learning depends on concentrated recreation of memory within new biocultural realizations. Default memory systems also helped some students understand why they tend to prefer familiar kinds of music, literature, performances, or plastic arts rather than explore new ones. All agreed that with more mindful exposure to new forms they could increase self-awareness and growth rather than simply returning to their default choices. As always, use of familiar, contemporary examples helped them understand their varying levels of self-realization. They attributed much of Pharrell Williams' success as a songwriter and vocalist to his self-acknowledged synesthesia. Discussion of how Williams associates numbers, colors, and other perceptions such as scent or touch was supported by our reading neuroscientist Ramachandran on the topic and by a class member explaining how his synesthesia boosts his memory. Finally, the plastic arts helped students connect visually with their own autopoiesis. Kandel's study of mirroring in Velázquez's "Las Meninas" engaged them in biocultural self-realization in the context of Cervantes' times and *Don Quixote*'s artistry. In the seminar as well as the *Quixote* class, the biocultural approach to chapters, such as those I have analyzed in this essay, afforded all students opportunities to enrich their individual development by engaging with Cervantes' masterpiece.

20. See Starr; Connor-Swietlicki, "Beyond Cognition."

WORKS CITED

Armstrong, Paul B. *How Literature Plays with the Brain: The Neuroscience of Reading and Art*. Baltimore: Johns Hopkins UP, 2013.

Canavaggio, Jean. *Cervantes*. Trans. J. R. Jones. New York: Norton, 1990.

Capra, Fritjof, and Pier Luigi Luisi. *The Systems View of Life: A Unifying Vision*. Cambridge: Cambridge UP, 2014.

Cervantes Saavedra, Miguel de. *Don Quixote*. Trans. Edith Grossman. New York: Harper Collins, 2003.

Cervantes Saavedra, Miguel de. *El ingenioso hidalgo don Quijote de la Mancha*. Ed. Tom Lathrop. Newark: European Masterpieces, 2003.

Connor (Connor-Swietlicki), Catherine. "Beyond Cognition: Don Quijote and Other Embodied Minds." *Cognitive Cervantes*. Ed. Julien Simon, Barbara Simerka, and Howard Mancing. Spec. cluster of essays of *Cervantes: Bulletin of the Cervantes Society of America* 32.1 (2012): 231–61.

Connor (Connor-Swietlicki), Catherine. "Bridging the Performance Gap: The Body, Cognitive Studies and *Comedia* Theory." *Bulletin of the Comediantes* 55.2 (2003 [2004]): 11–53.

Connor (Connor-Swietlicki), Catherine. "Embodying Rape and Violence: Your Mirror Neurons and 2RC Teatro's 'Alcalde de Zalamea'." *Comedia Performance* 7.1 (Spring 2010): 9–52.

Damasio, Antonio. *The Feeling of What Happens: Body, Emotion and the Making of Consciousness*. London: Heinemann, 1999.

Damasio, Antonio. *Looking for Spinoza: Joy, Sorrow, and the Feeling Brain*. New York: Harcourt, 2003.

Damasio, Antonio. *Self Comes to Mind: Constructing the Conscious Brain*. New York: Pantheon, 2010.

Davidson, Richard J. with Sharon Begley. *The Emotional Life of Your Brain*. London: Penguin-Hudson Street P, 2012.

De Tapia, Serafín. "Los moriscos de Castilla la Vieja, ¿una identidad en proceso de disolución?" *Sharq al-Ándalus* 12 (1995): 179–95.

Dehaene, Stanislas. *Reading in the Brain: The New Science of How We Read*. New York: Random, 2010.

Edelman, Gerald. *Bright Air, Brilliant Fire: On the Matter of the Mind*. New York: Basic, 1992.

Edelman, Gerald. *The Remembered Present: A Biological Theory of Consciousness*. New York: Basic, 1989.

Iacoboni, Marco. *Mirroring People: The New Science of How We Connect with Others*. New York: Farrar, 2008.

Kandel, Eric. *The Age of Insight: The Quest to Understand the Unconscious in Art, Mind and Brain, From Vienna 1900 to the Present*. New York: Random House, 2012.

Kandel, Eric. *In Search of Memory: The Emergence of a New Science of the Mind*. New York: Norton, 2006.

Kandel, Eric, and Larry Squire. *Memory: From Mind to Molecules*. New York: Holt, 1999.

Keen, Suzanne. *Empathy and the Novel*. Oxford: Oxford UP, 2007.

Keysers, Christian. *The Empathic Brain: How the Discovery of Mirror Neurons Changes Our Understanding of Human Nature*. N.p.: Social Brain P, 2011.

López-Muñoz, Francisco, Cecilio Álamo, and Pilar García-García. "Locos y dementes en la literatura cervantina: A propósito de las fuentes médicas de Cervantes en materia neuropsiquiátrica." *Revista de Neurología* 46.8 (2008): 489–501.

Martín-Araguz, A., and C. Bustamante-Martínez. "*Examen de ingenios*, de Juan Huarte de San Juan, y los albores de la neurobiología de la inteligencia en el Renacimiento español." *Revista de Neurología* 38.12 (2004): 16–30.

Maturana, Humberto, and Francisco Varela. El *árbol del conocimiento: Las bases biológicas del entendimiento humano.* Santiago: Edición Universitaria, 1976.

Maturana, Humberto, and Francisco Varela. *Autopoiesis and Cognition: The Realization of the Living.* London: Reidel, 1980.

Maturana, Humberto, and Francisco Varela. *De máquinas y seres vivos*: Autopoiesis, *la organización de lo vivo.* 6th ed. Santiago: Editorial Universitaria, 1994.

Maturana, Humberto, and Francisco Varela. *The Tree of Knowledge: The Biological Roots of Human Understanding.* Trans. Robert Paolucci. Rev. ed. Boston: Shambhala, 1998. Orig. published in 1980.

Menocal, María Rosa. *The Ornament of the World: How Muslims, Jews and Christians Created a Culture of Tolerance in Medieval Spain.* New York: Little Brown, 2002.

Naidoo, N., M. Ferber, M. Master, Y. Zhu, and A. Pack. "Aging Impairs the Unfolded Protein Response to Sleep Deprivation and Leads to Pro-apoptotic [cell-death] Signals." *Journal of Neuroscience* 26 (June 28, 2008): 6539–48.

Palma, José-Alberto, and Fermín Palma. "Neurology and Don Quixote." *European Neurology* 68 (2012): 247–57.

Quian Quiroga, Rodrigo. *Borges and Memory: Encounters with the Human Brain.* Trans. Juan Pablo Fernández. Cambridge: MIT P, 2012.

Ramachandran, V. S. *The Tell-Tale Brain: A Neuroscientist's Quest for What Makes Us Human.* New York: Norton, 2011.

Rizzolatti, Giacomo, and Corrado Sinigaglia. *Mirrors in the Brain: How Our Minds Share Actions and Emotions.* Trans. Frances Anderson. Oxford: Oxford UP, 2008.

Starr, G. Gabrielle. *Feeling Beauty: The Neuroscience of Aesthetic Experience.* Cambridge: MIT P, 2013.

Stone, Robert S. "Moorish Quixote: Reframing the Novel." *Cervantes: Bulletin of the Cervantes Society of America* 33.1 (2013): 81–112.

Thompson, Evan. *Mind in Life: Biology, Phenomenology, and the Sciences of the Mind.* Cambridge: Harvard UP, 2007.

Varela, Francisco, Evan Thompson, and Eleanor Rosch. *The Embodied Mind: Cognitive Science and Human Experience.* Cambridge: MIT P, 1991.

Zeki, Semir. *Splendors and Miseries of the Brain: Love, Creativity, and the Quest for Human Happiness.* West Sussex: Wiley-Blackwell, 2009.

CHAPTER 4

The Janus Hypothesis in *Don Quixote*: Memory and Imagination in Cervantes

JULIA DOMÍNGUEZ

The memory of the past is not made to remember the past; it's made to prevent the future. Memory is a prediction instrument.

Alain Berthoz

The autobiographical self is built on the basis of past memories and memories of the plans that we have made; it's the lived past and the anticipated future.

Antonio Damasio

Ausente, en la memoria la imagino;
Mis espirtus, pensando que la vían
Se mueven y se encienden sin medida

Absent, I image her in my memory;
my spirits, imagining seeing her,
move and turn without measure

Garcilaso de la Vega

I will start this essay with suggestive and thoughtful parting words by Daniel Schacter at the end of his book *Searching for Memory*: "Our memories are the fragile but powerful products of what we recall from the past, believe about the present, and imagine about the future"

(308).[1] Upon reading this quote for the first time, I immediately recalled how Cervantes' *Don Quixote* unfolds time and again: the protagonist's memories are created from his past chivalric readings and are the essence of his beliefs, actions, and desire to seek adventures. Those memories also guide his decisions and actions, becoming the principal subject written by the fictional historian, Cide Hamete Benegeli, who immortalizes the knight's adventure. Based on his reading experience, Don Quixote relives the past throughout the novel in order to construct an imagined future.

In Cervantes scholarship, studies abound on the "diseased" mind of the knight caused by humoral imbalances. Less studied, however, is the relevance of memory in the novel, and even less its relationship to imagination or the symbiotic workings between memory and imagination. In this essay, I argue that the intimate link between these two internal senses is central to Cervantes' novel. Following both the ancients and such early modern thinkers as Juan Huarte de San Juan in his *Examen de ingenios* [The Examination of Men's Wits] (1575), Cervantes came to realize how memory is not separate from present or future creative processes. The novel tells the story of a gentleman who goes mad from reading too many chivalric romances and whose actions seemingly pit his imagination against his bookish memory. However, the source of Alonso Quijano's problem is embedded in imagination and its relation to memories that are rooted in the past but available for future recall. I base my suppositions on Yadin Dudai and Mary Carruthers' "The Janus Face of Mnemosyne," which explores the latest scientific advances related to memory's capacity to both record the past and imagine the future—an idea somehow intuited in ancient and medieval times. Cervantes' character, Don Quixote, exemplifies that idea, as it embodies the characteristics of the Janus face, a visual representation of one who looks at the past and the future simultaneously, thereby intertwining seemingly dissimilar timeframes into a continuum. Using this metaphor as a point of departure, I will discuss how memory was believed to function in early modernity. I aim to provide a unique perspective on how the past directs Don Quixote's future. Close examination of the nuances between early modern ideas and recent scholarship on memory helps us understand more deeply Cervantes' contemplation of the human mind.[2]

1. I would like to express my sincere gratitude and appreciation to Isabel Jaén and Julien Simon for believing in this project when it was only a very abstract idea.
2. My study does not seek to connect the early modern ideas about the mind with the mechanics of what we know about the brain today, nor do I intend to compare them, which would be impossible. Instead, I seek to use the latter as a starting point to appreciate the former.

Recent research in cognitive neuroscience strongly suggests that past recollection and future prospection are closely related functions. Neuroimaging studies indicate that when a subject recalls the past and considers the future, similar networks in the brain are activated simultaneously, a phenomenon also known in scientific circles as the "Janus hypothesis."[3] Those neuroimaging studies also reveal that future event simulations are constructed by "extracting and recombining stored information into a simulation of a novel event" (Schacter, Addis, and Buckner 660). As Schacter and Addis note, the memory system is built based on constructive principles: "it can draw on the elements and gist of the past, and extract, recombine, and reassemble them into imaginary events that never occurred in that exact form" (27). Hence, memory serves as a simulator in that the core network used to recall past experiences can create future scenarios based on those past experiences.

Cognitive neuroscience has come to treat retrospection and prospection as twin functions of the same neural system, and they are closely related to episodic memory—in our ability to imagine nonexistent events and future happenings: "Important in this planning effort is not *accuracy of reproduction, but the act of imaginative recreation itself* as a totally sensed and felt experience" (Dudai and Carruthers 567; my emphasis). Some researchers tie prospective thinking to very specific brain functions involving memory. Ironically this new line of research in memory science manifests what Alan Richardson has called "a remarkable deficit in long-term (historical) memory" (673) as such theories regarding "mental time travel" have been around since ancient times.[4]

3. Currently researchers, after focusing entirely on the role of memory to preserve and recover the past, are trying to understand memory's errors by looking at its adaptive and constructive nature, as argued by Daniel Schacter and Donna Rose Addis: "There is also another important function for constructing memory, one that emerges from an idea that a growing number of researchers are embracing—that memory is important for the future as well as the past . . . people draw on past experiences in order to imagine and simulate episodes that might occur in their personal futures" (27).

4. As Richardson has pointed out, current memory researchers have begun to use the word "imagination" to express this ability of the mind to construct future scenarios (out of memories) and project itself "into other times, places, perspectives, and even invented worlds" (666). However, as Richardson notes in his reading of Daniel Gilbert's *Stumbling on Happiness*, the term "imagination" has been part of history since antiquity: "By imagination, cognitive psychologists and neuroscientists do not intend some highly specialized sense of the term, remote from common usage . . . rather they mean roughly what philosophers, poets, and literary theorists have meant by imagination and its equivalents since Plato" (665) or, as Gilbert puts it, "[the unique human] ability to imagine episodes and objects that do not exist in the realm of the real" (qtd. in Richardson 665).

Such figures as Hippocrates, Galen, and Aristotle (and their medieval commentators) as well as Renaissance scholars who studied the mind (Huarte and Juan Luis Vives in Spain) were quite aware of the important role of memory and its relation to imagination. To further grasp this intrinsic connection, it is imperative to understand two notions: since ancient times until the seventeenth century, first, it was believed that memories were formed out of *phantasms* (*imagines* in Latin), which originated in the complex process of perception; and second, there existed mechanisms that converted memory into an active player in the role of imagination and simultaneously in the construction of future scenarios.

JANUS HYPOTHESIS IN HISTORY: MEMORY AND IMAGINATION

hacer memoria de las cosas y acordarse dellas después de sabidas es obra imaginativa, como el escribir y tornarlo a leer es obra del escribano, y no del papel

to remember things and recall them afterwards is a work of imagination just like writing and returning to read it is a work of a writer and not of his page
Juan Huarte de San Juan

In his *Margarita Philosophica* (1503), a compendium of grammar, science, and philosophy, Gregor Reisch included what later would be one of the most popular portrayals of the brain and its functions. Reisch was following the ideas of Hippocrates, "The Father of Medicine," Herophilus of Chalcedon, Erasistratus of Ceos, and other important figures of the School of Alexandria (300 B.C.). Hippocrates' ideas were later followed by Galen. According to the Greek tradition and the Galenic anatomical description, memory (in the posterior ventricle of the brain) was believed to be a part of the internal senses along with imagination and intellect.[5] It was thought that through the physiological process of perception, the information entering the brain derived from the external senses through different channels—whether tactile, olfactory, visual, or auditory—ended up in the form of an image in memory (a copy or *eikon* in the words of Aristotle)

---

5. For more information on internal and external senses, see Wolfson's "The Internal Senses in Latin, Arabic, and Hebrew Philosophic Texts" and Summers' *The Judgment of Sense*. See also my forthcoming article "The Internal Senses in *Don Quixote* and the Anatomy of Memory," where I describe in greater detail the inner senses within the framework of the psychological model of Cervantes' time.

that could be visualized in the act of retrieval by the eye of the mind. The Spanish humanist and philosopher Juan Luis Vives also developed this idea in his writings:

> La sede de la memoria, a modo de taller, la ha colocado la naturaleza, con admirable previsión en el occipucio, por cuanto ve las cosas pasadas; de este modo tenemos allí una especie de ojo mucho más excelente que un ojo material que allí se hubiera podido incorporar, como el de la frente que en la fábula se atribuye a Jano. (II.2)

> Memory's workshop-like home was placed by nature with admirable anticipation in the occiput [the posterior part of the head] through which one sees past things; in this way, there we have a sort of eye which is much better than a physical eye that could have been placed there, like an eye embedded on the forehead attributed to the fable of Janus.

The information gathered by the external senses was received in the *sensus comunis* (or common sense area) and transformed into images in the *imaginativa*. Simultaneously, the experience was also "estimated" emotionally (like an instinct) in the *cogitativa*, where it was considered as benevolent or malevolent (Dudai and Carruthers 567). The final resulting image was then considered a product of the imagination charged with emotional overtones. Thought was therefore an activity of the imagination since memory inventoried these products in a way that made them accessible to the recreative action of remembering (Dudai and Carruthers 567). Consequently, a memory was considered a mental picture, a *phantasm* or image previously created by the *imaginativa* and stored in memory for future recall that had come about in the first place as a result of the process of sense perception. Hence, remembering was seen as a mental process by which one could visualize or "read" those images.

As Guillermo Serés reminds us in his edition of *Examen*, according to Huarte, imagination is in charge of creating the image in memory: "La memoria está directamente relacionada con la imaginación: es la que guarda los 'fantamas' con los que ha de 'hacer figura' la imaginación" (568n122) ["Memory is directly related to imagination: it is what stores the images that will be used by imagination"].[6] Huarte was clearly indicating that memory and imagination rely on one another, an idea that was shared by Plato, Aristotle, Avicenna, Albertus Magnus, and Roger Bacon.[7]

---

6. Unless otherwise noted, translations are mine.
7. See Bundy.

Consider, for example, Aristotle's thoughts on the proximity of memory to imagination in the soul:

> It is apparent, then, to which part of the soul memory belongs, namely the same part as that to which imagination belongs. And it is the objects of imagination that are remembered in their own right, whereas things that are not grasped without imagination are remembered in virtue of an incidental association. (450a 22)[8]

For Aristotle, a past action is an interior object that is not absent but rather one that is imprinted upon us forever, and it has the power to resurface in future creation or in imagination, and to foresee the future. In connection to this idea Galen similarly argues in his Book II *De motu muscularum* that, "The part of the soul that imagines, whatever it is, is the same that remembers."[9]

MEMORY AND IMAGINATION IN *DON QUIXOTE*

Cervantes wrote *Don Quixote* during a period that saw the continuation of the Galenic understanding of the brain and was familiar with the scientific and medical literature of his day. Among the 214 books that the writer owned in his personal library, there were well-known medical treatises from the period, including Huarte's *Examen*.[10] The writer also was aware of the influence of popular medical treatises and manuals related to the mind science of the time, fashionable reading during that era in Spain. Among these, it is worth mentioning, for example, Antonio Gómez Pereira (1500–1588) and his *Antoniana Margarita* (1554) and Miguel de Sabuco y

---

8. Translation by Richard Sorabji in *Aristotle on Memory* 49.

9. Cited by Huarte in Latin and translated by Serés in Spanish: "La parte del alma que imagina, cualquiera que sea, es la misma que recuerda" (363n46). My English translation.

10 Among the medical treatises that Cervantes owned were also the *Libro de las quatro enfermedades cortesanas* [Book of the Four Courtly Diseases] (1544) by Luis Lobera de Ávila (1480?–1551), the *Práctica y theórica de cirugía en romance y latín* [Practice and Theory of Surgery in Romance and Latin] (1584) by Dionisio Daza Chacón (1513–1596), the *Practica in arte chirurgica copiosa* [Practice in the Abundant Surgical Art] by Giovanni da Vigo (1450–1525), the *Dioscórides* (1555) commented by Andrés Laguna (1499–1560), and the *Tratado nuevamente impreso de todas las enfermedades de los riñones, vexiga, y carnosidades de la verga* [Newly Printed Treatise on All the Diseases of the Kidneys, Bladder and Fleshiness of the Penis] (1586) by Francisco Díaz. For a full listing of the texts kept by Cervantes, see Eisenberg, "La biblioteca de Cervantes."

Álvarez (1525–1588) and his study about emotions in *Nueva filosofía de la naturaleza del hombre* [New Philosophy of Human Nature] (1587). Of special mention is *De anima et vita* (1538) by Juan Luis Vives (1492–1540) in which the author considers the emotions as possible sources of instability in the judgment.

Cervantes was witness to a growing interest during his time in human psychology and the composition of the human wit. Based on the books he possessed and his own writings, in which references to medical topics of all sorts appear, there is little doubt that he was familiar with the humoral theories and the ideas about the mind that characterized the period. The depiction in some cases of mental insanity along with the imbalance of humors and the different types of melancholy (*Don Quixote, El Licenciado Vidriera*) indicate that Cervantes had good knowledge of medicine.[11] It is important to remember that he came from a family in which several members worked in a medical profession, including his father, who was a barber-surgeon.[12]

The word *memory* appears 134 times in *Don Quixote*, and this frequency should not be surprising if one considers that nearly everything the protagonist does is drawn from his memory of reading. In Cervantes' time memory had long been a valued and honored faculty, and that characterization changed only slightly between ancient times and the early modern period. Cervantes seemed to realize that memory's philosophical value had great potential in literary creation, especially through the literature-distorted mind of a character like Don Quixote. By considering the *Quixote* in relation to some of the scientific ideas of the period, especially Huarte's most important work, one can see the impact of these writings on the author.[13] In the *Examen*, Huarte summarizes the memory process (with a clear Aristotelian influence) by using the wax tablet metaphor described in Aristotle's *De anima*, where sensory impressions are imprinted like a stamp in the wax once they become images:

> Porque así como el escribano escribe en el papel las cosas que quiere que no se olviden y después de escritas las torna a leer, de la mesma manera se ha de entender que la imaginativa escribe en la memoria las figuras de las cosas que

11. See Soufas; Palma and Palma; López-Muñoz, Álamo, and García-García; García Barreno; and Peset.
12. Barber-surgeon was a medical profession of low prestige.
13. On the relationship between Huarte and Cervantes, see the works by scholars and scientists such as Iriarte; Jaén; Salillas; and López-Muñoz, Álamo, and García-García.

conocieron los cinco sentidos y el entendimiento y otras que ella misma fa-
brica. Y cuando quiere acordarse de ellas, dice Aristóteles que las torna a mirar
y contemplar. . . . Esto mismo hace la imaginativa: escrebir en la memoria y
tornar a leer cuando se quiere acordar. (363)

Just as the scribe writes on paper the things he does not want to forget and
reads them again (to remember), in the same way it is understood that the imagination inscribes in memory the visualization of things that the five senses
realize and the intellect and other things that imagination itself creates. And
when one wants to remember them, according to Aristotle, one should return
to contemplate them and consider them anew. . . . Imagination does this, too:
inscribing in memory and returning to read when one wants to remember.

A similar process plays out in *Don Quixote*. It is important to remember
that *Don Quixote* is a novel about reading, remembering what was read,
and acting upon reading by imposing oneself into a narrative that exists
only in imagination. Memories for the knight are not just signatory traces
of the past precisely because they are also closely connected to the faculty
of the imagination. According to Huarte:

El hombre . . . tiene tres potencias para conocer todas tres diferencias de
tiempo: memoria para lo pasado, sentidos para lo presente, imaginación y entendimiento para lo que está por venir. Y así como hay hombres que hacen
ventaja a otros en acordarse de las cosas pasadas, y otros en conocer lo presente, así hay muchos que tienen más habilidad natural en imaginar lo que
está por venir. (317)

Man . . . possesses the possibility of knowing three differences about time:
memory for what has passed, senses for the present, imagination and understanding for what is to come. Hence, there are those who take advantage of the
senses in remembering the past and others who do so in understanding the
present while still there are many more who have a natural ability in imagining what will come.

The protagonist of the novel is who he is because of his constant retrieval
of his bookish memories. His memories define him, they belong to him,
they shape his knowledge; and he makes them his because they are rooted
in his everyday life, they are part of his personal history, and each episode
is related to the stories he has read and that he has made his own. His
memory is what gives him a sense of personal identity, of self-awareness.
In fact, everything he does depends on his bookish memory, and that is
how he builds his identity.

It is necessary to keep in mind how important a book and the act of reading was in an early modern culture still rooted in the oral tradition that was itself dependent upon memory. The process by which one reads and imagines, or one listens and imagines, is a process that shapes the story, as Mary Carruthers indicates in *The Book of Memory*: "Whether the words come through the sensory gateway of the eyes or the ears, they must be processed and transformed in memory—they are made our own" (14). Later on, she explains, "What is read as well as what is seen is transformed into a mental signal that is read by the eye of the mind" (34). Reading was therefore considered a way of transferring the text into memory by means of images. In fact, the Latin verb *lego* ("to read") means to collect or gather, which has a fairly obvious connection to memory as the recollection of gathered material (Carruthers 11). If one considers the value of books in the early modern period, it should come as no surprise that some of the most used metaphors to describe memory were those linking memory to writing, such as a wax tablet, a written page, an inventory, or a library, among others.[14]

Don Quixote constructs himself as a character through the memories of what he remembers of chivalric novels. His life is composed of bits and pieces of reading memories that he subsequently uses to imagine future scenarios, and this process of memory retrieval and construction of self dictates how the novel unfolds. For example, he constantly uses his memories to justify his behavior and guarantee his future as a knight. In this sense, and remembering Schacter's words at the beginning of this essay, his memories are the fragile and powerful product of the past, they represent beliefs about the present, and they express an imagined future.

Don Quixote's knowledge base is derived from his close readings. The associated images he creates have been filtered, mediated, and influenced by a psychological imbalance that leads the knight to relate his circumstances to his personal situation, willfully leaving aside all objectivity. In moments when there is an unbalance in the hierarchy of the functions of the brain, the senses too are disordered, which leads to the protagonist's confusion, as the narrator indicates: "Siendo, pues, loco, como lo es, y de locura que las más veces toma unas cosas por otras y juzga lo blanco por negro y lo negro por blanco" (II.10.703) ["Then, being crazy, which is what he is, with the kind of craziness that most of the time takes one thing for another, and thinks white is black and black is

14. For more information on metaphors of memory and memorial objects, see Carruthers 44–54.

white" (515)].[15] Some of this can be accounted for by keeping in mind the principles of the Galenic humoral theories. According to the Galenic tradition, the melancholic humor is a product of the black bile that attacks the brain, affecting especially the internal senses such as memory and its functions. When this imbalance appears, the power of imagination increases while the intellect suffers dysfunction. Such a scenario would explain Don Quixote's heightened use of perception and the senses as well as his exalted imagination, often to the detriment of his intellect. For example, Aurora Egido writes that Don Quixote forcibly adjusts reality to his memory, and she explains the process in the following manner:

> No se trata, por tanto, de que el proceso de percepción de la realidad sufra una tergiversación posterior en la imaginativa, sino que ésta actúe sobre el presente en una permanente adulteración de lo percibido, por obra y gracia de la omnipresente memoria y del ejercicio de la fantasía. La memoria hace de filtro constante entre la percepción sensitiva y la imaginativa, obligándola a representar lo recordado y no aquello que captan los sentidos en el momento presente. (12)

> It has nothing to do, therefore, with the process of the perception of reality which suffers a posterior distortion in the imagination, but instead imagination acts upon the present in a permanent adulteration of what was perceived, by force and grace of memory's omnipresence and by fantasy's imposition. Memory becomes a constant filter between sensitive perception and imagination, obliging it to represent what was remembered and not what the senses capture in the present. (12)

In other words, as Don Quixote processes reality, memories stored from his readings are activated and his imagination runs wild, as if the process of perception and cognition inverted the traditional order. Although imagination is often valued more than memory, without memory imagination simply does not work, since the former provides the material for the latter. Huarte, among others, believed that in human psychology memory played a significant role: "el entendimiento no puede obrar sin que la memoria esté presente (representándole las figuras y fantasmas conforme aquello: *oportet intelligentem phantasmata speculari*) ni la memoria sin que asista con ella la imaginativa . . ." (325) ["The intellect

15. All English translations of *Don Quixote* come from Grossman. For the Spanish text, I use Rico's edition.

cannot work without memory's presence (representing the conforming figures and images: *oportet intelligentem phantasmata speculari*) nor can memory function without the imagination"]. To this, Huarte adds that memory "sólo sirve de guardar y tener en custodia las formas y figuras que las otras potencias han concebido" (195) ["only serves to store and have in its custody the forms and figures that other faculties have conceived"]. Indeed, for him, the principal function of memory is "guardar estos fantasmas para cuando el entendimiento los quisiere contemplar; *y si ésta se pierde, es imposible poder las demás potencias obrar*" (336; my emphasis) ["to store the images for when the intellect needs to contemplate them; *if memory is lost, it is impossible for the other faculties to work correctly*"].

Don Quixote's memory is connected to experience. As his story unfolds, individual experiences immediately connect to a similar image he has already stored in memory. The process connects experience and memory in interesting and novel ways, but such a process can cloud, even shape, reality. Don Quixote is therefore subject to the past since his memories override his perceptions—suggesting, as Egido has stated, that without memory, there cannot be invention: "La imaginativa del héroe opera siempre a partir de la memoria que es continuo pasto de sus invenciones. Memoria e imaginación trabajan conjuntamente a la hora de recrear las lecturas" (10) ["The hero's imagination always operates from memory, which is a continous product of his inventions. Memory and imagination work together when recreating readings"]. The words "memory" and "imagination" often appear in tandem throughout *Don Quixote*, as if Cervantes understood that both faculties needed to coexist and that their interdependence was so well regarded in literary and scientific circles during the period. At other points in the work, "imagination" is a substitute for "memory": "Llenósele la fantasía de todo aquello que leía en los libros . . . y asentósele de tal modo en la imaginación que era verdad toda aquella máquina de aquellas soñadas invenciones que leía" (I.1.39) ["His fantasy filled with everything that he read in his books . . . and he became so convinced in his imagination of the truth of all . . . he read that for him no history in the world was truer" (21)]. The interconnectedness of imagination and memory in *Don Quixote* clearly coincides with Huarte. For him, memory stores information, but it is imagination that imprints upon memory and then recalls "De manera que hacer memoria de las cosas y acordarse dellas después de sabidas es obra imaginativa" (364) ["In such a way that making a memory and storing it afterwards is a work of imagination"]. As one recollects a past experience, one is also reconstructing such an experience and imagining future ones: "Reminiscence is an act of interpretation, inference, investigation, and reconstruction, *an act like reading*" (Carruthers 29; my emphasis). Memory serves as a filter for Don Quixote's sensory perception, representing the recalled object instead of what his senses capture in the present:

> y como a nuestro aventurero todo cuanto pensaba, veía o imaginaba le parecía ser hecho y pasar al modo de lo que había leído, luego que vio la venta se le representó que era un castillo con sus cuatro torres y chapiteles de luciente plata, sin faltarle su puente levadiza y honda cava, con todos aquellos adherentes que semejantes castillos se pintan. (I.2.49)

> and since everything our adventurer thought, saw, or imagined seemed to happen according to what he had read, as soon as he saw the inn it appeared to him to be a castle complete with four towers and spires of gleaming silver, not to mention a drawbridge and deep moat and all the other details depicted on such castles. (26)

Don Quixote's dominant memory supersedes everything in his present. The images that he perceives and the places he visits are immediately identified with, and subsumed by, the places and images stored in his memory (Egido 11). As Aristotle pointed out long ago in his writings on reminiscence, memory leads to a representation of something that is not present (50–51 in Sorabji's translation; originally appears in Aristotle, *De memoria* 450b 11–20), implying that association and recollection can be intimately linked. In fact, recollection is therefore subordinate to the associational character of memory. As in the earlier example from chapter II, the knight arrives at the inn and immediately converts what he experiences into something else, which he draws from memory. Whatever he touches, sees, hears, eats, or drinks is subservient to what he imagines those objects should be: the inn and its welcoming prostitutes become a castle governed by a warden with damsels who welcome him with music and a scrumptious meal befitting his status. His judgment is warped by memories drawn from his readings, which he then endeavors to imitate at all times. When his external senses permit him to see, smell, hear, and touch, he does not conceive what is before him but rather retrieves a mental image stored in his memory. The resulting action is therefore a product of the images formed from his readings and subsequently used to create imagined scenarios.

Arguably the most symbolic episode of the novel—the one featuring the adventure of the windmills—is a fitting example, among so many others, to demonstrate the deformation of reality due to the knight's recall from memory. When Don Quixote sees the windmills, their enormous size and quick-moving blades are not an example of an early modern technology that dotted the landscape of central Spain but rather dreadful giants derived from the phantasmagorias he created when reading his books. He is incapable of differentiating between what he sees before him and what his readings have long told him they should be. This is essentially Don Quixote's foremost problem throughout the text. The objectiveness of memory is lost and the knight becomes unable to discriminate between his past and his present. He does not accurately see, hear, smell, or touch whatever appears before him, but rather these external sensorial images direct his future, a future distorted by the past.

Several other examples throughout the text emblematize the interchangeability of memory and imagination, and the two concepts even appear together often as if distinguishing between them were impossible. An example of the substitution at a lexical level can be found in the second part of the novel when Sancho responds to the fantastic tale of Don Quixote's adventure in the Cave of Montesinos by equating imagination ("magín") with memory: "Creo—respondió Sancho—que aquel Merlín, o aquellos encantadores que encantaron a toda la chusma que vuestra merced dice que ha visto y comunicado allá bajo, le encajaron en el magín o la memoria toda esa máquina que nos ha contado, y todo aquello que por contar le queda" (II.23.825) ["I believe, responded Sancho, that Merlin, or those enchanters who enchanted that whole crowd your grace says you saw and talked to down there, put into your mind or memory the whole story that you've told us, and the rest that you will have to tell" (611)]. As Sancho points out, on a very basic level, imagination and memory are the same—here used as synonyms.

Other instances in the story likewise indicate this close relationship between memory and imagination. In the opening chapters, Don Quixote spends a great deal of time creating a name for his lady and himself, and even longer coming up with a name befitting his steed: "Y así, después de muchos nombres que formó, borró y quitó, añadió, deshizo y tornó a hacer en su memoria e imaginación, al fin le vino a llamar Rocinante: nombre, a su parecer, alto, sonoro y significativo de lo que había sido" (I.1.42) ["And so, after many names that he shaped and discarded, subtracted from and added to, unmade and remade in his memory and imagination, he finally decided to call the horse Rocinante: A name, in his opinion, that was noble, sonorous and, reflective of what it had been" (22)]. At another point, during his first adventure, when the innkeeper reminds the knight of the necessity of carrying money and clean undergarments, the suggestion triggers recollection of also needing a squire, just as he read in his books: "Mas, viniéndole a la memoria los consejos de su huésped cerca de las prevenciones tan necesarias que había de llevar consigo, especial la de los dineros y camisas, determinó volver a su casa y acomodarse de todo, y de un escudero, haciendo cuenta de recebir a un labrador vecino suyo" (I.4.62) ["But calling to mind the advice of his host regarding the necessary provisions that he had to carry with him, especially money and shirts, he resolved to return to his house and outfit himself with everything, including a squire, thinking he would take on a neighbor of his, a peasant" (35)]. The laborer in question of course is Sancho Panza, who will act as Don Quixote's squire for the remainder of both parts of the novel. Here, the espousal of this particular squire corresponds more to his present than to his bookish past: Sancho is a somewhat dimwitted man of humble origins unable to read or write and who has absolutely no experience in the world of knight-errantry—but he is available and up to the task at hand. However, he is nothing like the typical young apprentices in the chivalric romances who are plucked from the nobility to serve great knights before becoming one themselves. Moreover, Sancho's physical presence—he is nearing middle age, short and stout, and driven by life's simple pleasures such as eating and sleeping—compares with Don Quixote's advanced age and frailness, but neither of them compares favorably to their models. Don Quixote even searches his memory for a previous instance in which a squire rode an ass: "imaginando si se le acordaba si algún caballero andante había traído escudero caballero asnalmente, pero nunca le vino alguno a la memoria" (I.7.92) ["wondering if he recalled any knight-errant who had with him a squire riding on a donkey, and none came to mind" (56)]. Here and elsewhere, composite memories serve as a reference point to recontextualize the present and shape the future.

Other examples likewise bear this out. After Don Quixote is knighted by the innkeeper and returns home to employ his squire, he confronts a group of travelers who refuse to admit that his lady, Dulcinea, is the most beautiful in the world. A fight ensues and Rocinante trips, leaving Don Quixote badly hurt and senseless on the path. His physical inability to get up does not impede his rather active imagination and he quickly compares his plight to what he once read—except that he gives the story a new context in which he is now the unfortunate star:

Viendo, pues, que, en efeto, no podía menearse, acordó de acogerse a su ordinario remedio, que era pensar en algún paso de sus libros; y trújole su locura a la memoria aquel de Valdovinos y del marqués de Mantua, cuando Carloto le dejó herido en la montiña, historia sabida de los niños, no ignorada de los mozos, celebrada y aun creída de los viejos; y, con todo esto, no más verdadera que los milagros de Mahoma. (I.5.71)

Seeing, then, that in fact he could not move, he took refuge in his usual remedy, which was to think about some situation from his books, and his madness made him recall that of Valdovinos and the Marquis of Mantua, when Carloto left him wounded in the highlands, a history known to children, acknowledged by youths, celebrated, and even believed by the old, and, despite all this, no truer than the miracles of Mohammed. (41)

These examples illustrate how Don Quixote's entire profession depends on what was read, stored, and then recalled. However, his present circumstances drive his interpretation of these memories so that they become relevant to the situation at hand.

CONCLUSIONS

Recent research in cognitive neuroscience indicates that remembering the past and imagining the future are linked ("Janus hypothesis") and helps us understand how early modern thinkers viewed this connection.[16] I have discussed early theories of memory and imagination and their central role in Cervantes' conception of narrative as can be seen in Don Quixote's actions. Following both the ancients and such contemporaneous thinkers as Huarte, the novelist seemed to understand that retained memory is not separate from present or future creative processes. In the novel, Don Quixote goes mad from reading too many chivalric romances. However, time and again, the source of his problem is embedded in imagination, a memory-bound construct rooted in the past but available for future recall. Through his creation of Don Quixote, Cervantes puts a human face on this clinical problem. Memory dictates how the knight will carry out his adventures, and his imagination adapts his literary models to his present and future circumstances, such as in his depiction of Maritornes: "y finalmente, él la pintó en su imaginación, de la misma traza y modo, lo que había leído en sus libros de la otra princesa" (I.16.173) ["in short, he depicted her in his imagination as having the form and appearance of another princess he had read about in his books" (113)].

16. For other examples of the connection between current technology-based research and prescientific views, see Herrmann and Chaffin 5; Morris; and Tulving.

I would like to finish with the words of a great admirer of Cervantes' work, Jorge Luis Borges, from his essay "El libro" [The Book]:

De los diversos instrumentos del hombre, el más asombroso es, sin duda, el libro. Los demás son extensiones de su cuerpo. El microscopio, el telescopio, son extensiones de su vista; el teléfono es extensión de la voz; luego tenemos el arado y la espada, extensiones de su brazo. Pero el libro es otra cosa: el libro es una extensión de la memoria y de la imaginación. (177)

Of all man's instruments, the most wondrous, no doubt, is the book. The other instruments are extensions of his body. The microscope, the telescope, are extensions of his sight; the telephone is the extension of his voice; then we have the plow and the sword, extensions of the arm. But the book is something else altogether: the book is an extension of memory and imagination.

And this is how *Don Quixote* unfolds: by swinging back and forth between memory and imagination, Cervantes weaves the structure of the novel, of a book that departs from the bookish memory of its protagonist: "Dichosa edad y siglo dichoso aquel adonde saldrán a luz las famosas hazañas mías, dignas de entallarse en bronces, esculpirse en mármoles y pintarse en tablas, para memoria en lo futuro" (I.2.47) ["Fortunate the time and blessed the age when my famous deeds will come to light, worthy of being carved in bronze, sculpted in marble, and painted on tablets as a remembrance in the future" (25)].

WORKS CITED

Borges, Jorge Luis. "El libro." *Obras completas 1975–1988*. Madrid: Emecé, 2005, 177–84.

Bundy, Murray Wright. *The Theory of Imagination in Classical and Mediaeval Thought*. Urbana: U of Illinois P, 1927.

Carruthers, Mary. *The Book of Memory*. Cambridge: Cambridge UP, 2008.

Cervantes, Miguel de. *Don Quijote de la Mancha*. Ed. Francisco Rico. Barcelona: Crítica, 1998.

Cervantes, Miguel de. *Don Quixote*. Trans. Edith Grossman. New York: Ecco-HarperCollins, 2003.

Domínguez, Julia. "The Internal Senses in *Don Quixote* and the Anatomy of Memory." *Beyond Sight*. Ed. Ryan Giles and Steven Wagschal. Toronto: U of Toronto P, 2016. Forthcoming.

Dudai, Yadin, and Mary Carruthers. "The Janus Face of Mnemosyne." *Nature* 434 (March 2005): 567.

Egido, Aurora. "La memoria y el *Quijote*." *Cervantes: Bulletin of the Cervantes Society of America* 11.1 (1991): 3–44.

Eisenberg, Daniel. "La biblioteca de Cervantes: Una reconstrucción." *Studia in Honorem prof. Martín de Riquer*. Vol. 2. Barcelona: Quaderns Crema, 1987, 271–328.

García Barreno, Pedro. "La medicina en *El Quijote* y su entorno." *La ciencia y* El Quijote. Ed. José Manuel Sánchez Ron. Barcelona: Crítica, 2005, 155–80.

Herrmann, Douglas J., and Roger Chaffin. "Introduction." *Memory in Historical Perspective*. Ed. Douglas J. Herrmann and Roger Chaffin. New York: Springer-Verlag, 1988, 1–15.

Huarte de San Juan, Juan. *Examen de ingenios para las ciencias*. Madrid: Cátedra, 1989.

Iriarte, Mauricio de. *El doctor Huarte de San Juan y su* Examen de ingenios: *Contribución a la historia de la psicología diferencial*. Madrid: C.S.I.C., 1948.

Jaén, Isabel. "Cervantes and the Cognitive Ideas of His Time." *Cognitive Cervantes*. Ed. Julien Simon, Barbara Simerka, and Howard Mancing. Spec. cluster of essays of *Cervantes: Bulletin of the Cervantes Society of America* 32.1 (2012): 71–98.

López-Muñoz, Francisco, Cecilio Álamo, and Pilar García-García. "Locos y dementes en la literatura cervantina: A propósito de las fuentes médicas de Cervantes en materia neuropsiquiátrica." *Revista de Neurología* 46.8 (2008): 489–501.

Morris, Peter Edwin. "Theories of Memory: An Historical Perspective." *Theoretical Aspects of Memory*. Ed. Peter E. Morris and Michael Gruneberg. New York: Routledge, 1994, 1–28.

Palma, José Alberto, and Fermín Palma. "Neurology and Don Quixote." *European Neurology* 68 (2012): 247–57.

Peset, José Luis. "Melancólicos e inocentes: La enfermedad mental entre el Renacimiento y el Barroco." *La ciencia y* El Quijote. Ed. José Manuel Sánchez Ron. Barcelona: Crítica, 2005, 181–8.

Richardson, Alan. "Defaulting to Fiction: Neuroscience Rediscovers the Romantic Imagination." *Poetics Today* 32.4 (2011): 663–92.

Salillas, Rafael. *Un gran inspirador de Cervantes, el doctor Juan Huarte y su* Examen de ingenios. Madrid: E. Arias, 1905.

Schacter, Daniel. *Searching for Memory: The Brain, the Mind and the Past*. New York: Basic Books, 1996.

Schacter, Daniel, and Donna Rose Addis. "The Ghosts of Past and Future." *Nature* 445 (January 2007): 27.

Schacter, Daniel, Donna Rose Addis, and Randy Buckner. "Remembering the Past to Imagine the Future: the Prospective Brain." *Nature* 8 (2007): 657–61.

Serés, Guillermo, ed. *Examen de ingenios*. By Juan Huarte de San Juan. Madrid: Cátedra, 1989.

Sorabji, Richard. *Aristotle on Memory*. Chicago: U of Chicago P, 2004.

Soufas, Teresa S. *Melancholy and the Secular Mind in Spanish Golden Age Literature*. Columbia: U of Missouri P, 1990.

Summers, David. *The Judgment of Sense: Renaissance Naturalism and the Rise of Aesthetics*. Cambridge: Cambridge UP, 1990.

Tulving, Endel. *Elements of Episodic Memory*. New York: Oxford UP, 1983.

Vives, Juan Luis. *El alma y la vida*. Valencia: Biblioteca Valenciana Digital, 1992.

Wolfson, Harry. "The Internal Senses in Latin, Arabic, and Hebrew Philosophic Texts." *Harvard Theological Review* 28.2 (1935): 69–133.

SECTION III

Embodied Cognition and Performance

CHAPTER 5

Cognitive Theatricality: Jongleuresque Imagination on the Early Spanish Stage

BRUCE R. BURNINGHAM

In my 2007 book *Radical Theatricality* I propose a theory of medieval Iberian street theater to partially explain the rise of the Spanish *comedia* in
the absence of a strong tradition of medieval liturgical drama on the Iberian Peninsula. Taking as its point of departure the longstanding debate
over the exact nature of medieval Iberian theater, *Radical Theatricality*
argues that the traditional search for extant medieval play scripts depends on a definition of theater far more literary than performative. This
literary definition—largely established, I argue, by the myth of Thespis'
supposed "invention" of Western theater in his dialogic interaction with
his dithyrambic chorus—pushes aside evidence of Spain's medieval performance traditions because this evidence is considered either intangible
or "un-dramatic" (which is to say, it does not look like a "play" when viewed
on the printed page).[1] Such an emphasis on written, dialogue-based texts
has left researchers unprepared to deal with the clowns, mimes, acrobats,
jugglers, troubadours, and singers that, in one way or another, have continued to perform their arts from well before the fall of Rome up through
the present day. By focusing on the dialogic relationship that exists in performance between performer and spectator—rather than on the kind of
literary dialogue between characters that is traditionally associated with
drama—*Radical Theatricality* examines the performative poetics of what I

1. For a more detailed discussion of these debates, see Burningham 17–25.

call the jongleuresque tradition and traces this tradition's performative impact on the development of the Spanish theater of the sixteenth and seventeenth centuries. Borrowing terminology from Albert Lord and Hollis Huston, I not only suggest that the essence of theater can be found among "singers of tales on simple stages," but that jongleuresque performance represents, quite literally, *the* popular theater of medieval Europe with or without liturgical drama.[2]

My project in *Radical Theatricality* is nothing less than to redefine our critical notions of what constitutes "acting" and what counts as legitimate "theater" in order to encompass a far wider variety of premodern performance activities that have long been ignored, activities that both theater history and literary criticism have considered as something less than truly theatrical and whose exclusion from these critical discourses has largely contributed to the notion that medieval Spain somehow lacked theater. And to accomplish this redefinition of theater I deliberately call into question those critical definitions that require some surplus element beyond the act of performance itself. In other words, I argue that a performance does not become legitimate theater *only* if it includes more than one performer dialoguing with other performers, or *only* if the performance occurs on some kind of architectural stage (however rudimentary), or *only* if there is mimesis, or *only* if the performance leaves behind some kind of preestablished literary text that critics can later point to as a piece of "drama." The essence of theater—which is fundamentally jongleuresque— is simply one person watching another person do something interesting. In short, my redefinition of legitimate theater insists that theater is much more about perception and imagination in performance than it is about sets, costumes, and props.[3]

Thus, in the years since publishing *Radical Theatricality* I have come to realize that many of my basic theoretical arguments about jongleuresque performance are essentially cognitive in nature since these arguments largely depend on notions of embodied cognition (even if I did not

2. As I note in *Radical Theatricality*, I do not dispute the connection between the *Quem quaeritis* trope and the rise of liturgical drama (37). Nor do I mean to suggest that liturgical drama itself was somehow alien to a larger medieval popular culture that also involved festivals, carnivals, processions, and so forth. What I reject is the notion that European theater "died out" with the fall of Rome, that it was only "reborn" several centuries later in the *Quem quaeritis* trope, and that the liturgical drama that evolved from this trope is the Ur-form from which all modern European theater ultimately derives.

3. As Mark Pizzato argues, "Theatre as an art form enables actors to externalize the inner performance realms of memory, dream, and fantasy through mimetic and narrative skills" (13).

recognize this when I first started writing *Radical Theatricality* in the early 1990s). As Amy Cook rightly points out (in a comment that can be applied both to my own approach to medieval theater and to my initial lack of appreciating my approach's cognitive underpinnings), "the problem is not with making our thinking or our performing more 'embodied.' The challenge is coming up with the language to articulate what it has been all along" (84). The purpose of this present essay, then, is to essentially revisit some of my arguments from *Radical Theatricality* in the light of what has been called the "cognitive turn" (McConachie and Hart 1). I revisit these arguments here for two reasons. First, such a backward glance allows me to properly reframe *Radical Theatricality* both for myself and for readers who may come to my book after having read this present essay first. Second, by revisiting my original arguments in the light of more recent research on embodied cognition, I am able to advance my project even further than I could before precisely because the field of cognitive literary studies provides me with a more precise theoretical apparatus for analyzing and describing those activities that I see as essentially theatrical despite the general unwillingness of the traditional critical discourses to view them as such.

To give just one example of how my original arguments in *Radical Theatricality* related to the issue of embodied cognition, I call into question the conventional notion that theater necessarily emerges out of religious ritual by interrogating the hubristic assumption that

> "ancient" humans—that is, anyone who lived before recorded history, which essentially means prior to the invention of writing less than 5,500 years ago— were essentially nothing "like us," despite the fact that their physical characteristics as *homo sapiens* (including the capacity for language and abstract thought) had been fully evolved for tens of thousands of years. And hence, we tend to assume that these noble savages were so frightened by a universe they did not fully understand . . . as to be cognitively incapable of performing narrative simply for the pleasure of performing narrative. (40)

Moreover, I challenge the Thespis myth's declaration that theater emerges out of ritual. Such a declaration, I argue, only serves to marginalize a whole variety of contemporary non-Western performance traditions precisely because this paradigm assumes that "the indigenous cultures of today's so-called third and fourth worlds are still engaged in a progressive, evolutionary process that will eventually lead them to become more 'like us'" as their rituals supposedly become ever more "theatrical" over time (40). To counter such assumptions, I argue that "ritual is not the point of departure in an evolutionary chain that leads from lower to higher forms of representation, from 'primitive' to 'civilized' mimesis," but, rather is "one possible point of arrival among many" (41). Compare such comments from *Radical Theatricality* to those of Bruce McConachie in his recent work on cognition and the evolution of play, ritual, and performance:

> If religious rituals are understood from [an] evolutionary perspective, it is clear that they are an offshoot of other kinds of performances. Indeed, there is some evidence that performance activities preceded religious rituals in our evolutionary past. . . . Consequently there is good evidence to reverse the assumption of many theorists that performance and the arts grew out of religion. Rather, rituals tied to religious beliefs are the evolutionary offspring of play and performance. ("Evolutionary" 44–45)

What comments such as McConachie's demonstrate when juxtaposed against my own work is that my analysis of the jongleuresque tradition is tied to a whole set of ideas that are part of recent critical debates about embodied cognition in performance and cultural studies.[4] Indeed, as McConachie argues in an even more recent essay on "Enaction," the so-called origins of theater cannot be understood outside of cognitive evolutionary theory:

> An Enaction approach to spectatorship necessarily begins with the assumption that the capabilities that involve perceiving the performances of others must have evolutionary roots that play out in normal childhood development. Because making and watching theatre and other kinds of performance events occurred very recently in the history of our species, we know that there could not have been enough evolutionary time for humans to develop and pass down to their ancestors a special module in the human brain uniquely suited for enjoying and understanding performances. ("Spectating" 185–6)

To advance my ideas on jongleuresque performance within the context of embodied cognition, I want to offer two "case studies" here. The first involves a contemporary Spanish juggler named Pedro Elis. The second involves Benjamin Bagby's recent performances of *Beowulf* in the original Old English. Before examining either of these case studies, however, a quick overview of my notion of the "jongleuresque" is in order.

4. See also Zunshine.

JONGLEURESQUE PERFORMANCE

My use of the term "jongleuresque" refers to much more than just the quasi-literary activities associated with the medieval Iberian *mester de juglaría*.[5] It refers, really, to an entire mode of popular performance that ranges from minstrelsy to circuses, from vaudeville to street theater, from magicians to mountebanks. It is a performance tradition that—as the thirteenth-century Provençal poem *Flamenca* clearly demonstrates—encompasses balladry, music, storytelling, acrobatics, prestidigitation, juggling, and dancing (Blodgett 32–35). It is a performance tradition intimately tied to what Huston has called the "simple stage," which he defines as "the circle that the street performer opens in a crowd" (1), a space paradoxically constituted by the very performance it is said to contain:

> The *mimus* fills that space by keeping it empty, possessing it, making it impossible for us to enter. . . . The stage is the sign of a contract, and exists for precisely that length of time during which the contract is fulfilled. I will watch, says the viewer, as long as you do something that is worth watching. I will do something that is worth watching, says the actor, as long as you watch. (76)[6]

When I first cited Huston some twenty years ago, what struck me as important about this passage—based as it is on Peter Brook's notion of "empty space" (9)—is the reciprocity between performer and spectator that he invokes in his performative "contract," a reciprocity that I then characterize as a performative "dialogue" between performers and their

5. Within the field of Hispanic literary criticism the *mester de juglaría* (i.e., the oral poetry of the jongleurs) is generally contrasted with the *mester de clerecía* (i.e., the literate poetry of the clerics). The literary forms associated with the *mester de juglaría* include medieval epics such as the *Poema de mio Cid* as well as the ballads of the *Romancero* tradition. On the tendency of literature scholars to acknowledge the gamut of performance activities associated with the *mester de juglaría* (i.e., acrobatics, prestidigitation, music, etc.) only to dismiss such activities out of hand because they are not sufficiently literary, see Burningham 23–25. See also Menéndez Pidal.

6. Huston uses the term *mimus* to denote his generic performer. Others prefer "rhapsode" (Else), "clown" (Preiss), "shaman" (Schechner), or "fool" (Willeford). My own preference for the term "jongleur" stems not only from its specific relevance for medieval Iberian performance, but also because it is the most expansive of all the terms, involving both literary and nonliterary activities, as well as mimetic and nonmimetic performances. On the "spectator's gaze," see also Furse (66). On the dynamic between performer and spectator, see Lutterbie 103.

audio-spectators (*Radical Theatricality* 45–46).[7] And while I still think Huston's reciprocity is crucial to any definition of theater, I have become much more interested—precisely through contact with cognitive cultural studies—in the implied question of *why* we watch; which brings me to Pedro Elis and Benjamin Bagby.

CASE STUDIES

Elis, who was born in Jerez de la Frontera, is best known for holding the *Guinness Book of World Records* title for juggling five basketballs simultaneously. Having grown up in a well-respected circus family now in its fifth generation, Elis' training is entirely jongleuresque, not just because he was trained in a variety of activities such as juggling, acrobatics, and other circus genres, but also because his training occurred precisely through the process of apprenticeship in which the knowledge and skills of the craft are handed down from one generation to the next.[8] The family's "Circo Continental" website highlights the history of "Los Bassy" (as they are called) and their longstanding jongleuresque traditions, which also include clownery, animal acts, magic tricks, trapeze performance, and so forth (*Circo Continental*). More to the point, Elis' own webpage includes a fourteen-minute video clip of a 2013 show that demonstrates his own versatility within a performance that includes the juggling of various balls, plastic rings, umbrellas, clubs, and flaming torches, all alongside his Guinness world record act of juggling five basketballs at once.

Taking seriously Huston's notion of the simple stage, Elis' relatively simple act of minor acrobatics represents the essence of theater. Nothing else is required. We don't need a second performer. We don't need "dialogue." We don't need narrative (unless you count the implicit narrative of "Will any of the suspended objects fall to the ground?"). We don't even need language. Elis simply does something and we watch because this something is—apparently—worth watching. Now, the question remains, of course: why do we consider this worth watching? Why, for instance,

---

7. Daniel Nettle also conceives of Brook's "empty space" theory as a kind of performative conversation: "Brook's formulation, designed as it was to unclutter a theater overly concerned with sets and settings, contains an important truth: someone has to walk across the empty space. All drama involves a social interaction between and among one or more characters and an audience. This interaction typically involves a conversation, as a result of which their social relationships are transformed" (68). Likewise, Naomi Rokotnitz speaks of a "productive economy of reciprocity" (118).

8. I would hasten to note that the words "jongleur" ("juglar" in Spanish) and "juggler" are etymologically related.

might we stop, if only momentarily, on a downtown sidewalk if we were to happen upon this very same act of juggling on our way to work? The answer, I think, lies in the much-discussed functioning of "mirror neurons," which are neurons that fire in our brains whenever we do something *or* whenever we watch someone else do something.[9] In other words, when we watch Elis masterfully juggling five basketballs, a large part of the pleasure we derive from watching this activity may stem from the mirror neurons in our own brain firing as if we were equally adept at juggling these five balls. As Matthew Reason and Dee Reynolds note in their study of kinesthetic empathy, "The virtuosic performance elicits a 'wow' factor, often linked to a very embodied engagement, and for some spectators it is this thrill that forms a very strong drive and reward in watching" (58). Moreover, since the implied narrative of Elis' act of juggling is the drama of whether he will drop any of the objects, our sense of relief at the end of the act when none of them has landed on the ground is also caused by the way in which we cognitively mirror ourselves into Elis' precarious situation. As Gabriele Sofia reminds us in the context of performance studies, "we activate the same motor neurons both to perceive and to perform an action. Our motor system shapes not only our actions but also our perception and therefore our cognition" (174). Or, as McConachie again argues,

> neuroscientific work on mirror neurons validates the reality and importance of empathy for human performance. Networks of such neurons in the frontal lobe of the brain, evident in many higher mammals as well as humans, respond to intentional motor action initiated by others. If an actor/character onstage in a murder melodrama grabs for a gun, the grabbing motion will be picked up by the mirror networks of those sitting in the auditorium: the spectators' mirror networks will fire in the same way that they would have if each of them had done the grabbing. ("Evolutionary" 37)

In short, mirror neurons are an important component of our ability to experience empathy (i.e., feel with others), whether this empathy involves watching a performer engage in a relatively low-stakes game of juggling, or whether we are watching an actor play Oedipus in a relatively high-stakes game of finding out who is responsible for the plague in Thebes.[10] In both cases, the "catharsis" that we experience at the end—fear and relief

9. See, among others, Rizzolatti and Craighero; and Iacoboni. On the controversy surrounding mirror neurons, see Gallese et al.
10. On empathy and its different dimensions, see Batson.

in the case of Elis, fear and pity in the case of Oedipus (to quote Aristotle [58])—is intimately connected to this aspect of our neurophysiology.[11]

But this brings us to our second example: Benjamin Bagby's performance of *Beowulf*. Now, in moving from Pedro Elis to *Beowulf*, some may consider that we are moving upward within some kind of presumed artistic hierarchy. I do not. From a jongleuresque perspective, moving from Elis to *Beowulf* is simply a lateral move, as again *Flamenca* demonstrates by placing both acrobats and narrative singers side by side within the performative context of the same banquet entertainment. The fact that the residual literary epic of *Beowulf* just happens to be one of the foundational texts of what has become the institution of English literature is merely an accident of history.

To set up this discussion, I will only mention that Bagby is a classically trained musician who is a founding member of the early music ensemble Sequentia and has been a visiting professor at a number of universities, including Harvard, Michigan, and NYU. He has performed *Beowulf* at a number of locations, including New York City's Lincoln Center for the Performing Arts. I have selected Bagby's performance for two reasons. First, insofar as Bagby's "reconstruction" of this medieval performance tradition can be considered "authentic" (or, at least, as authentic as possible all these centuries later), his performance provides us a unique glimpse into the workings of this performance tradition from the inside out. (And please note that Bagby's performance does not appear, at least to me, to be an attempt to impersonate a medieval scop; rather, Bagby simply appears to be attempting a reconstruction of the scop's jongleuresque mode of performance.) And second, in contrast to Elis' acrobatic performance, which is primarily visual, the singing of an epic is primarily—although not exclusively—oral in nature.

Early in *Radical Theatricality* I discuss the relative importance of the physical accessories that accompany any theatrical performance:

> the stage does not exist apart from the performance itself; on the contrary, the performance space comes into being at the behest of the performer, and anything that is then added to that space—from simple scenery to elaborate laser effects—remains nothing more than a supplement to the imaginary world created by the performer. . . . For, even in an elaborately staged production, the initial and most important work of the actor is to create the reality of the imaginative world through voicing, gesture, and gaze. The sets, costumes,

11. On mirror neurons and the evolutionary basis for empathy, see Blair 137–8; McConachie, "Spectating" 191; and Tribble and Sutton 31–33.

and stage properties that enter this world do so incrementally and only come together in their totality at the dress rehearsal shortly before the production opens for an audience. Yet, even when all of these elements have been added to the performance, their referential effectiveness is still very much a product of the actor's original creation of the imaginary object. (27)

Again, as is clear from this citation, my own sense of theater is fundamentally cognitive. It is a sense of theatricality that undergirds a Shakespearean line such as the one from *Henry V* where the character named Chorus says, "Think when we talk of horses, that you see them" (I.1.27). Or, as Juan Ruiz de Alarcón points out in *La verdad sospechosa* (following a lengthy description of a party that never happened): "¡Por Dios, que la habéis pintado de colores tan perfetas, que no trocara el oírla, por haberme hallado en ella!" (I.7.749) ["By God, you have painted such a perfect picture that I could easily exchange hearing about it for having been there" (my translation)].[12]

David Eagleman explains the neuroscience behind such dramatic lines using a thought experiment. "[S]hut your eyes," he says, "and imagine an ant crawling on a red-and-white tablecloth toward a jar of purple jelly. The low-level parts of your visual system just lit up with activity. Even though you weren't actually seeing the ant, you were seeing it in your mind's eye" (46–47). The visual perceptions we experience when going through Eagleman's thought experiment entail what are called "rich images," which F. Elizabeth Hart describes as "concrete, specific, fleeting, and ephemeral [and which occur] to us by virtue of either the linguistic medium (as a function of text or speech) or direct (generally visual) perception" (42). Such is the underlying cognitive activity that allows for what Christopher Collins calls, in his aptly named book *The Poetics of the Mind's Eye*, the basic process of diegetic monologue where, he says, "the unbounded protean narrator . . . invites us to imagine he is now one character now another, now in one place and now hundreds of miles removed" (5).[13]

Bagby's performance, I think, amply demonstrates the importance of these cognitive processes, particularly as they relate to our perception of "rich images." He changes his vocal inflection both to modulate the mood of the narration as well as to imitate the character voices embedded within the poem itself; he speaks certain passages while singing others in order to make more direct contact with his audience; he makes both facial and manual gestures. In fact, during the following passage Bagby even

12. See also Hildy; and Thacker.
13. See also Esrock.

pantomimes a bow and arrow using his Anglo-Saxon harp, imaginatively converting his musical instrument (the only physical object present with him on stage) into a temporary weapon:

þa wæs Hroðgare   heresped gyfen,
wiges weorðmynd,   þæt him his winemagas
georne hyrdon,   oðð þæt seo geogoð geweox,
magodriht micel. (0:07:07–0:07:18)

The fortunes of war favoured Hrothgar.
Friends and kinsmen flocked to his ranks,
young followers, a force that grew
to be a mighty army. (Heaney 7)

Thus, despite the fact that Bagby is trained as a musician, his performance here is as much that of an actor as it is that of a "mere" singer. But this, in and of itself, demonstrates one of the fundamental drawbacks of examining the oral tradition from a strictly literary perspective—even one labeled "oral literature"—rather than as elements of a larger jongleuresque performance tradition.[14]

In fact, the fundamentality of gesture in performance is central to the so-called oral tradition both for performers and spectators.[15] On the performer's side of the equation, gesture is intimately tied not just to speech, but to cognition as well. As Evelyn Tribble and John Sutton note, "bodily movements are themselves the vehicles of thinking rather than mere external supplements to it" (36). Moreover, in his own discussion of the connection between language and gesture, John Lutterbie argues that "gestures or the impulse to gesture are complicit in the retrieval of the words necessary to communicate thought" (109). Indeed, for a performance tradition where the "archive" is housed only in the minds of those performers trained in the tradition, gesture is an indispensable component of memory itself. As Neal Utterback points out, "memory is a physical act" and "gesture is remarkably important to how and to what degree of success the actor is able to store and remember text" (148). Meanwhile, on the

14. My comments regarding *Beowulf* here should in no way be taken as a dismissal of the decades of erudite study (both philological and critical) that has been dedicated to examining the epic and other such medieval texts as part of the evolving manuscript and print traditions. On medieval epic and cognition, see Leverage. On orality and manuscript culture, see Huot.

15. For one of the earliest comprehensive attempts to study gesture, see Bulwer. For more recent studies of performance and gesture, especially with regard to medieval theater, see Dromgoole 64–82; Jousse; and Peters 147–65.

spectator's side of the equation, gesture is fundamental to what Matthew Reason, Dee Reynolds, Marie-Hélène Grosbras, and Frank Pollick call "kinesthetic empathy" through which our own embodied experience allows us to make deeper cognitive connections when we observe already familiar actions (46–47). Such embodied cognition, precisely through the workings of our mirror neurons, helps to create among spectators what has been called "emotional contagion" (McConachie, "Spectating" 194).[16] For this reason, *Beowulf* is really an incomplete text not just without performance, but without a performance that includes gesture and all other markers of embodied cognition.

Of course, it may seem somewhat odd, in a collection of essays ostensibly devoted to cognitive approaches to early modern Spanish literature, to devote so much attention to a performer (Bagby) and to a performance text (*Beowulf*) neither of which has any apparent connection to the Hispanic tradition. One might ask why I have not chosen instead to analyze embodied cognition and its connection to some other one-man show from the Spanish-speaking world, given that everything I have just said about *Beowulf* and cognition would be equally true for a solo performance of, say, *Don Quixote* or *El Buscón*. The answer to this question takes us directly back to my main project in *Radical Theatricality*.

Any text can be turned into an act of theater simply by performing it (with or without some kind of textual adaptation when necessary). However, my central argument in *Radical Theatricality* is not that medieval epic poetry can become a kind of theater when performed, but rather that medieval epic—as a fundamentally jongleuresque genre—was always already theater *in performance*. Thus, Bagby's performance of *Beowulf* functions as a stand-in for a hypothetical performance of the *Poema de mio Cid* that, to my knowledge, does not currently exist.[17] In other words, while we can certainly find YouTube videos of a musician singing a few lines from the

16. McConachie borrows this phrase from Elaine Hatfield and her colleagues, who define "emotional contagion" as "the tendency to automatically mimic and synchronize expressions, vocalizations, postures, and movements with those of another person's and, consequently, to converge emotionally" (Hatfield et al. 96).

17. The *Poema de mio Cid* is a medieval Castilian epic poem consisting of some 3,700 verses that narrate the feats of Rodrigo Díaz de Vivar (d. 1099) during the "Reconquest" of Spain from the Moors. The lone surviving copy of the poem was composed circa 1207 and was written down (probably copied from an earlier version) in the fourteenth century. Interestingly, even this written manuscript is tied to the jongleuresque performance tradition, for it includes a short appendix (written in a different hand) that invites the audience to buy the performer a cup of wine as payment for the performance, thus suggesting that the extant document itself once served as a theatrical "script."

Poema de mio Cid while playing the guitar, or of U.S. undergraduates reading various passages of the text aloud, there is simply no performer in the Spanish-speaking world (at least not to my knowledge) currently doing the same kind of reconstructive performance of the *Poema de mio Cid* that Bagby has been doing with *Beowulf.* Nothing currently available even comes close to Bagby's recuperation of the "radical theatricality" of medieval epic. And for this reason, Bagby's reconstructive performance of *Beowulf* can teach us much about the cognitive workings of the *Poema de mio Cid*, especially in segments such as the following one where a weapon and its violent usage are even more strongly evoked than they are in the passage from *Beowulf* that I cited earlier:

> Martín Antolínez   mano metió al espada,
> rrelumbra tod' el campo,   tanto es linpia e clara;
> diol' un colpe,   de traviéssol tomava,
> el casco de somo   apart ge lo echava,
> las moncluras del yelmo   todas ge las cortava,
> allá levó el almófar,   fata la cofia llegava,
> la cofia y el almófar   todo ge lo levava,
> rraxól' los pelos de la cabeça,   bien a la carne llegava,
> lo uno cayó en el campo   e lo ál suso fincava. (Raffel 240)

> Martín Antolínez drew his sword,
> Shining so clear and bright it lit the whole field.
> He struck a sideways blow
> That smashed the top of Diego's helmet,
> Slicing through the metal and all the straps,
> Reaching the woolen lining, cutting it away,
> Scraping off much hair and not a little flesh. (Raffel 241)

Indeed, Bagby's performance of *Beowulf* opens up a window on an entire pan-European jongleuresque performance tradition that lies at the heart of Western theater.

COGNITIVE THEATRICALITY

I offer earlier the two examples in order to demonstrate why it is a mistake to view theater history from a predominantly literary perspective. The object of literary study, by definition, is the literary text. And for this reason, most literary analysis—even analysis that takes into account the importance of performance—seeks to ultimately isolate the literary object from its performative context, separating out (for instance) the text of an epic poem from the jongleuresque act of juggling that (perhaps) accompanied it simply because the epic is seen as a work of high verbal art while the act of juggling is seen as little more than a brief moment of low spectacle. In the end, whether we are talking about Albert Lord and Milman Parry's theories of the oral-formulaic composition of Homer's *Odyssey*, or of Colin Smith's "individualist" interpretation of the *Poema de mio Cid*, all literary approaches to the oral tradition are ultimately dedicated to explaining those linguistic elements that scholars first encounter in the written documents: Is this turn of phrase evidence of oral composition?[18] Do these specific lexical elements indicate that the author was a monk from Salamanca who was trained in Thomistic philosophy?

My own approach, in contrast, at least within the confines of this particular project, is to consider the residual written documents associated with the oral tradition as just one piece of evidence among many—including visual representations in illuminated manuscripts, written descriptions found in historical documents, and archeological evidence culled from the record of material culture—of a larger performance tradition within which events rather than texts are the primary object of study. And thus, for a variety of reasons related to embodied cognition, I make no distinction between epic poems and magic tricks, between mystery plays and somersaults. In fact, I make very little distinction between professional performers and amateurs. Not all acts of theater are public events; not all acts of theater take place on recognized stages; not all acts of theater involve performers who see themselves as performers. As I argue in *Radical Theatricality*, "the oral tradition is not just a history of stories handed down from one generation to the next for the mere sake of remembering these narratives. . . . Instead, the oral tradition is the continued history of countless evenings of simple entertainment, countless moments of intensely personal theater" (60).

Cognitive psychologists speak of "procedural memory," the almost unconscious—but learned—body of knowledge that allows us to drive cars, fold clothes, snap beans, and so forth, without having to pay too much attention to everything that we are doing.[19] If you have ever left the house to go to the store and suddenly found yourself driving to work, you have been the victim of your own procedural memory. And procedural memory is important for what I just said about "countless

18. For a recent cognitive study of orality in the medieval Spanish epic, see Bailey.
19. On "procedural memory," see Eagleman 56.

moments of intensely personal theater" because it is the existence of procedural memory that both allows for and—in fact—requires something like an oral tradition. When folklorists interview people they later call "respondents" and ask them to recite any folkloric songs that they may have learned as children, such scholars are engaged in the literary separation activity that I described earlier. In their attempt to collect "specimens" of these oral texts, they are necessarily isolating these songs from the performative context within which they were originally learned and performed.

And what exactly were the original performative contexts of these events? They were contexts created by procedural memory. For most of human history (by which I mean prior to the invention of electronic media) working people spent long hours engaged in manual labor, accomplishing a set of tasks that essentially ran on autopilot thanks to procedural memory: hunters skinning a deer; farmers harvesting grain; shepherds shearing sheep; cobblers mending shoes; servants washing clothes on the banks of a river. And because these people had no radios or portable TVs to distract them from the tedium of what was literally "mindless" labor, they performed for each other (or even for themselves alone) in ways that allowed them to keep working while also engaging in personal entertainment. These working people performed for each other in order to satisfy what Ellen Spolsky has called "cognitive" or "representational hunger," which she defines as a biological, evolutionary need by humans to engage in storytelling (ix–x, 15–16, 32–33, 63–72). Indeed, Denis Dutton speaks of what he calls a "fiction instinct": "Human beings across the globe expend staggering amounts of time and resources on creating and experiencing fantasies and fiction. . . . The love of fiction—a fiction instinct—is as universal as hierarchies, marriage, jokes, religion, sweet, fat, and the incest taboo" (109).[20] Moreover, as Steven Mithen argues in *The Singing Neanderthals: The Origins of Music, Language, Mind and Body,* our capacity (and biological propensity) to make music may very well be an evolutionary vestige of the hominid communication systems that existed prior to the evolution of language per se in *homo sapiens* (266)—which may partially explain why so many of humanity's oldest narratives are intimately tied to the performance of music.[21]

But getting back to the topic of oral traditions and their importance for working people, particularly the people of medieval Iberia: Did these

---

20. See also Gottschall; and Gottschall and Wilson.
21. See also Mithen, *Prehistory.*

people always sing ballads to entertain themselves? Probably not. I am sure that they also recounted anecdotes, told jokes, and exchanged gossip. They probably also engaged in occasional feats of skill to impress each other: "Hey, Miguel, look what I can do with my hammer." And I am also fairly certain that somewhere at some time someone sang or recited a few lines from the *Poema de mio Cid* (lines that had perhaps been picked up from a professional jongleur just the day before). But whatever these people chose to sing at any given moment, these now-anonymous amateur performances (along with the reception of these performances by whoever may have been present) were cognitively no different from the performances effectuated by the professional jongleurs. These amateur performance events—like those of the professionals—opened up a simple stage in whatever physical space the performers inhabited at the time. The amateur performers' gestures, gazes, and vocal inflections—again, as with the professional performances—caused someone else's mirror neurons to fire. Such amateur performance events created "rich images" inside someone else's head, and along the way, gave these other people a few moments of pleasure while they worked. Such performance events—however amateur and anonymous they may seem to us at a distance—were very real, very personal, and very important to the people involved, because these real people had very limited access to any other forms of entertainment. Such intimate, personal performance events represent the essence of theater.

CONCLUSION

Performance, of course, is ephemeral. Therefore, our knowledge of medieval theater is limited to what we can glean from the few written records that exist. Still, unless we are prepared to simply declare large portions of medieval theatrical culture to be irretrievable (and hence unknowable), we have to make provisional conjectures about this culture based on what we already know. For this reason, cognitive approaches to such questions are indispensable because they help us reconstruct a more complete picture of the medieval stage by allowing us to see that medieval audiences were probably drawn to street theater for the same reasons we are attracted to it today. More importantly, these approaches not only allow us to better understand the underlying evolutionary impulses—Dutton's fiction instinct—that connect medieval epic to liturgical drama, but also allow us to see that medieval theater was a much bigger phenomenon than what literary history usually allows.

WORKS CITED

Aristotle. *Aristotle's* Poetics. Ed. and trans. James Hutton. New York: Norton, 1982.

Bagby, Benjamin, perf. *Beowulf.* Charles Morrow Productions, 2006. DVD.

Bailey, Matthew. *The Poetics of Speech in the Medieval Spanish Epic.* Toronto: U of Toronto P, 2010.

Batson, C. Daniel. "These Things Called Empathy: Eight Related But Distinct Phenomena." *The Social Neuroscience of Empathy.* Ed. Jean Decety and William Ickes. Cambridge: MIT P, 2009, 3–15.

Blair, Rhonda. "Introduction: The Multimodal Practitioner." *Affective Performance and Cognitive Science.* Ed. Nicola Shaughnessy. London: Bloomsbury, 2013, 135–46.

Blodgett, E. D., ed. and trans. *The Romance of Flamenca.* New York: Garland, 1995.

Brook, Peter. *The Empty Space.* New York: Athenaeum, 1984.

Bulwer, John. *Chirologia.* London: Printed by Tho. Harper, 1644. *Internet Archive.* Web. May 19, 2015. <http://www.archive.org>.

Burningham, Bruce R. *Radical Theatricality: Jongleuresque Performance on the Early Spanish Stage.* West Lafayette: Purdue UP, 2007.

Circo Continental. Web. Jan. 14, 2015. <http://www.circocontinental.com>.

Collins, Christopher. *A Poetics of the Mind's Eye: Literature and the Psychology of Imagination.* Philadelphia: U of Pennsylvania P, 1991.

Cook, Amy. "Introduction: Texts and Embodied Performance." *Affective Performance and Cognitive Science.* Ed. Nicola Shaughnessy. London: Bloomsbury, 2013, 83–90.

Dromgoole, Nicholas. *Performance Style and Gesture in Western Theatre.* London: Oberon, 2007.

Dutton, Denis. *The Art Instinct: Beauty, Pleasure, and Human Evolution.* New York: Bloomsbury, 2009.

Eagleman, David. *Incognito: The Secret Lives of the Brain.* New York: Vintage, 2012.

Elis, Pedro, perf. *Pedro Elis, performance. Plus malabarista Pedro Elis.* Web. May 19, 2015. <http://www.pedroelis.com/videos.htm>.

Else, Gerald F. *The Origin and Early Form of Greek Tragedy.* Cambridge: Harvard UP, 1965.

Esrock, Ellen J. *The Reader's Eye: Visual Imaging as Reader Response.* Baltimore: Johns Hopkins UP, 1994.

Furse, Anna. "Retracing our Steps . . . On *When We Were Birds*, a Work in Progress." *Affective Performance and Cognitive Science.* Ed. Nicola Shaughnessy. London: Bloomsbury, 2013, 57–68.

Gallese, Vittorio, Morton Ann Gernsbacher, Cecilia Heyes, Gregory Hickok, and Marco Iacoboni. "Mirror Neuron Forum." *Perspectives on Psychological Science* 6.4 (2011): 369–407.

Gottschall, Jonathan. *The Storytelling Animal: How Stories Make Us Human.* Boston: Houghton Mifflin Harcourt, 2012.

Gottschall, Jonathan, and David Sloan Wilson, eds. *The Literary Animal: Evolution and the Nature of Narrative.* Forewords by E. O. Wilson and Frederick Crews. Evanston: Northwestern UP, 2005.

Hart, F. Elizabeth. "Performance, Phenomenology, and the Cognitive Turn." *Performance and Cognition: Theatre Studies and the Cognitive Turn.* Ed. Bruce McConachie and F. Elizabeth Hart. London: Routledge, 2006, 29–51.

Hatfield, Elaine, John T. Cacioppo, and Richard L. Rapson. "Emotional Contagion." *Current Directions in Psychological Science* 2.3 (1993): 96–99.

Heaney, Seamus, trans. *Beowulf.* New York: Norton, 2000.

Hildy, Franklin J. "'Think when we talk of horses, that you see them': Comparative Techniques of Production in the Elizabethan and Spanish Golden Age Playhouses." *Text & Presentation: The Journal of the Comparative Drama Conference* 11 (1991): 61–68.

Huot, Silvia. *From Song to Book: The Poetics of Writing in Old French Lyric and Lyrical Narrative Poetry.* Ithaca: Cornell UP, 1987.

Huston, Hollis. *The Actor's Instrument: Body, Theory, Stage.* Ann Arbor: U of Michigan P, 1992.

Iacoboni, Marco. *Mirroring People: The New Science of Empathy and How We Connect with Others.* New York: Farrar, Straus and Giroux, 2008.

Jousse, Marcel. *The Oral Style.* Trans. Edgard Sienaert and Richard Whitaker. New York: Garland, 1990.

Leverage, Paula. *Reception and Memory: A Cognitive Approach to the Chansons de Geste.* Amsterdam: Rodopi, 2010.

Lord, Albert B. *The Singer of Tales.* Ed. Stephen Mitchell and Gregory Nagy. 2nd ed. Cambridge: Harvard UP, 2000.

Lutterbie, John. "Wayfaring in Everyday Life: The Unraveling of Intricacy." *Affective Performance and Cognitive Science.* Ed. Nicola Shaughnessy. London: Bloomsbury, 2013, 103–15.

McConachie, Bruce. "An Evolutionary Perspective on Play, Performance, and Ritual." *TDR: The Drama Review: A Journal of Performance Studies* 55.4 [T212] (2011): 33–50.

McConachie, Bruce. "Introduction: Spectating as Sandbox Play." *Affective Performance and Cognitive Science.* Ed. Nicola Shaughnessy. London: Bloomsbury, 2013, 183–97.

McConachie, Bruce, and F. Elizabeth Hart. Introduction. *Performance and Cognition: Theatre Studies and the Cognitive Turn.* Ed. Bruce McConachie and F. Elizabeth Hart. London: Routledge, 2006, 1–25.

Menéndez Pidal, Ramón. *Poesía juglaresca y juglares.* 5th ed. Madrid: Espasa-Calpe, 1962.

Mithen, Steven. *The Prehistory of the Mind: The Cognitive Origins of Art, Religion and Science.* London: Thames and Hudson, 1996.

Mithen, Steven. *The Singing Neanderthals: The Origins of Music, Language, Mind and Body.* Cambridge: Harvard UP, 2006.

Nettle, Daniel. "What Happens in *Hamlet*? Exploring the Psychological Foundations of Drama." *The Literary Animal: Evolution and the Nature of Narrative.* Ed. Jonathan Gottschall and David Sloan Wilson. Evanston: Northwestern UP, 2005, 56–75.

Peters, Julie Stone. *Theatre of the Book, 1480–1880: Print, Text, and Performance in Europe.* Oxford: Oxford UP, 2000.

Pizzato, Mark. *Inner Theatres of Good and Evil: The Mind's Staging of Gods, Angels, and Devils.* Jefferson: McFarland, 2011.

Preiss, Richard. *Clowning and Authorship in Early Modern Theatre.* Cambridge: Cambridge UP, 2014.

Raffel, Burton, trans. *The Song of the Cid: A Dual-Language Edition with Parallel Text.* Introd. by María Rosa Menocal. New York: Penguin, 2009.

Reason, Matthew, and Dee Reynolds. "Kinesthesia, Empathy, and Related Pleasures: An Inquiry into Audience Experiences of Watching Dance." *Dance Research Journal* 42.2 (2010): 49–75.

Reason, Matthew, Dee Reynolds, Marie-Hélène Grosbras, and Frank E. Pollick. "Researching Dance Across Disciplinary Paradigms: A Reflective Discussion of the Watching Dance Project." *Affective Performance and Cognitive Science*. Ed. Nicola Shaughnessy. London: Bloomsbury, 2013, 39–56.

Rizzolatti, Giacomo, and Laila Craighero. "The Mirror-Neuron System." *Annual Review of Neuroscience* 27.1 (2004): 169–92.

Rokotnitz, Naomi. "Between Faulty Intellects and Failing Bodies: An Economy of Reciprocity in *Wit* and *33 Variations*." *Affective Performance and Cognitive Science*. Ed. Nicola Shaughnessy. London: Bloomsbury, 2013, 117–31.

Ruiz de Alarcón, Juan. *La verdad sospechosa*. Ed. Alva V. Ebersole. Madrid: Cátedra, 1977.

Schechner, Richard. *Performance Theory*. New York: Routledge, 1988.

Shakespeare, William. *The Riverside Shakespeare*. Ed. G. Blakemore Evans and J. J. M. Tobin. 2nd ed. Boston: Houghton Mifflin, 1997.

Smith, Colin. *The Making of the* Poema de mio Cid. Cambridge: Cambridge UP, 1983.

Sofia, Gabriele. "The Effect of Theatre Training on Cognitive Functions." *Affective Performance and Cognitive Science*. Ed. Nicola Shaughnessy. London: Bloomsbury, 2013, 171–80.

Spolsky, Ellen. *Word vs Image: Cognitive Hunger in Shakespeare's England*. Basingstoke: Palgrave Macmillan, 2007.

Thacker, Jonathan. "'Puedo yo con sola la vista oir leyendo': Reading, Seeing, and Hearing the *Comedia*." *Comedia Performance* 1.1 (2004): 143–73.

Tribble, Evelyn B., and John Sutton. "Introduction: Interdisciplinary and Cognitive Approaches to Performance." *Affective Performance and Cognitive Science*. Ed. Nicola Shaughnessy. London: Bloomsbury, 2013, 27–37.

Utterback, Neal. "Embodied Memory and Extra-Daily Gesture." *Affective Performance and Cognitive Science*. Ed. Nicola Shaughnessy. London: Bloomsbury, 2013, 147–58.

Willeford, William. *The Fool and His Scepter: A Study in Clowns and Jesters and Their Audience*. Evanston: Northwestern UP, 1969.

Zunshine, Lisa, ed. *Introduction to Cognitive Cultural Studies*. Baltimore: Johns Hopkins UP, 2010.

CHAPTER 6

A Mindful Audience: Embodied Spectatorship in Early Modern Madrid

ELIZABETH M. CRUZ PETERSEN

Madrid's first permanent public theaters or *corrales*, Corral de la Cruz (1579) and Corral del Príncipe (1583), presented a unique architecture and organization that very much influenced how spectators from diverse social backgrounds experienced drama. Unlike the playhouses of Paris, the Théâtre de l'Hôtel de Bourgogne and the Théâtre du Marais, which were built in a converted indoor tennis court, and the English playhouses that were either custom-built or used converted buildings, like churches or inns with yards, the *corral*'s stage, adapted from a courtyard framed by blocks of houses, intimately connected the representation to the owners of the surrounding buildings, some of whom were also residents. These owners opened windows in chambers to accommodate paying viewers from their houses, as in the case of a don Rodrigo de Herrera y Ribera, who requested authorization to break a bedroom wall for a window to the Corral del Príncipe (Shergold, *Los corrales* 16). At times, these windows served as a gateway to the rooftop for unauthorized viewing of the *comedias* by servants or young people. Owners also added *rejas* [grilled windows] and *aposentos* [boxes], which were elaborately decorated rooms located in their homes. Similarly, they converted the attic space on the fourth floor of the buildings to theater boxes called *desvanes* for additional observation space. Eventually, more benches and entrances were also incorporated to the *corral* to further accommodate audiences.

The structure of the *corral* made it possible for all classes to share in the theatrical experience, although from different vantage points. The ground floor or pit housed spectators from high and low economic classes—young noblemen and *mosqueteros* (similar to England's groundlings). The platform, which resembled the orchestra of the French and Italian theaters, did not obstruct the view of the spectator standing in the pit or patio, or the view of those sitting on the *gradas* (stands attached to the lateral walls of the *corral*) (Shergold, *History* 411–12; Allen, *Reconstruction* 20). Literary critics, and at times playwrights, sat on *taburetes* [stools or seats] for a better view of the *comedia*.[1] The clergy who frequented the *corrales* sat at the west end of the third floor in a separate section called the *tertulia*, signaling their distance from the rest. Melveena McKendrick points out: "Friars and lesser clerics crowded in the *tertulia* although attendance for them was in theory forbidden by a succession of unheeded edicts" (*Theatre* 193–4). The *cazuelas*, balconies or partially grilled boxes located on the second floor facing the stage, were designated for women of lower social and economic classes since they were required to sit separately from the men. The design and mutable structure of the *corrales* described earlier—coupled with the unstable economic, social, and political circumstances—contributed to the natural evolution of the Spanish playhouse. This dynamic context led to an increasingly complex experience for the spectators, who responded in a variety of ways to the theater by embodying the performances in the physical space of the *corral*.

Within cognitive literary studies, we find multiple approaches to theater and performance centered on "embodied spectatorship."[2] Here, I will focus on the embodied experience of the audience that attended the *corrales* in Madrid by framing my discussion within Richard Shusterman's somaesthetics, a discipline of theory and practice[3] that offers an inclusive

1. See McKendrick, *Theatre* 197.
2. See McConachie and Hart's *Performance and Cognition* (2006) and McConachie's *Engaging Audiences* (2008), as well as, more recently, Shaughnessy's *Affective Performance* (2013) and Johnson, Sutton, and Tribble's *Embodied Cognition and Shakespeare's Theatre* (2014). In the context of early modern Spanish performance, see the work of Connor-Swietlicki, "Bridging the Performance Gap" and "Embodying Rape & Violence."
3. Somaesthetics was founded by Shusterman in the late 1990s, as a new philosophical discipline concerned not only with the body's external representation, but also with its lived experience ("Somaesthetics" 302). Shusterman's somaesthetics is rooted in ancient philosophy on bodily care. It is the first systematic framework structured for somatic care or enhancement of it, useful in examining art and performance. Somaesthetics includes feelings and insight, creative thinking, ethical action, and communicative expressions or physical signs. It offers pragmatic practices as a means to improve embodied experiences and somatic awareness: how you perceive your body and how you perceive others.

and innovative understanding of the relationship between mind and body. The term "somaesthetics" is the combination of "soma," a body that is something more than flesh and blood, something that lives and is lived by, and "aesthetics," a sensorial perception that links the mind and the emotions to the sense of beauty (Shusterman, *Body* 1). There are three basic branches of somaesthetics. First, analytic somaesthetics examines the impact of epistemological, ontological, and sociopolitical issues relating to "bodily perceptions and practices and their function in our knowledge and construction of reality" (*Performing Live* 141); second, pragmatic somaesthetics not only presupposes the theoretical branch but prescribes various methods to enhance somatic awareness as a means of changing or remaking the body; and third, practical somaesthetics applies somatic awareness and experiential embodiment for "heightened somatic sensibility and mastery" (153), used in practices such as Zen meditation, yoga, and the Feldenkrais Method.[4]

Shusterman further divides pragmatic somaesthetics—the specific branch that constitutes the framework of my essay—into three dimensions: representational, experiential, and performative. Representational somaesthetics orients itself toward external appearance, dealing with the body's surface forms. On the other hand, experiential somaesthetics emphasizes the aesthetic quality of the body's inner experience. These two dimensions are not mutually exclusive; instead, they work interdependently. The third dimension, performative somaesthetics, concentrates primarily on improving inner and/or outer strength, well-being, or skill. Depending on the goal—whether for external appearances or inner senses of power and skill—the performative discipline may be linked to or assimilated into the representational or experiential dimensions. Furthermore, all three dimensions of pragmatic somaesthetics interconnect with both theory and practice, enhancing "not only our discursive knowledge of the body but also our lived somatic experience and performance" (*Performing Live* 21). On a sociopolitical level, somaesthetics brings the understanding of the encoded somatic habits imposed by hierarchies of power and enforced by laws and social norms; for example, how a woman should walk, speak, and so forth (*Performing Live* 140). In this sense, Shusterman contends with Foucault that the "repressive identities that are encoded and sustained in our bodies . . . can be challenged by alternative somatic practices" (Shusterman, "Somaesthetics and Care" 535).

4. The Feldenkrais Method focuses on the relationship between movement and thought, using movement to teach one how to improve and maximize one's daily motor functions.

As I will demonstrate, a somaesthetics approach to Spanish *comedia* is particularly useful to discuss how human beings engage in the early modern theatrical experience, to account for the dynamic interactions that occur among those embodied minds in the physical and social environment of the *corral*. First, it allows us to go beyond discourse-based *comedia* studies, which tend to neglect or do not pay sufficient attention to the performative-experiential aspects of drama.[5] Second, conducting this discussion in the context of Shusterman's pragmatic dimension of somaesthetics provides us with the methodological framework to both systematize and further understand the embodiment aspects of the theatrical experience, particularly those related to socio-normative aspects and how individuals of certain social groups push, as audience members, the limits of prescribed behavior. Although I have chosen to focus on this pragmatic dimension for the purpose of placing spectatorship at the core of this discussion, the essay will evidence the permeability among all the dimensions outlined by Shusterman. Theory, norm, representation, experience, and skill are inseparable elements of the early modern theatrical experience in the same manner that actorship, spectatorship, and environment are intrinsically linked and cannot be considered in isolation.

MINDFUL SOMATIC PRACTICES IN THE SPANISH *CORRAL*

In early modern Madrid, theatergoers practiced a form of somaesthetics, playing an active role in the live experience of the playhouse. Spectators exercised an embodied aesthetics by merging their own experiences with representational forms such as attire, mannerisms, and expressions of feeling they adopted from actors and fellow playgoers they observed in the *corrales*: "The spectators not only watch persons acting in front of them, but are also aware of the other members of the audience around them. Personal experience becomes embedded in a triangular relationship between oneself, the other spectators and the performers" (Sauter 174). Hence, the theater is not only about watching the performance; it is about *being in the space* (both physical and social), where playgoers become active participants, actively engaging in the events on and off-stage.

As Evelyn Tribble reminds us, "the design of a physical environment influences how agents behave within it. . . . In the case of the early modern theater, the most important element of the environment was the playhouse itself" (142). This is particularly relevant in the case of Madrid's

5. See also Burningham and Reed in this volume.

playhouses, which resembled a melting pot of heterogeneous elements, all of which conspired to intensify the aesthetic experience. The design of the *corral* was meant to separate the classes and the sexes, reflecting the seventeenth-century Spanish society. Ironically, however, the topography of the theater enabled the uninhibited vociferation from lower classes, which ultimately influenced the plays' direction and success. The heterogeneous nature of the *comedia* audience[6] influenced changes in the theater space as well—for example, adding windows for more viewing of *comedias*, as mentioned earlier, or at times adding *gradas*, or side benches, in order to accommodate women spectators when the *cazuelas* were full.[7] The manager of the *corral* optimized the space of the *cazuela* by doubling the seating, ergo making it amiable to larger groups. In fact, Jonathan Thacker notes that "there were times when women started queuing at dawn for the seats at the front of the *cazuela* for the afternoon's performance" (127), as perception from the first or last row would differ immensely. Interestingly, the number of women frequenting the *corrales* at times surpassed the 350 public spaces available to them for seating, especially if one considers playwright Juan de Zabaleta's observation of an attendant known as an *apretador* [pusher] packing as many female spectators as possible into the *cazuela* (119). These women, having full view of the actors on stage, exercised somatic control by voicing their disapproval and by banging their keys against the railings or throwing lemon peels at the performers, regardless of social norms that advocated the practice of passive behavior from women.[8] As McKendrick points out, female spectators exerted "a degree of unsupervised freedom that released them from the traditional polarized categories of virtuous woman (silent, reticent, passive, house-bound) and whore" ("Breaking the Silence" 23). In other words, the parameters of the entire playhouse permitted a change in status or an ambiguous zone in terms of behavior and social decorum. Similar to the women in the *cazuela*, the *mosqueteros* had a better view of the *comedias* than most of those sitting in the *aposentos* or *gradas*. The close proximity

6. On the socioeconomic composition of the theatrical audience in early modern Madrid, see Albrecht; and Fischer-Lichte and Riley.

7. See Granja's study, "Sin los pies en la cazuela."

8. Franciscan friar Francisco Ortiz Lucio's devotional works preached: "There is nothing more gracious in the eyes of God and man than silent women, friends of enclosure, cloistering, and withdrawal" (*Lugares* fol. 5r; trans. Fink de Backer 19). Similarly, Fray Luis de León insisted that as a norm, women "must always practice silence" (71). According to Nancy LaGreca, women were considered "inherently simple and impulsive creature[s] prone to laziness who [were] to be kept enclosed, busily tending to the economy of the household" (7), a stark contrast to the freedom women exercised in the theater.

to the stage permitted them to voice their likes and dislikes more directly with the actors, thus exerting control over the plays. In 1690, José Alcázar described the groundlings as "los sastres, los zapateros, los cocheros, los litereros y otros semejantes, que por el ruido que meten se llaman 'mosqueteros'" (237) ["tailors, shoemakers, coachmen, sedan chair carriers and the like, who, because of the noise they make, are called *mosqueteros*"].[9] Jodi Campbell remarks that a play's success or failure oftentimes depended on audience reception, especially that of the *mosqueteros*, who verbally and physically attacked the actors on stage with "a torrent of insults, rotten fruit, and any other objects on hand" (*Monarchy* 40). The noble classes sitting in the *aposentos* that were located in the homes framing the sides of the stage did not enjoy the same level of direct engagement, as it was more difficult for them to follow a play (either visually or aurally). However, regardless of the audiences' social status or seating arrangements, "everyone from illiterate poor to the cultured and wealthy" found ways to view the *comedias* (McKendrick, *Theatre* 196). As I argue here, the *corral*'s space served as an impetus for spectators to become active participants in the world of theater. In sharp contrast to passive observation, the *corral*'s playgoers responded to the theater through physical awareness, employing somaesthetic practices that empowered them.[10]

REPRESENTATIONAL SOMAESTHETICS

The exercise of altering the body's external form and cultivating habits of certain individuals or groups of people to comply with or diverge from social norms, a form of representational somaesthetics, played an important role in seventeenth-century Spain. During the early modern period, many treatises and devotional works regarding social decorum circulated in Spain. In addition to Juan Luis Vives' *De institutione feminae christianae* [Of the Instruction of the Christian Woman] (1523) and Fray Luis de León's *La perfecta casada* [The Perfect Wife] (1583), treatises such as Francisco de Osuna's *Norte de los estados* [The North Star of Ranks] (1531) and

9. All translations from Spanish in this essay are mine, unless indicated otherwise.
10. As opposed to the *corrales*, court theaters and street theater in the plazas had different agendas. McKendrick writes: "The crucial difference between court and public theatre, however, lay in the nature of the occasion. In the presence of the monarch, the audience observed rather than participated, and observed in an atmosphere of formality and silence quite foreign to the *corrales*" (*Theatre* 224). In court theaters, the royal family was "the prime object of attention." For more information on the space of the street and court theater, see also Rull Fernández; and Greer.

Antonio de Guevara's *Letra para recien casados* [Letter to Newlyweds] (1524) advised their readers on proper dress codes and habits.[11] Moreover, sumptuary laws were put in place to control dress.[12] At a time when treatises of behavior and dress code prescriptions were emphasized for common citizens' social decorum, it was also a matter of importance on stage. For example, in 1615, a decree was issued prohibiting women actors from dressing provocatively, which included dressing as a man (Bravo Villasante 152).

A representational aspect of theater could also be found in the actors' costumes, which captured the spectators' attention. Seventeenth-century theater treatises emphasized the importance of the costume to match the proper social status and age of the characters. For José Pellicer de Tovar, "la gala y el adorno en los que la representan es elocuencia muda que escuchan los ojos" (226) ["the actors' dress and adornment is mute eloquence heard by the eyes"]. Alonso López Pinciano established this rule early in his treatise on the process of acting: "En la persona, después de considerado el estado, se debe considerar la edad, porque claro está que otro ornato y atavío o vestido conviene al príncipe que al siervo, y otro, al mozo que al anciano" (500) ["After considering the social state of the character, you should consider the age, because clearly the movement and attire or dress of a prince is different than that of a servant, as well as that of a young person is different than that of an elder"]. In 1690, José Alcázar gave the following counsel to the actors: "En el traje se deben considerar la propiedad y la riqueza" (245) ["In the dress one should consider property and wealth"], encouraging extravagant spending habits in regards to costumes by actors.[13] Consequently, sumptuary laws were put in place to curtail expenditures of luxury apparel for actors, such as the decrees in 1615 (mentioned earlier) and in 1644 that restricted the amount of costumes actors could wear during the course of a play, which, as Laura Bass observes, "offered further testimony that the stage was the fashion runway of seventeenth-century Spain" (46).[14] At the same time,

11. For several examples of other conduct manuals that deliver similar messages, see Dopico Black 17.
12. Martínez Bermejo's study, "Beyond Luxury," shows that from 1563 to 1691 sixteen luxury laws were passed (97).
13. Detailed accounts of costumes and wardrobes purchased by actors can be found in Greer and Varey. For examples of actors' extravagant spending habits in regards to costumes, see Ruano de la Haza and Allen 297.
14. Bass reminds us: "As early as 1563, Tomás de Trujillo's treatise *Reprobación de trajes* [Condemnation of Clothing] had connected sartorial habits offstage with their equivalents onstage. For Trujillo, the person who wore a different outfit for every occasion was like the actor who, playing multiple roles in a single play, constantly changed his costume" (45).

emboldened by the performers' attire, spectators attended the theater "*lucidas*" [well dressed] in the case of women, as Zabaleta observed (119), or as P. Juan Ferrer witnessed, wearing expensive outfits or accessories such as "*zapato pintado y aun bordado*" (qtd. in Cotarelo y Mori 254) ["painted and embroidered shoes"].[15] Thus, spectators empowered by these representational somaesthetic practices donned attire that permitted them a certain degree of confidence to defy dress codes that stressed social decorum.

The playgoers' external appearance and cultivation of habit extended beyond the dress. For instance, an important component of the *corral's* aesthetic experience was the food and drink. In another form of representational somaesthetics, spectators used *aloja*,[16] fruits, and wine bought from the concession stands as props to represent a certain status. The *aloja* became so popular with playgoers that contracts and legislations were put into place in order to ensure its proper making and selling (Ball 71–73). The spices, such as pepper, cinnamon, cloves, and nutmeg found in the *aloja*, were considered precious commodities during the Middle Ages and early modern period (Malanima 162),[17] placing particular social importance on the beverage.

The drinks, as well as the fruit and snacks sold at the *alojero*, served as a visual cue of one's place in the social order. In her recent study on food and performance in early modern Spain, Campbell underscores the important role food plays in social settings, arguing that "food works as a display of power" and "as performance of elite identity" ("Foods" 2). In fact, nobles went to great lengths to defend the elite status of specific foods, having the courts add certain city regulations to sort food by social categories (4–5). In hopes of making an impression, young men would often send sweet snacks, such as "ciruelas de Génova" (Zabaleta 120), to women sitting in the *cazuela*. Doing so, spectators expressed their sense of empowerment through representational somaesthetics that included rituals or habits related to aspects such as dress and refreshments. This form of

15. In his 1613 treatise, P. Juan Ferrer saw theaters as "escuelas donde se enseña todo género de torpeza con ingenio, agudeza y disimulación" (qtd. in Cotarelo y Mori 252) ["schools where every kind of stupidity is taught with wit, sharpness and dissimulation"]. The Catalan Jesuit warned that spectators who imitated actors and their manner of dress posed a moral danger to society.
16. *Aloja* was a mixture of honey, spices, and water sold at the refreshment booths called *alojería* or *alojero*.
17. Nutmeg, for example, was a luxury product until the end of the Dutch monopoly in 1770. It seemed to become a symbol of elite status for the wealthy who, according to Ken Albala, "often took their own portable container and grater with them wherever they went" (46).

embodiment enhanced their sense of aesthetic agency, enabling them to both comply with and challenge social codes.

EXPERIENTIAL SOMAESTHETICS

In early modern Spain, a number of theatrical treatises emphasized the importance of the actors' inner experience in bringing their characters to life and making the audience feel with them. In his *Nueva idea de la tragedia antigua* [New Idea of Ancient Tragedy] (1633), Jusepe Antonio González de Salas stresses the actor's role in facilitating spectators' inner emotional experience by embodying the character—imagined by the poet—who is the mediator between the emotions of the playwright and those of the audience or the "arcaduz i conducto, por donde comunicará el Poeta al Auditorio sus passiones i affectos" (86) ["means and conduit through which the poet will communicate his passions and affections to the audience"]. Lope de Vega—one of the most prolific playwrights of early modern Europe and the author of *Arte nuevo de hacer comedias* [The New Art of Writing Plays] (1609), in which he gathers his innovative ideas for the new *comedia*— directs the playwright to depict characters with emotions that transform the actor, since it is through the actor's embodiment that the audience will be moved (vv. 272–6). He puts this advice into practice, for instance, in his *comedia Lo fingido verdadero* [The Feigned Truth]. The protagonist, Ginés, speaks of an actor portraying the pains of love, saying that only when he feels love's passion can he convincingly perform a man in love, because "no los sabrá hacer si no los siente" (232) ["if he doesn't feel them, he won't know how to play them" (69; Trans. by McGaha)]. These words echo the advice of Quintilian, the celebrated Roman orator and rhetorician from Hispania (c.35–c.100), who states that, if one wishes to arouse emotions in others, one first needs to "feel those emotions oneself" (6.2.26).[18] Following this line of thought, seventeenth-century rhetoricians acknowledged the intrinsic connection between mental and bodily states and believed that "the actor's inward state of mind" easily influenced the outward shape of the body (Roach 49). Consequently, proper exercise was key for the actor in preparing for her role. Corporeal exercises, such as breathing to strengthen the voice and lungs, helped the actor to control visceral movements connected to her emotional state. Through these physical exercises, the actor strived to increase her awareness of bodily states and

18. All citations from Quintilian's *Institutio Oratoria* refer to book, chapter, and section.

feelings to facilitate greater insight of sentiments. Such awareness of somatic functions allowed the actor to make adjustments and portray her character in a natural and realistic manner, as demanded by Lope's new precepts. López Pinciano lays out some physical movements actors should consider in preparation for their specific roles, insisting that they follow the natural movement of the person they will represent, whose gestures vary depending on the individual's mood. He recommends to focus on body parts such as the hand to communicate the character's emotion: "si está desapasionado puede mover la mano con blandura, agora alzándola, agora declinándola, moviéndola al uno y al otro lado; y si está indignado la moverá más desordenadamente, apartando el dedo vecino al pulgar, llamado índice, de los demás como quien amenaza" (505) ["if he is dispassionate, he can move the hand with gentleness, raising it now, dropping it now, moving it now from side to side; and if the mood is outraged, moving it more wildly, pressing the thumb to the forefinger, called the index finger, in a threatening manner"].

Affective embodiment in the *corral* was also mediated in great part by the eyes. For Quintilian, they are a critical element of expression, "since they, more than anything else, reveal the temper of the mind, and without actual movement will twinkle with merriment or be clouded with grief" (11.3.75). Therefore, makeup that exaggerated the actor's eyes or the expressive movement of her eyes was a necessary component of acting, especially in large spaces such as the *corrales* or the palace stages.[19] The eyes were also a key symbol in Baroque art and literature as windows to the soul and, thus, possessed not only a representational value but also an experiential one, as they were both portrayers of emotion and vehicles of emotional transformation. In connecting the eyes to the soul, López Pinciano lists the array of emotions this "small organ" exhibits: "ira, odio, venganza, amor, miedo, tristeza, alegría, aspereza y blandura" (505) ["anger, hatred, revenge, love, fear, and sadness, tough and tender joy"]. Moreover, Juan de Guzmán argues in the *Primera parte de la Rhetorica* [First Part of the Rhetoric] (1589) that with one's eyes one can easily communicate "cualquier afecto o pasión" (148) ["any affect or passion"]. Playwrights placed great importance on the eyes, rendering them the culprit for inciting emotions in others. For example, in *Lo fingido verdadero*, Marcela's eyes cause Ginés to feel aroused: "¡Por Dios, que por sus ojos me abraso!" (264) ["My God, her eyes drive me crazy!"]. In *La serrana de la Vera* [The Mountain Woman of La Vera], Luis Vélez de Guevara goes further by

19. Evidence of woman actors wearing stage makeup can be found quoted in Cotarelo y Mori's *Bibliografía de las controversias*, pp. 216, 264, 349, and 401.

emphasizing the protagonist's "ojos hermosos rasgados" (vv. 213) ["beautiful, almond-shaped eyes"] throughout the play, specifying both their movements and effect on others, which equally seduce and instill fear. On the power of the eyes to move the audience, Quintilian explains:

> By far the greatest influence is exercised by the glance. For it is by this that we express supplication, threats, flattery, sorrow, joy, pride or submission. It is on this that our audience hangs, on this that they rivet their attention and their gaze, even before we begin to speak. It is this that inspires the hearer with affection or dislike, this that conveys a world of meaning and is often more eloquent than all our words. (11.3.72)

In this sense, the eyes connect the inner experience of the actors to that of the audience, illustrating the interconnectedness of representational and experiential somaesthetics: they not only allow actors to depict emotion but are also the open "windows of the soul" that allow the audience to connect to the actors' inner emotional states, thus enabling the spectators' emotional experience. Along with the voice, gestures, movements, hands, and all the other elements that form the actor's body, the eyes are the vehicle through which both actors and spectators actively experience drama, participating in the third dimension of pragmatic somaesthetics: performative somaesthetics.

PERFORMATIVE SOMAESTHETICS

To increase their chances of succeeding in their profession, early modern Spanish actors became themselves spectators of life. Female actors, for example, observed the behavior of real-life models of respectable women, who at times ventured outside their homes to attend to religious functions or to visit family. McKendrick remarks that "respectable women of the nobility and often of the wealthy bourgeoisie in Madrid (and to some extent other large cities like Barcelona and Seville) had a reputation for liveliness and wit" (*Woman and Society* 27), a behavior foreign travelers often commented on, as in the case of Tomé Pinheiro da Veiga. McKendrick informs us that in 1605 the Portuguese traveler reacted with shock at the public behavior displayed by decent women. Especially incredible to him was how the women were "treated as people and as Christians" by the Spanish men (26).[20] His disapproval of women's social freedom resonated

20. See Pinheiro da Veiga's diary *Fastiginia o fastos geniales*, p. 85.

with those who subscribed to the manuals on proper behavior mentioned earlier. Interestingly, Theresa Ann Smith points out that "texts promoting women's enclosure and praising male rule—two antidotes to women's capricious nature—more likely constituted reactions to, rather than shapers of, women's behavior. [Queen] Isabel and countless other Spanish women lived more public and more active lives than promoters of patriarchy desired" (19).

Consequently, when seen through a somaesthetics lens, early modern Spanish actresses emerge, as McKendrick asserts, "as forceful spokeswomen." She writes:

> Their behavior on stage might belong to the world of imagination and popular entertainment, but from within that protected fictional space the words they spoke revealed what it was like to be a woman, and specifically what it was like to be a woman in a man's world. . . . as a result of their profession and their peripatetic lives they knew more about the world than most of their sex and were amply equipped to act as forceful spokeswomen for a wide range of female causes. ("Representing their Sex" 73)

The words and actions of these spokeswomen and their male counterparts would have resonated with the spectators, who learned to articulate similar meanings in their daily contact with others. Ros King proposes that "the unique, unseen, and unknown play in the head of each spectator . . . may not be just concerned with what is being performed but may include reflection on that individual spectator's current concerns, or previous and immediate life experiences, combined with conscious awareness of the performance as distinct from the story" (32). The actors' artistic energies engaged the viewers, who by the end of the play actually believed them to be the characters they played and not the actors, even though they comprehended the difference. Thus, not only were the actors agents whose embodied emotions mediated the spectators' theatrical experience, but they also became models of behavior through which spectators challenged the social rigidity of early modern Spain. Consider William Egginton's description of audience members' behavior in relation to embodied aesthetics:

> [*Mosqueteros*] put on airs as well as noble clothing to come to the theater, a place where they could exercise an importance and power which they desired and identified with, but to which they had no access in everyday life. In this way, the gestural, verbal, and sartorial codes that the audience learned so well in order to project an alternate reality on the screen of the stage became equally an integral part of everyday personal interaction. (409)

This example highlights how the theater influenced the spectator's somatic awareness, especially considering, as Laurie Johnson reasons, that in early modern plays "the language that maps gestures to words becomes wholly internalised, fitting play texts more perfectly to the environment in which bodies and voices will be used to convey the text" ("Cogito Ergo Theatrum" 228). By incorporating the gestures in their daily relationships with others, spectators practiced experiential/performative somaesthetics. They interpreted their role in society, not by mirroring the reflection presented to them in literature or books of manners, or by Church or government authorities, but instead in relation to their own experience, effectively moving from object to subject to establish their subjectivity.

Women sitting in the *cazuela* or the *mosqueteros* in the pit observed other individuals' movements and "empathetically" connected with them. Spectators responded to performances by synchronizing their physical and vocal expressions with audience members among them. However, they did not merely imitate other audience members, but instead interpreted every movement with their own personal experience. They physically and emotionally connected to the events surrounding the performances, often feeling seduced and overwhelmed, as witnessed by an anonymous playgoer in 1620, who describes his experience in the *corral* as a continual battery to all his senses: "Los ojos ven tanto aderezo y adorno, los oidos oyen tantas agudezas, el olfato tanto olor y perfumes, el tacto tanta blancura y regalo, el gusto tantas colaciones y meriendas, que es milagro poder uno resistir á tan larga bateria y tan porfiada á una siempre y por tantas puertas" (qtd. in Cotarelo y Mori 214) ["The eyes see so much dressing and adornment; the ears hear so much witticism; the nose so many odors and perfumes; the touch so much whiteness and pleasure; the palate so many sweets and snacks; it takes a miracle to resist such a persistent and long battery of one's senses, which attack one from all sides"]. Through this performative (physical and emotional) engagement with all the different aspects that form part of the theatrical space, spectators undergo a transformation that is possible due to the fact that they "are not disembodied minds but rather embodied beings whose experience is conditioned by the body" (Mullis 106). As David Hillman and Carla Mazzio suggest, when studying early modern spectatorship one should think of the term "body-mind" as a "porous and inclusive entity that is constantly interacting with everything around it" (253). This active interaction contributes to the audience members' embodiment of the performances and theatrical experience, enhancing their sense of aesthetic agency.

CONCLUSIONS

Pragmatic somaesthetics offers a systematic framework helpful in furthering the discussion and understanding of embodiment in the field of early modern *comedia* studies, as well as that of cognitive studies. In early modern Spain, playgoers created a sense of self-stylization that not only permitted them to control the body, but to strengthen its expressive authority. They cultivated somatic habits through attire (i.e., clothing that denoted social prominences), gestures (actions and articulations that expressed personal character), and food (i.e., refreshments that served as props for defining aesthetic agency). Furthermore, they reacted to their environment by "empathetically" responding to others (be it prompted by actors, fellow playgoers, and/or the *corral*'s architectural design), displaying behavior and adopting habits that permeated their lives outside the theatrical realm, in a form of experiential/performative somaesthetics. Far from a passive mirror of society, theater established an active relationship between actors and audiences. The mirror through which the actors and spectators saw themselves was a composite of collective and individual experiences that resulted in a somaesthetic experience for all parties involved.

WORKS CITED

Albala, Ken. *Food in Early Modern Europe*. Westport: Greenwood, 2003.

Albrecht, Jane W. *Irony and Theatricality in Tirso de Molina*. Ottawa: Dovehouse, 1994.

Alcázar, P. José. "Ortografía castellana (ca. 1690)." *Preceptiva dramática española del Renacimiento y el Barroco*. Ed. Federico Sánchez Escribano and Alberto Porqueras Mayo. Madrid: Editorial Gredos, 1965, 236–50.

Allen, John J. *The Reconstruction of a Spanish Golden Age Playhouse: El Corral del Príncipe, 1583–1744*. Gainesville: UP of Florida, 1983.

Ball, Rachel. "Water, Wine, and Aloja: Consuming Interests in the Corrales de Comedias 1600–1646." *Comedia Performance* 10.1 (2013): 59–92.

Bass, Laura. *The Drama of the Portrait: Theater and Visual Culture in Early Modern Spain*. University Park: Pennsylvania State UP, 2008.

Bravo Villasante, Carmen. *La mujer vestida de hombre en el teatro español (Siglos XVI–XVII)*. Madrid: Mayo de Oro, 1988.

Campbell, Jodi. "Food and the Performance of Social Identity in Early Modern Madrid." Sixteenth-Century Society and Conference. Fort Worth, Texas. October 27, 2011. Conference Presentation.

Campbell, Jodi. *Monarchy, Political Culture, and Drama in Seventeenth-Century Madrid: Theater of Negotiation*. Burlington: Ashgate, 2006.

Connor-Swietlicki, Catherine. "Bridging the Performance Gap: The Body, Cognitive Studies and *Comedia* Theory." *Bulletin of the Comediantes* 55.2 (2003 [2004]): 11–53.

Connor-Swietlicki, Catherine. "Embodying Rape & Violence: Your Mirror Neurons & 2RC Teatro's *Alcalde de Zalamea.*" *Comedia Performance* 7.1 (2010): 9–52.

Cotarelo y Mori, Emilio. *Bibliografía de las controversias sobre la licitud del teatro en España.* Madrid: Rev. de archivos, bibliotecas y museos, 1904.

Dopico Black, Georgina. *Perfect Wives, Other Women: Adultery and Inquisition in Early Modern Spain.* Durham: Duke UP, 2001.

Egginton, William. "An Epistemology of the Stage: Theatricality and Subjectivity in Early Modern Spain." *New Literary History* 27.3 (1996): 391–413.

Fink de Backer, Stephanie. *Widowhood in Early Modern Spain: Protectors, Proprietors, and Patrons.* Leiden: Brill, 2010.

Fischer-Lichte, Erika, and Jo Riley. *History of European Drama and Theatre.* London: Routledge, 2002.

González de Salas, Jusepe Antonio. *Nueva idea de la tragedia antigua.* Madrid, 1633. *Hathi Trust Digital Library.* Web. Aug. 6, 2012.

Granja, Agustín de la. "Sin los pies en la cazuela: Público femenino y ruptura de normas en los corrales españoles de los siglos XVI y XVII." *En torno al teatro del siglo de oro: XV Jornadas de Teatro del Siglo de Oro [Almería, 5 al 15 de marzo 1998].* Ed. Irene Pardo Molina and Antonio Serrano Agulló. N.p.: Instituto de Estudios Almerienses, 2001. 177–86. *Dialnet.* Web. Sept. 11, 2014.

Greer, Margaret R. "Playing the Palace: Space, Place and Performance in Early Modern Spain." *A History of Theatre in Spain.* Ed. Maria M. Delgado and David T. Gies. New York: Cambridge UP, 2012, 79–102.

Greer, Margaret R., and J. E. Varey. *El teatro palaciego en Madrid, 1586–1707: Estudio y documentos.* Madrid: Tamesis, 1997.

Guevara, Antonio de. *A los recien casados: Letra para Mosen Puche, valenciano, en la cual se toca largamente como el marido con la mujer y la mujer con el marido se han de haber.* Madrid: Libreria de A. Duran, 1868.

Guzmán, Juan de. *Primera parte de la Rhetorica de Ioan de Guzman.* Impresso en Alcala de Henares, en casa de Ioan Yñiguez de Lequerica, 1589.

Hillman, David, and Carla Mazzio. Afterword. *Embodied Cognition and Shakespeare's Theatre: The Early Modern Body-Mind.* Ed. Laurie Johnson, John Sutton, and Evelyn Tribble. New York: Routledge, 2014. 253–56. *ProQuest.* Web. July 30, 2014.

Johnson, Laurie. "Cogito Ergo Theatrum: Redistributing Cognition on the Early Modern Stage." *Embodied Cognition and Shakespeare's Theatre: The Early Modern Body-Mind.* Ed. Laurie Johnson, John Sutton, and Evelyn Tribble. New York: Routledge, 2014. 216–34. *ProQuest.* Web. July 30, 2014.

Johnson, Laurie, John Sutton, and Evelyn Tribble, eds. *Embodied Cognition and Shakespeare's Theatre: The Early Modern Body-Mind.* New York: Routledge, 2014. *ProQuest.* Web. July 30, 2014.

King, Ros. "Plays, Playing, and Make-Believe: Thinking and Feeling in Shakespearean Drama." *Embodied Cognition and Shakespeare's Theatre: The Early Modern Body-Mind.* Ed. Laurie Johnson, John Sutton, and Evelyn Tribble. New York: Routledge, 2014. 27–46. *ProQuest.* Web. July 30, 2014.

LaGreca, Nancy. *Rewriting Womanhood: Feminism, Subjectivity, and the Angel of the House in the Latin American Novel, 1887–1903.* University Park: Pennsylvania State U, 2009.

León, Fray Luis de. *A Bilingual Edition of Fray Luis de León's* La perfecta casada: *The Role of Married Women in Sixteenth-Century Spain.* Trans. John A. Jones and Javier San José Lera. Lewiston: Edwin Mellen, 1999.

López Pinciano, Alonso, and Pena P. Muñoz. *Filosofía antigua poética*. Valladolid: Impr. y Librería Nacional y Extranjera de Hijos de Rodríguez, 1894.

Malanima, Paolo. *Pre-modern European Economy: One Thousand Years (10th–19th Centuries)*. Leiden: Rill, 2009.

Martínez Bermejo, Saúl. "Beyond Luxury: Sumptuary Legislation in 17th-Century Castile." *Making, Using and Resisting the Law in European History*. Ed. G. Lottes, E. Medijainen, and J. Viðar Sigurðsson. Pisa: Pisa UP, 2008. Web. March 4, 2015. <www.cliohworld.net/onlread/6/05.pdf>.

McConachie, Bruce. *Engaging Audiences: A Cognitive Approach to Spectating in the Theatre*. New York: Palgrave MacMillan, 2008.

McConachie, Bruce, and F. Elizabeth Hart, eds. *Performance and Cognition: Theatre Studies and the Cognitive Turn*. London: Routledge, 2006.

McGaha, Michael D., trans. *Acting Is Believing: A Tragicomedy in Three Acts by Lope de Vega (c. 1607–1608)*. By Lope de Vega. San Antonio: Trinity UP, 1986.

McKendrick, Melveena. "Breaking the Silence: Women and the Word in the *Comedia*." *Revista Canadiense de Estudios Hispánicos* 29.1 (2004): 13–30. *JSTOR*. Web. Aug. 29, 2011.

McKendrick, Melveena. "Representing their Sex: Actresses in Seventeenth-Century Spain." *Rhetoric and Reality in Early Modern Spain*. Ed. Richard Pym. London: Tamesis, 2006, 72–91.

McKendrick, Melveena. *Theatre in Spain, 1490–1700*. London: Cambridge, 1989.

McKendrick, Melveena. *Woman and Society in the Spanish Drama of the Golden Age: A Study of the* Mujer Varonil. London: Cambridge, 1974.

Mullis, Eric C. "Performative Somaesthetics: Principles and Scope." *Journal of Aesthetic Education* 40.4 (2006): 104–17. *Project Muse*. Web. Feb. 19, 2011.

Ortiz Lucio, Francisco. *Lugares comunes de la segunda impression muy corregida y emendada con una nueva tabla y compendio de todas las doctrinas, lugares y escripturas, de grande utilidad para todos los estados, especial para Predicadores, Curas, y Prelados*. 1592. *La biblioteca virtual Miguel de Cervantes*. Web. Aug. 15, 2014. <www.cervantesvirtual.com>.

Osuna, Francisco de. *Norte de los estados, en que se da regla de bivir a los mancebos y a los casados y a los biudos y a todos los continentes, y se tratan muy por estenso los remedios del desastrado casamiento*. Burgos: Juan de Junta, 1550.

Pellicer de Tovar, José. "Idea de la comedia de Castilla (1635)." *Preceptiva dramática española del Renacimiento y el Barroco*. Ed. Federico Sánchez Escribano and Alberto Porqueras Mayo. Madrid: Editorial Gredos, 1965, 217–27.

Pinheiro da Veiga, Tomé. *Fastiginia o fastos geniales*. Trans. Narciso Alonso Cortés. Valladolid: Imprenta del Colegio de Santiago, 1916. 85. U of Toronto. *Open Library*. Web. Dec. 27, 2014.

Quintilian. *Institutes of Oratory*. Trans. H. E. Butler. Loeb Classical Library, 1920–22. Web. Oct. 4, 2012. <http://penelope.uchicago.edu/Thayer/E/Roman/Texts/Quintilian/Institutio>.

Roach, Joseph R. *The Player's Passion: Studies in the Science of Acting*. Ann Arbor: U of Michigan P, 1993.

Ruano de la Haza, J. M., and John J. Allen. *Los teatros comerciales del Siglo de Oro y la escenificación de la comedia*. Madrid: Castalia, 1994.

Rull Fernández, Enrique. *Arte y sentido en el universo sacramental de Calderón*. Kassel: Reichenberger, 2004.

Sauter, Willmar. "The Audience." *The Cambridge Companion to Theatre History*. Ed. David Wiles and Christine Dymkowski. Cambridge: Cambridge UP, 2013, 169–83.

Shaughnessy, Nicola, ed. *Affective Performance and Cognitive Science Body, Brain and Being*. London: Bloomsbury, 2013.

Shergold, N. D. *Los corrales de comedias de Madrid, 1632–1745: Reparaciones y obras nuevas*. London: Tamesis, 1989.

Shergold, N. D. *A History of the Spanish Stage: From Medieval Times until the End of the Seventeenth Century*. Oxford: Clarendon, 1967.

Shusterman, Richard. *Body Consciousness: A Philosophy of Mindfulness and Somaesthetics*. Cambridge: Cambridge UP, 2008.

Shusterman, Richard. *Performing Live*. London: Cornell UP, 2000.

Shusterman, Richard. "Somaesthetics: A Disciplinary Proposal." *Journal of Aesthetics and Art Criticism* 57.3 (1999): 299–313. *JSTOR*. Web. Feb. 18, 2008.

Shusterman, Richard. "Somaesthetics and Care of the Self: The Case of Foucault." *The Monist* 83.4 (2000): 530–51.

Smith, Theresa Ann. "The Woman Question." *The Emerging Female Citizen: Gender and Enlightenment in Spain*. Los Angeles: U of California P, 2006, 17–39.

Thacker, Jonathan. *A Companion to Golden Age Theatre*. Woodbridge: Tamesis, 2007.

Tribble, Evelyn B. "Distributing Cognition in the Globe." *Shakespeare Quarterly* 56.2 (2005): 135–55. *Project MUSE*. Web. July 30, 2014.

Vega Carpio, Lope de. "Arte nuevo de hacer comedias en este tiempo, dirigido a la academia de Madrid." *Preceptiva dramática española del Renacimiento y el Barroco*. Ed. Federico Sánchez Escribano and Alberto Porqueras Mayo. Madrid: Editorial Gredos, 1965, 125–36.

Vega Carpio, Lope de. "Lo fingido verdadero." *Comedias*. Ed. Luis Guarner. Vol. 1. Barcelona: Iberia, 1967, 191–287.

Vélez de Guevara, Luis. *La serrana de la Vera*. Ed. William R. Manson and C. George Peale. Newark: Juan de la Cuesta, 2002.

Vives, Juan Luis. *De Institutione Feminae Christianae*. Ed. Charles Fantazzi and Constatinus Matheeussen. Trans. Charles Fantazzi. Leiden: Brill, 1998.

Zabaleta, Juan de. *El día de fiesta por la mañana y por la tarde*. Madrid: D. Pacheco y Latorre, 1885. *Ebook*. Web. Dec. 10, 2012.

Perceiving and Understanding Others

Wearing Gender on One's Sleeve: Cross-Dressing in Ángela de Azevedo's *El muerto disimulado*

JUDITH G. CABALLERO

At age fifteen, Francisco Loyola ran away from a cloister in Spain and embarked to the New World, where he joined the military efforts to subdue the Amerindian rebellions in Chile and Peru. Because of his bravery, he was promoted to ensign. However, his violent behavior led him to many fights; he was even incarcerated for killing a man, but was eventually released. When he returned to Europe, after approximately nineteen years of military service, he petitioned King Phillip IV for remuneration for his various contributions to the military and was granted a generous allowance. Francisco, who now went by the name of Antonio de Erauso, later returned to the Americas, where he lived until his death.

For the 1600s, this might seem a typical life of a prosperous *indiano* (a Spaniard who leaves Spain in search for fortune and fame in the Americas); however, what I omitted in this abridged biography is that Francisco's real name was Catalina de Erauso. Catalina—later known as *la monja alférez* (the nun ensign)—lived for over nineteen years dressed as a man.[1]

---

1. Enriqueta (Enrique) Faber, Mary (George) Hamilton, and James (Miranda) Barry are examples of European women who cross-dressed during the 1700s and 1800s. Both Faber and Hamilton married women and were later arrested for doing so. James Barry's biological sex was only discovered during his autopsy. For more information on Faber, Hamilton, and Barry, see the works of Ivonne Cuadra, Terry Castle, and June Rose, respectively.

After she revealed that she was not biologically male, Pope Urban VIII granted her a dispensation to use male garb. Likewise, King Phillip IV promised her an allowance and gave Catalina permission to travel to New Spain.[2] Although the details of Catalina's life are ambiguous—the official documents are not in complete agreement with her alleged autobiography—what remains certain is that for almost two decades she was successful in convincing her fellow soldiers that she was a man.[3] Through her manipulation of sartorial conventions, Catalina was able to adopt the norms of conduct that applied to men and was allowed to travel, to partake in military actions, and even to decide whether or not to get married.

To early modern Spanish critics, Catalina's life is inevitably reminiscent of *comedias*—full-length plays written in that era—because in many of them, characters cross-dress to gain access to a different social space.[4] Usually in *comedias*, women who have been deceived or who need to restore their family's honor dress as men to find their offender.[5] Men, on the other hand, typically dress as women to enter the private space of the home or to hide.[6] The characters' inability to correctly identify the sex of the cross-dressed character is thus interpreted as a necessary ploy to efficiently create tension or complication in the storyline. But, as I argue here, this device was likely effective for early modern Spaniards because biological sex was perceived as a social category that needed to be performed.

Sex (the biological manifestations of the reproductive system) was considered unstable during the early modern period. Behavior could potentially alter or reinforce sex, and thus adhesion to gender roles and the proper adoption of gendered garments served to stabilize it. Gender (the social construction of sex, which includes gendered clothes, gender roles, and engendered spaces) was not understood as a socially contrived

2. A transcribed copy of King Phillip's permission and other documents are compiled in "El Alférez Doña Catalina de Herausso."

3. Her purported autobiography, *Historia de la Monja Alférez, Catalina de Erauso, escrita por ella misma,* has sometimes been labeled a picaresque novel. Additionally, it is not clear if she commissioned the autobiography, if she dictated it, or if she wrote it herself (see Pérez Villanueva).

4. Catalina's life became in fact the subject of the *comedia La monja alférez,* attributed to Juan Pérez de Montalbán.

5. There are other less common reasons for which women in *comedias* cross-dress. For example, Semíramis, in Calderón's *La hija del aire,* cross-dresses to impersonate her son after she has been dethroned.

6. Cross-dressed men were far less common in *comedias* than cross-dressed women. There are still a few cases—for example, Aquiles in both Calderón de la Barca's *El monstruo de los jardines* and in Tirso de Molina's *El Aquiles.*

signifier, but as a sine qua non for distinguishing between male and female.[7] In this essay, I analyze the effect that the relationship between sex and gender has on the characters in *El muerto disimulado* (date unknown) by Ángela de Azevedo. I show that the characters' acceptance of the cross-dresser as a member of the opposite sex is not an outright theatrical device, but that it also probes the limitations of perception.

I approach this play through a combination of socio-historical analysis and cognitive studies.[8] I agree with Bruce McConachie in that "[s]ocial experiences [nurture] and genetic endowments [nature] come together in the construction of our brains and minds in so many ways that they are inseparable from infancy onward" (4). The brain (the biological organ) works in particular ways as to affect the mind (our thoughts, experiences). Studying only the historical context of the characters is insufficient because it disregards the crucial role that the brain has on our mind. On the other hand, a scientific approach that disregards the environment is also inadequate because daily experiences and previous knowledge heavily influence our minds. Adopting a cognitive approach to analyze literature enables us to explore the interrelatedness of the brain and the mind, thus allowing for the integration of a scientific approach to literature with a socio-historical one.

An understanding of the limitations of the human brain helps us to reinterpret paradigms that previously seemed unlikely. This is especially true with respect to human perception. *Seeing* (casting our eyes upon) something is not equivalent to *perceiving* it (interpreting it or even acknowledging its existence). In the field of cognitive psychology, it is thought that an individual's perspective is shaped in part by things that she cannot control and, in many cases, by things that she does not consciously perceive. Every stimulus, as Ann Marie Seward Barry asserts, is ambiguous and must be interpreted by the individual (27). Following J. J. Gibson's definition of the "visual field" as that which the retina captures, and the "visual world" as the brain's interpretation of that image, Seward states: "The visual world . . . is an interpretation of reality but not reality itself. It is an image created in the brain, formed by an integration of immediate multi-sensory information, prior experience, and cultural

---

7. Nowadays, gender also refers to the individual's perception of his/her own sexuality, which may or may not align with his/her own biological sex: "Gender is the sex we perceive ourselves to be and how we express our sexuality in our dress, our gait, and our very name. Gender is society's stereotype" (Potts 51).

8. For a previous cognitive approach to Azevedo's play, centered on how characters predict the behaviors of others (Theory of Mind), see Simerka 30–39.

learning" (15). Thus, perception depends not simply on casting our eyes upon something, but interpreting what we see.[9]

This interpretation is neither automatic nor conscious and is part of a mental process known as the perceptual cycle (Neisser 213). Steven Most's neurophysiological experiments support Ulric Neisser's notion that "[i] tems do not leap into awareness on initial attentional engagement. Rather, a cyclical process of visual interpretation and reinterpretation [the perceptual cycle] ultimately determines our conscious percepts" (Most, Scholl, Clifford, and Simons 224). The perceptual cycle starts with the creation of a schema, which is a sort of pattern for processing and codifying information, constructed through a combination of the observer's expectations and visual information.[10] The schema then forms an attentional set, which guides what is to be considered relevant information.[11] For Most and Daniel Simons, the attentional set is the most crucial part of the perceptual cycle because it is the means through which transient information can be gathered. By setting parameters and guidelines, the attentional set effectively determines what information to pick up from the environment. According to Simons, "Unless subjects adopt an attentional set for the appearance of a new object or they are not focused on any other objects, events, or locations, it is unlikely to capture attention exogenously" (154). Once this information is collected, it forms another rudimentary schema, which in turn modifies the initial attentional set and allows for the perception of new things (Most and Simons 167). This cycle gets stronger as it repeats, such that stimuli that contradict the prevalent

9. The traditional philosophical theory about perception stated that individuals passively receive information from the environment (LaBerge 20). It was believed that the intrinsic qualities of an object would capture the attention of the perceiver—what is now known as *Bottom-Up* theory. William James disagreed with this theory and placed in the individual complete control over what she observed (402). From this emerged the *Top-Down* theory, in which the individual's perception is influenced by her state of mind, previous experiences, and preconceptions. Frederic Bartlett later combined *Bottom-Up* and *Top-Down* theories and stated that for perception to occur one needs "(1) a specified sensory reaction, and (2) an attitude, or orientation" (191).

10. Bernard Baars, Marvin Minsky, Roger Schank, and Robert Abelson developed theories akin to the schema theory. Baars stated that previous events and experiences "prime" (prepare) the context for the following events to be understood (118). Minsky's theory regarding how humans understand events uses interconnected frames to create a system where input is placed within a preformed frame (212–21). Schank and Abelson conclude that: "The actions of others make sense only insofar as they are part of [a 'script'] a stored pattern of actions that have been previously experienced" (67).

11. Neisser divides schemata into two types: perceptual and anticipatory (55). In Most and Simons' model, "schema" corresponds to Neisser's "perceptual schema," while the "attentional set" corresponds to "anticipatory schema."

attentional set become less likely to be incorporated into the perception cycle and to be consciously perceived (Neisser 44).

Thus, an attentional set within a persistent perception cycle (one that has completed many cycles) is very likely to disregard information that does not conform to it, even though the same stimulus might seem obvious to people with a different attentional set. In *El muerto disimulado*, the characters' acceptance of the cross-dresser as a member of the other sex is a manifestation of an attentional set that assigns sex according to gendered behaviors. As stated by Thomas Laqueur, the common assumption of two clearly differentiated sexes—male and female—is a rather recent phenomenon and was not firmly adopted until the nineteenth century (5–6). Before that, people could, of course, distinguish between male and female genitalia; however, genitalia's relation to gender and sex was understood very differently than it is today.[12]

In *El muerto disimulado*, it becomes clear, through the characters' actions and dialogue, that there is a connection between Azevedo and the medical theories of her time regarding sex and gender. As an early modern educated Spaniard, Azevedo's notions of the physical body were in consonance with Juan Huarte de San Juan's *Examen de ingenios para las ciencias* [The Examination of Men's Wits], first published in 1575.[13] Following Galen, Huarte states that the reproductive organs are the same in males and females; the only difference is that males have the organs outside and females inside (315). Anatomically, then, women and men were thought to be identical, though their organs were in different configurations.

The main difference between men and women stemmed from the amount of heat and humidity contained in their bodies. Huarte explains that heat allows for things to expand, whereas cold contracts them. Therefore, since women have their genitals inside (contracted) they must be cold, and men must be warm because their genitals are outside (316). Women then, by definition, may not be hot, and men may not be cold (324). Women can fit into one of three categories (first, second, and third degree) depending on the amount of cold and humidity in their bodies (318). These degrees can be ascertained by the woman's appearance and behavior (318–9). He describes a woman in the third degree (high amount) of coldness/humidity as "boba, bien acondicionada; tiene la voz muy

---

12. See Laqueur.

13. Huarte's book was widely read and very influential. It was reprinted in Spain several times and was translated into other European languages within a few years after its original release (Torre 17). It was later included in the Index of Forbidden Books in Portugal, Spain, and Rome (27–28). In 1594 an expurgated version was printed to comply with Spain's censorship.

delicada; muchas carnes, blandas y blancas; no tiene vello ni bozo, ni es muy hermosa" (329) ["dumb, of good disposition, has a very delicate voice, heavyset, has soft and pale skin, does not have body hair or mustache, and is not too beautiful"].[14] In contrast, a woman in the first degree (low amount) of coldness/humidity is more masculine. She is "avisada, de mala condición, con voz abultada, de pocas carnes, verdinegra, vellosa y fea" (328) ["smart, of bad disposition, has a deep voice, is thin, is very dark-skinned, has too much body hair and is ugly"]. A woman in the second degree of coldness/humidity would have a combination of the characteristics of women in the first and third degree, yet she would be the most beautiful due to the balance of her composition (323). Similarly, men fall under three categories of heat and dryness. Men can be hot and dry, hot and humid, or lukewarm. A hot and dry man (third or high degree of heat/dryness) will be smarter, hairier, darker, and ugly. On the other hand, a hot and humid man (first or low degree of heat/dryness) is not as intelligent, he is pale, has soft skin, and lacks much body hair—not too far from a woman in the first degree of coldness/humidity. A lukewarm man, like a woman in the second degree, is a balanced type and tends to be wise, virtuous, and the most beautiful (323–7).

By doing this, Huarte reshapes Galen's one-sex continuum into a two-sex continuum determined by the degree of heat/humidity in a person and expressed through behavior and physical appearance. Moreover, this dependence on heat/humidity to categorize men and women had the result of destabilizing sex because an excessive heat alteration could potentially transform women into men and vice versa.[15] According to Huarte, if there is an increase of heat in the womb, the genitals of a woman could descend and thus be transformed into a male before she is born. The result of such transformation would be a man that has "ciertos movimientos . . . indecentes al sexo viril: mujeriles, mariosos, [con] la voz blanda y melosa; son los tales inclinados a hacer obras de mujeres, y caen ordinariamente en el pecado nefando" (315–6) ["certain indecent manifestations unfit of the male sex: he is womanish, effeminate, of soft and sweet voice. He is inclined to do women's chores, and usually commits sodomy"]. The contrary may also happen: excessive coldness may retract the genitals and transform a man into a woman. "Conócese después de nacida en que tiene el aire de varón, así en la habla como en todos sus movimientos y obras"

14. All the translations of quotes are mine.
15. In *El parto de Juan Rana* [Juan Rana Gives Birth] by Francisco Pedro Lanini y Sagredo, Juan Rana is accused of allowing his wife to order him around. The judge condemns Juan Rana to dress as a woman to show that he is no longer a man. He is paraded through town cross-dressed and proceeds to give birth on stage.

(316) ["This is known, after she is born, from the air of masculinity in her speech as well as in all her movements and deeds"]. Huarte later affirms that this sex change is not limited to the unborn child, and that in Spain there were reported cases in which young women became men by the spontaneous inversion and subsequent descent of their genitalia (316). Consequently, biological sex was understood as unstable. Being male or female was "based on gender distinctions—active/passive, hot/cold, formed/unformed, informing/formable—of which an external or an internal penis was only the diagnostic sign. Maleness and femaleness did not reside in anything particular" (Laqueur 135). The degree of coldness/heat and humidity/dryness could vary and change. This could push one person from one degree to the next, and potentially over the threshold that directly affects the positioning of the external or internal penis.

The Huartian sex continuum blurs sexual anatomical differences by defining sex as a combination of other physical and behavioral characteristics.[16] As a result, clothing has a richer and more profound meaning because sartorial conventions help individuals differentiate between sexes with ease. Ursula Heise points out that when there is a necessity to separate the genders socially but a difficulty in doing so biologically, clothing becomes greatly important and violations of sartorial conventions become more problematic (370). Cross-dressing displaces the individual within the sex continuum; consequently, a sartorial transgression is also interpreted as a transgression of gender and sex—and perhaps this is why we often see cross-dressed women in *comedias* automatically capable of sword fighting and other abilities that were thought of as masculine. According to Jean Howard, cross-dressing "opened a gap between the supposed reality of one's social station and sexual kind and the clothes that were to display that reality to the world" (421). In early modern society, where gender roles separated the sexes, people were well aware of the transformational functionality of clothes.[17] As Teresa Scott Soufas notes, Juan Luis Vives "went

16. These physical characteristics were facial and corporal hair and quality of the skin and voice. Huarte does not include breasts or genitalia to distinguish between the sexes.

17. The anti-theatricalists "feared the power of clothes to produce new subjects, to metamorphose boy into woman [in England], commoner into aristocrat" (Jones 216). In recognition of this, sartorial laws were implemented to clearly divide men and women, social classes, and even religions. In 1608, 1615, 1641, 1653, 1672, and 1675, Spanish laws addressed and reiterated the illegality of female cross-dressing on stage (Heise 359). Even though cross-dressing laws applied specifically to theater, there were certainly unspoken, social laws prohibiting non-actresses from dressing outside of their gender. That such laws tacitly existed was made apparent by the fact that Catalina de Erauso had to be granted papal permission to dress as a man.

on to insist that differentiated clothing allowed individuals to present their sexual identity, which, he implied might fade before the eyes of the gazing public if not clearly marked through the conventions of outward decorations" (114). Hence, the portrayal of the cross-dresser and his/her effect on the other characters reflects the reliance on clothing as a marker for sex and the confusion that results from sartorial transgression.

In most *comedias,* the cross-dresser or a *gracioso* immediately reveals through dialogue that cross-dressing has occurred. Thus, the audience is aware of the transgression from the start. In fact, the dramatic irony that results from it is one of the main sources of the humor in these *comedias.* However, the other characters typically find out about this transgression toward the end of the play. Their acceptance of the cross-dresser as a member of the opposite sex is an expected behavior, not simply due to a theatrical convention, but also because their schema (their previous knowledge and expectations about the relation between sex and gender) creates an attentional set that picks up information about sartorial conventions yet disregards anatomical peculiarities to distinguish between male and female. Additionally, because the cross-dressed character has already adopted male garb, and thus shifted her behavior (and her placement within the sex continuum), she starts displaying other gender-specific behaviors that contribute to the success of her disguise. Conversely, if she still displays behaviors or physical characteristics that might be considered of the opposite sex, these are not picked up by the other characters' attentional set (because they do not fit in the other characters' schema of the sex she is portraying, and thus they are not incorporated into the perceptual cycle) or are interpreted using Huarte's theory as degrees of heat and dryness within the male sex. In other words, if a cross-dressed woman has a soft voice or soft skin she is perceived as a man who is less dry/hot, rather than as a woman.

The connection between Huarte's medical theories and the characters' development is apparent from the beginning in *El muerto disimulado.* Lisarda cross-dresses to find her brother's murderer since she is the sole descendant of her family and it is her obligation to seek revenge. She wants to kill the murderer with her own hands and not relinquish him to the authorities. This portrayal immediately identifies her as a woman in the first degree of coldness and humidity—the least cold/humid type of woman and hence more similar to men. Lisarda's rage is unambiguous in her first speech:

No me hables de hermosuras,
sino en coriscos, en rayos,
en fierezas, en rencores,

en pasiones, en enfados
en pesadumbres, en iras,
en furores, en estragos
que la cólera mi pecho
hizo un incendio en que ardo. (98)[18]

Don't talk to me about beauty.
Talk to me in terms of lightning bolts, rays,
ferocity, resentment,
passion, exasperation,
sorrow, anger,
rage, ravages,
because the fury within my breast
started a fire in which I am burning.

Lisarda feels ablaze. The news of her brother's death has heated her temper and this newly found heat drives her to seek revenge. At the same time, cross-dressing encourages cross-behaving, thereby arousing the masculine within her, as shown by the forcefulness of her speech. Heat is even present in Lisarda's real and adopted name, as Papagayo, her servant, is sure to point out:

si ardo, es de Lisardo el eco,
¿qué mucho en tu nombre hablando,
que arda Lisarda también? (98)

if ardo (*ardent*) is the echo of Lisardo,
is it much of a stretch
that Lisarda also burns?

Arder means "to burn" in Spanish. Her name—in both feminine (Lisarda) and masculine (Lisardo) forms—contains this verb within it. In the feminine form, it is in the present subjunctive "arda" [may it burn], signaling a significant change in heat to come. In the masculine form, the present indicative "ardo" [I burn] signals Lisarda's current heat increase (or her decrease in coldness). This modification in heat displaces Lisarda within the sex continuum, thus blurring gender differences. According to Donna Chambers, even the etymology of Lisarda's name reflects gender ambiguity since it is derived from the *fleur-de-lis*, which "is as commonly associated with the masculine concept of heraldry as it is with the feminine image of the Virgin Mary" (56).

18. All quotations from this play come from Soufas' edition. All translations into English are mine.

When Lisarda arrives in Lisbon, she stumbles upon a fight and intercedes, showing her dexterity as a swordsman. Because of her actions and her attire, Álvaro, one of the swordfighters, fully accepts Lisarda as a gentleman. His reaction is to be expected because, as Teresa Ferrer Valls asserts, "Para la sociedad es la apariencia, no la esencia la que crea la identidad sexual" (12) ["For society, appearances create sexual identity; the essence does not"]. Álvaro, as a product of the era, has an attentional set that does not enable him to recognize Lisarda as a woman because she is cross-dressed. Furthermore, for Álvaro, her fighting skills serve to confirm her masculinity. According to Soufas, "the shift of a human being from her usual social guise of womanhood into a realm of manhood does not require any great suspension of disbelief in the early modern era, since what the cross-dressed individual must ultimately do is decide which behavioral characteristics need to be emphasized in order to obtain a different set of privileges" (108). Lisarda's cross-dressing allows her to emphasize her bravery, and this in turn tricks Álvaro's attentional set away from her physical characteristics.

Álvaro experiences a type of inattentional blindness, which, according to Most, "is a striking phenomenon in which people fail to notice stimuli appearing in front of their eyes when they are preoccupied with an attentionally demanding task. . . . Such failures within the visual modality . . . violate the intuition that people should see [perceive] whatever they direct their eyes to" (221). Most, Neisser, Simons, and other cognitive scientists have shown that people sometimes will simply not perceive something even if they are staring right at it. Following Mackand Rock, Simons and Chabris state that: "When attention is diverted to another object or task, observers often fail to perceive an unexpected object, even if it appears at fixation" (Simons and Chabris 1060). Álvaro is diverted by Lisarda's clothing, assertive behavior, and swordsmanship, and immediately places her in the category of male. Lisarda's feminine voice, her lack of facial hair, and possibly her breasts are incorporated into Álvaro's perceptual cycle as characteristics of a man in the first degree (low amount) of heat/dryness— closer to the feminine sex. Álvaro's attentional set deems Lisarda's physical characteristics as irrelevant for identifying her sex, which in turn reinforces the persistent cycle of sartorial conventions and keeps Álvaro from perceiving the woman behind the costume.

Blurring of gender also occurs with Lisarda's brother, Clarindo, who was not actually killed.[19] Papagayo runs into Clarindo and recognizes him but

19. Clarindo's liminality includes not only gender but also his existence (Chambers 58, Stoll 151). Stoll writes: "He is not really dead, but he is not really alive, either, because socially his death is accepted as a reality" (151).

believes he is a ghost. When Clarindo finds out that everyone believes him to be dead, he decides to cross-dress to see if Jacinta, his love interest, has been loyal to him. He changes his name to Clara and dresses as a woman who sells knickknacks so that he can have an excuse to talk to Jacinta.[20] Whereas Clarindo is successful at pretending to be a woman, "[h]is role breaks down across class lines . . . when everyone realizes that this individual knows nothing about selling ribbons and trinkets" (Soufas 134). When the other women start to suspect that "Clara" is not what she claims to be, Clarindo, rather than confessing that he is a man, invents a new story and tells Jacinta that he is a woman who, cross-dressed as a man, has traveled to find her lover, who abandoned her after taking her virginity (110). When Clara mentions that she cross-dressed as a man, she uses the phrase "de hombre el hábito tomado" (110) ["having taken a male habit"]. The decision to use the word *hábito* [habit] in place of *vestido* [clothing/garb]—even though *vestido* would fit within the rhyming scheme of the line—emphasizes the codification of clothing in early modern Spain. As Ann Rosalind Jones and Peter Stallybrass point out, "clothing as 'habit' implies a cultural way of life. This was perfectly clear in relation to the 'habits' that monks wore" (6). However, it also relates to the constraints that sartorial conventions imposed on the representation of gender. The intentionality of the word "habit" as a garment that has the potential to blur or reinforce sex is also highlighted by Papagayo's conversation with Clarindo, where he tells him that Lisarda became a monk and then clarifies that she became a nun, but since both nuns and monks "tienen hábitos todos / y viven en monasterios" (105) ["wear habits / and live in monasteries"], they are basically the same thing. "His claim," according to Soufas, "reiterates the insufficiency of discursive limits upon gendered identity" (132); it also reinforces clothing's capacity to befog gender distinction.

Even though Jacinta and Lisarda know Clarindo's face very well, neither of them is able to recognize him when he is cross-dressed as Clara. Likewise, Clarindo never suspects that Lisardo could be his sister because the gender does not match the clothes:

CLARINDO: . . .

> y si así como fue hembra
> mi hermana, fuera varón
> y fuera viva, dijera
> que era la misma.

20. For information about the carnivalesque aspect of social relations in this play, see Múzquiz-Guerreiro.

LISARDA: ¿No miras

lo mucho que se asemeja

con el semblante a Clarindo?

¡Ay, si mi hermano viviera,

y así como fue varón,

fuera mujer, ¡con firmeza

afirmara que era el mismo!

PAPAGAYO: Yo no, que aun me representa

el miedo aquí su persona,

y hallo mucha diferencia

de aquesta cara que mata

para aquella cara muerta. (114)

CLARINDO: And, if my sister would have been a man, and if she were alive, I
would say that she and this man were the same person.

LISARDA: Don't you see how much her countenance is similar to Clarindo's?
Oh, if my brother lived, and if he were a woman, I would firmly attest that
she and he were the same person!

PAPAGAYO: Not me. Fright still paints a clear picture of your brother in my mind.
And I find many differences between this face that kills and that dead face.

Even Papagayo, who has encountered Clarindo's supposed ghost, refuses
to recognize similarities between Clara and Clarindo: he "finds many differences" between the two faces. The fact that Papagayo mentions the face
is significant because it allows us to see that Clarindo is not hiding his face
and relies solely on his costume. In addition to this, we know that Papagayo was paying attention to Clara's features because he later runs into
her and recognizes her as Clara. Likewise, the siblings are not able to recognize each other because they believe the other to be dead and they know
that they do not belong to the gender portrayed by the person they are
observing. By equating these two parameters (death and sex) the author is
emphasizing the gravitas that clothing has on how a person is perceived: a
person who is dead cannot possibly be standing in front of us, just like a
person who is dressed as a man cannot possibly be a woman and vice versa.

At the end of the play, Azevedo does not simply allow the characters to
reveal that they belong to the opposite sex while they are still cross-
dressed: both Clarindo and Lisarda have to leave the stage, change clothes
and then state their gender and identities. They never reveal who they are
until they are appropriately dressed. In addition, before they come out,
one of the servants, Hipolita, sees each of them changing clothes and com-
municates that to the other characters: "Señores, ¿hay más encantos / que

los que hay en esta casa? / ¿Hay más confuso palacio? / ¿En qué más metamorfosis / los dioses se transformaron? / Una mujer se hizo hombre, / y agora (¡quién ha pensado / tal cosa!), ¿un hombre mujer / se ha hecho?" (130) ["Ladies and Gentlemen, is there any other house with more enchantments? Is there a more confusing palace? In what other metamorphoses did the gods transform themselves? A woman became a man, and now (who could have thought of this!) a man has become a woman?"]. This statement, which draws direct comparisons to magic and metamorphosis, allows the characters to realize that the person who just left is the same person who came back, though they are wearing clothes from the opposite sex. At the same time, as Mercedes Maroto Camino states, it emphasizes that it is not a mere wardrobe change but entails a recreation of gender and identity (322). The servant does not say that a man has cross-dressed as a woman, but that he has *become* one. It is a transformation and a re-gendering of the individual. The play shows how gender-specific clothing is not just a convention, but a crucial element for distinguishing between men and women during the early modern period. The fact that the cross-dressers are successful at navigating in the space designed for the opposite sex exemplifies that "Azevedo seeks to illustrate that gender difference is not innate, it is not inborn, it is socially constructed" (Gabriele 133).

Azevedo creates situations within her play that highlight sex as an unstable category that can be manipulated by the transgression of sartorial conventions. Azevedo's use of clothing reflects the theatricality of gender by playing on the ambiguity of biological sex. As Beatriz Cortez reminds us, cross-dressing impinges on the ability to create clear-cut definitions and categories (384). Clothing—as a gendered, prosthetic device that can intentionally distinguish between or blend together sex and gender—is crucial in this play because it is meant to transgress sexual and gender conventions.

In *El muerto disimulado*, the characters' acceptance of the cross-dresser as a member of the opposite sex is an expected and logical reaction because it reflects a schema that incorporates the medical theory of heat/coldness and dryness/humidity in the body and its interconnectedness with society's dependence on clothing to distinguish between sexes. Huarte's work reinforced the idea that women and men were anatomically identical in regard to their internal organs and that the internal or external penis was a mere manifestation of the level of heat in the body. Furthermore, the amount of heat in each person was manifested through a combination of physical and behavioral characteristics that allowed for variation within the sexes. Thus, a man who had qualities belonging to the opposite sex was not immediately identified as a woman, but as a man who is less dry and hot than other men. Conversely, a woman who displayed male behavior was identified as a woman in the first degree of coldness and humidity, not as a man. Azevedo signals from the beginning of her play that she will be drawing on this medical knowledge by indicating the change in heat level in her protagonist. Thus, the reactions of the characters that accept the new identity of the cross-dresser without reproach must be analyzed taking into consideration humoral theory. Due to the variation in men and women in regard to heat/coldness, dryness/humidity and to their connection to gendered behavior, the characters must rely on the clear manifestation of sex through clothing. Since the cross-dresser has identified himself as male (used a masculine name), is dressed accordingly, and exhibits male behavior, he is perceived as a male.

CONCLUSIONS

When discussing cross-dressing, we must take into account that it is not simply a theatrical device used to advance the storyline, but also "desnaturaliza lo que culturalmente tenemos aceptado como lógico y como ley natural" (Cortez 379–80) ["distorts what we culturally hold as logical and as natural law"]. Cross-dressing encompasses more than mere swapping of attires; it becomes an embodied way of commenting on the culture's preconceptions and expectations (schemata) regarding sex and gender formation, expression, and interpretation.

Perception in humans is not automatic, and it is not completely voluntary. Our schemata (previous beliefs and experiences) have a firm anchoring effect in what we can perceive. For the characters displayed in this *comedia*, their schema includes Huarte's views on maleness and femaleness (which fuse behaviors and physical characteristics to separate genders) and, on the other hand, sartorial conventions that neatly bifurcated between sexes. These concepts form an attentional set that guides the attention of the characters, who gather information about the costumes and behavior. The visual (or auditory) clues that conform to the attentional set are used to reinforce the notion that the character is a male; the clues that question the masculinity of the character are either ignored or integrated into the perceptual cycle as a mere variation within the male sex.

Taking into account the process through which the brain acquires visual information, and the medical history of the time, we can see in *El muerto disimulado* that the characters' reactions to the cross-dresser are expected and logical within their framework. By dismissing the impact that cross-dressing has on the other characters as a mere theatrical device, scholars privilege their own notions of biological sex and gender as a schema that neatly bifurcates the biological sexes.

WORKS CITED

Azevedo, Ángela de. *El muerto disimulado. Women's Acts: Plays by Women Dramatists of Spain's Golden Age*. Ed. Teresa Scott Soufas. Lexington: UP of Kentucky, 1997, 91–132.

Baars, Bernard J. *In the Theater of Consciousness*. New York: Oxford UP, 1997.

Bartlett, Frederic C. *Remembering: A Study in Experimental and Social Psychology*. Cambridge: Cambridge UP, 1961.

Castle, Terry. "Matters Not Fit to Be Mentioned: Fielding's *The Female Husband*." *English Literary History* 49.3 (1982): 602–22. *JSTOR*. Web. Aug. 28, 2014.

Chambers, Donna M. *From within the Birdcage: Societal Revelations in the Works of Angela de Azevedo*. MA thesis. Georgetown U, 2007. Ann Arbor: UMI, 2007. *ProQuest*. Web. Dec. 14, 2014.

Cortez, Beatriz. "El travestismo de Rosaura en *La vida es sueño* y de Leonor en *Valor, agravio y mujer*: El surgimiento de la agencialidad femenina y la desnaturalización del binarismo del género." *Bulletin of the Comediantes* 50.2 (1998): 371–85. Web. *Project Muse*. Dec. 23, 2014.

Cuadra, Ivonne. "Entre la historia y la ficción: El travestismo de Enriqueta Faber." *Hispania* 87.2 (2004): 220–26. *JSTOR*. Web. Aug. 28, 2014.

"El Alférez Doña Catalina de Herausso: Documentos correspondientes á sus servicios militares en el Reino de Chile y el Perú." N.d. MS. Archivo General de Indias, Contratación, 5408, N.41, 1630–37–11. *Pares: Portal de Archivos Españoles*. Web. Aug. 10, 2014.

Erauso, Catalina de. *Historia de la Monja Alférez, Catalina de Erauso, escrita por ella misma*. Ed. Ángel Esteban. Madrid: Cátedra, 2002.

Ferrer Valls, Teresa. "Del oratorio al balcón: Escritura de mujeres y espacio dramático." *Espacios domésticos en la literatura áurea. Insula* 714 (June 2006): 8–12. *Entre Siglos: Portal de literatura a cargo de Joan Oleza y Teresa Ferrer Valls*. Web. Dec. 22, 2014.

Gabriele, John P. "Engendering Narrative Equality in Ángela de Azevedo's *El muerto disimulado*." *Bulletin of the Comediantes* 60.1 (2008): 127–38.

Heise, Ursula K. "Transvestism and the Stage Controversy in Spain and England, 1580–1680." *Theatre Journal* 44.3 (1992): 357–74. *JSTOR*. Web. Nov. 14, 2012.

Howard, Jean E. "Crossdressing, the Theatre, and Gender Struggle in Early Modern England." *Shakespeare Quarterly* 39.4 (1988): 418–40. *JSTOR*. Web. Aug. 20, 2008.

Huarte de San Juan, Juan. *Examen de ingenios para las ciencias*. Ed. Esteban Torre. Madrid: Editorial Nacional, 1976.

James, William. *Principles of Psychology*. New York: Holt, 1890.

Jones, Ann Rosalind, and Peter Stallybrass. *Renaissance Clothing and the Materials of Memory*. Cambridge: Cambridge UP, 2000.

LaBerge, David. *Attentional Processing: The Brain's Art of Mindfulness*. Cambridge: Harvard UP, 1995.

Laqueur, Thomas. *Making SEX: Body and Gender from the Greeks to Freud*. Cambridge: Harvard UP, 1992.

Maroto Camino, Mercedes. "Transvestism, Translation, and Transgression: Ángela de Azevedo's *El muerto disimulado*." *Forum for Modern Language Studies* 37.3 (2001): 314–25.

McConachie, Bruce. *Engaging Audiences: A Cognitive Approach to Spectating in the Theater*. New York: Palgrave Macmillan, 2008.

Minsky, Marvin. "A Framework for Representing Knowledge." *The Psychology of Computer Vision*. Ed. Patrick Henry Winston. New York: McGraw-Hill, 1975, 211–77.

Most, Steven B., Brian J. Scholl, Erin R. Clifford, and Daniel J. Simons. "What You See Is What You Set: Sustained Inattentional Blindness and the Capture of Awareness." *Psychological Review* 112.1 (2005): 217–42.

Most, Steven B., and Daniel J. Simons. "Attention Capture, Orienting, and Awareness." *Attraction, Distraction and Action: Multiple Perspectives on Attentional Capture*. Ed. Charles L. Folk and Bradley S. Gibson. New York: North-Holland, 2001, 151–73. Advances in Psychology.

Múzquiz-Guerreiro, Darlene. "Symbolic Inversions in Ángela de Azevedo's *El muerto disimulado*." *Bulletin of the Comediantes* 57.1 (2005): 147–63. *Project Muse*. Dec. 23, 2014.

Neisser, Ulric. *Cognition and Reality: Principles and Implications of Cognitive Psychology*. San Francisco: Freeman, 1976.

Pérez de Montalbán, Juan. *La monja alférez: Comedia famosa*. N.d. MS. Biblioteca Nacional de España, Madrid.

Pérez Villanueva, Sonia. "Historia de la Monja Alférez: ¿Escrita por ella misma?" *Actas del VI Congreso de la Asociación Internacional Siglo de Oro: Burgos—La Rioja 15–19 de julio 2002*. Ed. María Luisa Lobato and Francisco Domínguez Matito. Madrid: Iberoamericana, 2004. 1443–52. *Centro Virtual Cervantes*. Web. Aug. 21, 2014.

Potts, Malcolm, and Roger Short. *Ever since Adam and Eve: The Evolution of Human Sexuality*. Cambridge: Cambridge UP, 1999.

Rose, June. *The Perfect Gentleman: The Remarkable Life of Dr. James Miranda Barry, the Woman Who Served as an Officer in the British Army from 1813 to 1859*. London: Hutchinson, 1977.

Schank, Roger C., and Robert P. Abelson. *Scripts, Plans, Goals and Understanding: An Inquiry into Human Knowledge Structures*. Hillsdale: Lawrence Erlbaum, 1977.

Seward Barry, Ann Marie. *Visual Intelligence: Perception, Image, and Manipulation in Visual Communication*. New York: State U of New York P, 1997.

Simerka, Barbara. *Knowing Subjects: Cognitive Cultural Studies and Early Modern Spanish Literature*. West Lafayette: Purdue UP, 2013.

Simons, Daniel J. "Attentional Capture and Inattentional Blindness." *Trends in Cognitive Sciences* 4.4 (2000): 147–55.

Simons, Daniel J., and Christopher F. Chabris. "Gorillas in Our Midst: Sustained Inattentional Blindness for Dynamic Events." *Perception* 28.9 (1999): 1059–74.

Soufas, Teresa Scott. *Dramas of Distinction: A Study of Plays by Golden Age Women*. Lexington: UP of Kentucky, 1997.

Stoll, Anita. "'Tierra de en medio': Liminalities in Ángela de Azevedo's *El muerto disimulado.*" *Engendering the Early Modern Stage: Women Playwrights in the Spanish Empire.* Ed. Valerie Hegstrom and Amy Williamsen. New Orleans: UP of the South, 1999, 151–64.

Torre, Esteban. Introducción. *Examen de ingenios para las ciencias.* By Juan Huarte de San Juan. Ed. Esteban Torre. Madrid: Editorial Nacional, 1976, 9–45.

CHAPTER 8

Don Quixote's Response to Fiction in Maese Pedro's Puppet Show: Madman or Transported Reader?

DOMINGO RÓDENAS DE MOYA AND JOSÉ VALENZUELA

Real y verdaderamente os digo, señores que me oís, que a mí me pareció todo lo que aquí ha pasado que pasaba al pie de la letra: que Melisendra era Melisendra, don Gaiferos don Gaiferos, Marsilio Marsilio, y Carlomagno Carlomagno. Por eso se me alteró la cólera, y por cumplir con mi profesión de caballero andante quise dar ayuda y favor a los que huían, y con este buen propósito hice lo que habéis visto.

I tell you really and truly, you gentlemen who can hear me: it seemed to me that everything that happened here was actually happening, that Melisendra was Melisendra, Don Gaiferos Don Gaiferos, Marsilio Marsilio, and Charlemagne Charlemagne; for that reason I was overcome by rage, and to fulfill the obligations of the knight errantry I profess, I wanted to give my help and favor to those who were fleeing, and to this worthy end I did what you have seen.

Miguel de Cervantes

For Giorgio Agamben, the most beautiful six minutes of the history of cinema are provided by Don Quixote in a provincial movie theater. The theater is full and the top gallery is overcrowded with children. A historical movie is being projected and suddenly some armed knights and a woman in danger appear on screen. Don Quixote draws his sword, rushes toward the screen, and reduces its fabric to tatters; the adult audience is angered and children frantically celebrate the mayhem. Agamben is thinking about Orson Welles and the episode is, obviously, that of Maese Pedro's puppet show in chapter XXVI of *Don Quixote (Part II)*. The knight-errant has been completely transported by fiction and has put his real arm at the service of an imaginary salvation. This gesture is neither useless nor absurd but instead heroic. Unlike what happens in Woody Allen's *The Purple Rose of Cairo*, Don Quixote enters the possible world of the light reflected on the screen. "What are we to do with our imaginations?" wonders Agamben, and he doesn't hesitate to answer himself: "Love them and believe in them to the point of having to destroy and falsify them," even though they reveal themselves as illusory. "But when, in the end, they reveal themselves to be empty and unfulfilled, when they show the nullity of which they are made, only then can we pay the price for their truth and understand that Dulcinea— whom we have saved—cannot love us" (93–94). This doesn't prevent us, however, from loving her, and we continue to do so with real passion.

INTRODUCTION

One of the commonplaces of Cervantes scholarship is that Quixote's madness, caused by his unhealthy engagement with fiction, prevents him from seeing the world as it is. George Haley, in his seminal essay on the Maese Pedro episode in *Don Quixote (Part II)*, says as much: "Because of his madness, Don Quijote cannot clearly distinguish literature from life" (251). The underlying assumption is that readers maintain at all times a healthy cognitive and emotional distance between what they read and their environment, between the world of fiction and the reality of the world. Their engagement with fiction is akin to what Samuel Taylor Coleridge termed the "suspension of disbelief" or "willing suspension of disbelief." In other words, the world of fiction is "fake" or implausible; we willingly accept this fact in order to engage in it without acting upon it. For Haley (a view shared by many a Cervantes scholar), Don Quixote is a fiction-overdosed reader, whose madness "is responsible for transforming empathy into belief and belief into overt action" (260). However, as we will argue in this essay, Don Quixote exemplifies instead the way that readers experience fictional worlds: readers are in fact active participants and Quixote-like rather than passive spectators.

Informed by cognitive psychological research, in particular the work of Richard Gerrig, we would like to draw an analogy between the episode of Maese Pedro's puppet show and readers' engagement with fiction. Our goal is twofold. First, we want to provide cognitive literary scholars with a case study that builds upon the premise that readers tend to engage in fictional events as if they were real until they make an effort to reject them as such (i.e., Gerrig's "willing *construction* of disbelief;"[1] emphasis is ours) and then inhibit their impulse to act upon those events.[2] To do so, we will employ the metaphor of transportation to fictional worlds, to ultimately show how the Maese Pedro episode in *Don Quixote* not only illustrates but also enriches this metaphor by directing our attention to discursive and experiential aspects of the transportation phenomenon.[3] Second, in the context of Cervantes studies, we would like to propose an alternative view of Don Quixote's inability to distinguish reality from fiction as stemming from his madness, through an interdisciplinary view that helps us shed light on how Cervantes portrays the psychology of reading.

Over the last decades, the research at the intersection of literary studies and the cognitive sciences has rapidly grown. This interface is allowing specialists who work at this crossroads to make progress in both directions, thanks to the fruitful collaboration between humanistic and scientific approaches. Literature is, for cognitive scientists, a repository of complex and paradigmatic examples of creation and a record not only of thought but also of human experience. Keith Oatley asserts, "Fiction is an excellent test-bed for understanding mind" ("Fiction and Its Study" 155), while Gerrig stresses the importance of the cooperation of very diverse disciplines: "Cognitive science aspires to understand the full range of human experience. To do so, its practitioners draw upon a variety of domains, including psychology, linguistics, philosophy, and neuroscience" ("Why Literature" 36). Literature is also a nearly inexhaustible source of human emotions. According to Suzanne Keen, for some time social psychology has been considering narrative "as one type of cultural artifact possessing dynamic structuring techniques for the elicitation of emotions" (22), thus turning it into a privileged object of analysis.[4]

1. See Gerrig, *Experiencing* 230, 240.
2. We agree with Howard Mancing in his defense of Gerrig's criticism of the separation of our behavior toward fictional events or real events ("Against Dualisms," "Response"). According to Gerrig, readers are participants in narrative worlds and they produce cognitive and emotional responses as if the events were real, so the main difference between confronting real/fictional situations is that during reading we inhibit our impulses. As Mancing reminds us, in Gerrig's view, narrative engagement is an active process where we as readers "first accept what we read as true and only later, and through a conscious and effortful process, reject some or all of it as false" ("Against Dualisms" 159).
3. For a discussion on the importance of including these and other relevant features to readers' experiences in the transport metaphor, see Bortolussi and Dixon.
4. Hogan, in *What Literature Teaches Us about Emotion* (2011), elaborates on the place of literature in affective science and how literature can help us understand our experience of emotion.

To better know how literary fiction works requires knowing how the human mind works. The study of the cognitive processes that take place in a reader's mind, heir to Roman Ingarden and Wolfgang Iser's phenomenology and reader response criticism, is based on the responses of subjects before a text. In this area of study the contributions of empirical research have been shedding light on individual differences between readers (Gerrig, "Individual Differences"; Gibbs), the elicitation of emotions (Mar, Oatley, Djikic, and Mullin; Miall, "Feeling," "Emotions"), the use of memory during the reading of pieces of texts that evoke resonance in the reader (Gerrig, "Readers' Experiences"), or the process by which we feel inside the story when reading literary fiction: the transportation into a narrative possible world (Gerrig, *Experiencing*; Green; Green and Brock, "The Role"; Appel and Richter), among other themes.

In this essay, we will discuss how the episode of Maese Pedro's puppet show in *Don Quixote* exemplifies the process of transportation into a fictional world. In 1965, Haley emphasized that the novel is full of readers—everyone reads: Don Quixote, the priest, Sansón Carrasco, and the narrators, as the second author reads the translator and the translator reads Cide Hamete Benengeli. He concludes, in his classical analysis of the Maese Pedro episode, that "Cervantes demonstrates a complementary concern with the effect of a story upon its readers, which leads him to dramatize the act of reading as well" (244). What Cervantes dramatizes goes, indeed, beyond the act of reading: he dramatizes readers' transportation and the behavioral aspects involved in the reception of fictional discourses.

The Maese Pedro episode represents the main roles involved in the experience of fiction: the author (the puppeteer and his assistant), the text (the representation of Gaiferos and Melisendra's legend), and the receptor (Don Quixote and the rest of the audience).[5] It ultimately serves as a paradigmatic example of reader transportation gone too far that culminates in action instead of inhibition. We will focus here on the receptive experience of Don Quixote as an analogy not only of the novel's main theme of fictional engagement but of the general experience of reading fiction.

This episode pertains to the domain of self-representation or metafiction, where fiction "draws attention to its status as an artifact in order to

---

5. This episode has been thoroughly analyzed by Cervantes scholars due to its relevance for the inner workings of the novel. See Forcione 146–51; Allen; Moner 101–4; Riley 63–71; among others. In the words of Haley, it "reproduces on a miniature scale the same basic relationships among storyteller, story and audience that are discernible in the novel's overall scheme" (261).

pose questions about the relationship between fiction and reality" (Waugh 2). It is important to remember that the novel itself is a self-conscious narration about the nocive consequences of an "inadequate use" of fiction or, to put it in Aristotelian terms, the damages of reading poetry as if it were history, in this case of taking chivalry stories as if they were chronicles, real stories of real medieval knights. As a self-conscious novel, *Don Quixote* "flaunts its own condition of artifice and . . . by so doing probes into the problematic relationship between real-seeming artifice and reality" (Alter x). In this sense, Cervantes disturbs his readers in relation to their notions of truth and fiction, allowing them to be fully transported by his fictional world while awaking them to the evidence that what they were reading was a verbal artifact and that this "partial magic" they were enjoying was a product of his talent and effort.

MAESE PEDRO'S PUPPET SHOW

Chapters XXV and XXVI of *Don Quixote (Part II)* take place in an inn where Ginés de Pasamonte, disguised as the puppeteer Maese Pedro, is going to perform for his hosts the medieval legend of Don Gaiferos and his bride Melisendra. The boy who accompanies Maese Pedro is narrating the first part of the story when Don Quixote interrupts him for the first time to give him style advice: to continue with the story in a straight line and not succumb to divagations or digressions. Maese Pedro sides with our knight-errant, adding that the child should not lose himself in rhetorical subtleties—"no te metas en contrapuntos, que se suelen quebrar de sotiles" (II.26.928) ["don't get involved in counterpoints that usually break because they are so refined" (630)][6]—and ordering him to follow the knight's suggestions. Soon after, Don Quixote interrupts the narrator again to urge him not to break the story's verisimilitude since "entre moros no se usan campanas, sino atabales" (II.26.928) ["the Moors do not use bells but drums" (632)]. These two intromissions reveal Don Quixote's initial awareness of being in front of an artifice, since he is comparing the adequacy of the illusory world of Don Gaiferos to the legend that for him is historical reality. Nothing leads us to expect what is about to happen and, until this moment, Don Quixote's behavior has simply bordered on insolence.

6. All citations from *Don Quixote* are from the edition by Rico and refer to part, chapter, and page. The translations are from Grossman, citing page only.

After those two interruptions, a third one triggers the genuine content of the chapter. When the narrator or *trujamán* arrives at the point of the story where Don Gaiferos rescues Melisendra and, being persecuted by Moorish King Marsilio de Sansueña's chivalry, they escape on horseback, Don Quixote suddenly acts upon the events that he is witnessing: "Viendo y oyendo, pues, tanta morisma y tanto estruendo don Quijote, pareciole ser bien dar ayuda a los que huían" (II.26.928) ["And Don Quixote, seeing and hearing so many Moors and so much clamor, thought it would be a good idea to assist those who were fleeing" (632)]. What Don Quixote sees and hears ceases to be for him an artistic simulacrum to become part of his reality, possessing the same ontological status as himself. The hero stands up excitedly, draws his sword, and "con acelerada y nunca vista furia comenzó a llover cuchilladas sobre la titerera morisma" (II.26.929) ["with swift and never before seen fury began to rain down blows on the crowd of Moorish puppets" (632)].

The torrent of "cuchilladas, mandobles, tajos y reveses" (II.26.929) ["slashes, two-handed blows, thrusts, and backstrokes" (632–33)] breaks and ruins the puppets, but not even then does Don Quixote acknowledge the fictional nature of the puppet show. On the contrary, he rather proudly justifies his actions as a proof "de cuánto provecho sean en el mundo los caballeros andantes" (II.26.930) ["how much good knights errant do in the world" (633)] because without his intervention the good Gaiferos and the beautiful Melisendra would have been caught by the pursuing horde. Maese Pedro's desolation touches the heart of Sancho Panza, who tries to comfort him saying that his lord, "tan católico y escrupuloso cristiano" (II.26.930) ["so Catholic and scrupulous a Christian" (634)], will repair this mess "si él cae en la cuenta de que te ha hecho algún agravio" (II.26.930) ["if he realizes he's done you any harm" (634)]. This "caer en la cuenta" [realization] refers to Don Quixote's ability to recognize fiction as such, which should have inhibited his disruptive behavior before causing so much harm.

The knight's realization, his construction of disbelief, is untimely. He is initially resistant to accepting that he is in debt to Maese Pedro: "hasta ahora yo no sé que tenga nada vuestro, maese Pedro" (II.26.930) ["until now I did not know that I had anything of yours, Master Pedro" (634)], he says. But the eloquence of the puppeteer's complaints ends up convincing Don Quixote that something strange has happened there and that he (Quixote) has been a victim: the invisible *encantadores* [enchanters] that harass him have intervened again, transforming the surrounding reality to confuse him. So he regrets: "estos encantadores que me persiguen no hacen sino ponerme las figuras como ellas son delante de los ojos, y luego

me las mudan y truecan en las que ellos quieren" (II.26.931) ["the enchanters who pursue me simply place figures as they really are before my eyes,
and then change and alter them into whatever they wish" (634)]. The sin-
ister enchanters, therefore, operate for Don Quixote as catalyzers of both
his recognition of the puppet show as such and his return to his original
state of belief in the fictional world of chivalry. Anchored now in this explanation of what happened, Don Quixote stands in awe again before the
intense sensation of truth of the fictional experience that he has under-
gone within the chivalric fiction that he inhabits: "Real y verdaderamente . . . a mí me pareció todo lo que aquí ha pasado que pasaba al pie de
la letra" (II.26.931) ["really and truly . . . it seemed to me that everything
that happened here was actually happening" (634)]. The hero, ashamed,
resolves to pay for the damage. As Agamben had said: when fiction shows
us the vacuum from which it is made, we have to pay the price for this
truth. This is what Don Quixote does literally.

DON QUIXOTE'S JOURNEY TO THE PUPPETEER'S WORLD

Umberto Eco summed up the experiencing of fictional worlds by stating
that fiction "encloses us within the boundaries of its world and leads us,
one way or another, to take it seriously" (78). More recently, psychologist
Melanie Green has defined fictional transportation as follows: "A transported individual is cognitively and emotionally involved in the story and
may experience vivid mental images. . . . Readers of compelling stories
may lose track of time, fail to observe events going on around them, and
feel that they are completely immersed in the world of the narrative"
(247). In other words, readers disengage, lose the notion of time, and in a
way disconnect their senses, feeling isolated from the objective world that
surrounds them to completely get transported into the narrative world.

For transportation to occur, "some narrative world must be created;
characters and settings must be evoked, not merely emotions" (Green
248)—that is, a figurative discourse is required. In the Maese Pedro episode, the elements that transportation requires are present in the play:
the puppets and the stage serve as characters and setting so that spectators "may not only enter a narrative world, they may also become highly
involved with the people they find there" (Green and Brock, "The Role"
702). Recently, Marisa Bortolussi and Peter Dixon have emphasized the
importance of discourse style features when discussing readers' engagement with fiction and have denounced the fact that "research on transport
privileges story at the expense of discourse" (529). In this regard, the case

of Maese Pedro's performance is particularly relevant for scholars to reconsider the importance of how the story is told and the effect of discourse on readers.

Cervantes constructs this episode using a multimodality medium that combines a visual-figurative-performative realm (through the puppets and the show itself) and a verbal-visual one (through the boy's narrative that interweaves references to visually presented scenes with his diegetic narration). Haley points at the hybrid style of the scene, which is at the same time dramatic and narrative: the boy begins the story "in the present, the tense of all drama . . . occasionally shifts into the imperfect, usually used to describe events evolving in the past . . . sometimes even lapses into the preterit, the tense of completed history or of legend" (249). He alternates his narration, which includes quotations from actual ballads, with instructions for the audience to focalize on relevant aspects: "Miren vuestras mercedes. . . . Vuelvan vuestras mercedes los ojos a aquella torre" (II.26.925) ["look, your graces. . . . Your graces turn your eyes to the tower" (629–30)]. Such discursive arrangement results in a vivid description of the narrative, which is potentiated by its visual-performative feedback. The combination of these media makes Don Quixote's attack ultimately possible, since verbal narration itself would not have supported Cervantes' depiction of the behavioral results of the knight's transportation gone too far.

Let us go back to the premise that the cognitive processes we use in our engagement with fiction are the same as those involved in our day-to-day lives (Gerrig, *Experiencing*). In 2008, Raymond Mar and Oatley found that four of the five brain areas commonly related to narrative processing are also related to studies of social processing (180). This finding points to the possible shared neural basis between our way to make sense of the behavior of real people and our processing of fictional representations of persons. The resources we use to interpret people's behavior may overlap with the ones we use to read a novel but, in the second case, we willingly create disbelief and inhibit ourselves from reacting to fictional characters. The magic resides in the fact that we feel emotions toward them before we realize they are illusory.

Maese Pedro's episode shows us the creation of a narrative world (through the verbal narration of the assistant and the movement of the puppets) with its characters (Gaiferos, Melisendra, the Moors) and its adventures (the Christians' escape) in front of a disparate audience completely enthralled by the artist's magic: "pendientes estaban todos los que el retablo miraban de la boca del declarador de sus maravillas" (II.26.924) ["all those looking at the stage were waiting to hear the words of the narrator regarding its marvels" (628)]. The level of transportation of Don Quixote's fellow show-goers is impossible to assess, but his has a devastating intensity. He feels literally transported to the performed world of the show, to the point of not seeing puppets nor characters but people in danger.[7] And he acts accordingly, true to the laws of chivalry. But what prevents Don Quixote from disbelieving this fictional event and inhibiting his behavior?

Pointing at Haruki Murakami's literary depiction of fictional entrancement in *Kafka on the Shore*, Norman Holland delineates the basic points of the state that we experience while reading a story: (1) we cease to be aware of our surroundings or our bodies; (2) we tend not to judge the reality of whatever fabulous story or film or play or poem we are "lost in"; and (3) we feel real emotions[8] toward fictional people and events (*Literature* 40). Don Quixote, like any standard reader, goes through these stages and reaches the affective one. However, his emotional reaction results in a behavioral response that is typically suppressed in readers as they acknowledge the fictional nature of the witnessed events.[9]

As we mentioned earlier, Cervantes scholars have viewed Don Quixote's inability to distinguish literature from life as stemming from his madness, a view echoed by Haley, who reminds us that the knight "is convinced that the heroes of romance were once people of flesh and blood and that the account of their deeds given in chivalric novels is history" (251). Cognitive literary scholar Lisa Zunshine has proposed that "Cervantes' protagonist suffers from a selective failure of source-monitoring" (75), a failure in the cognitive mechanism essential to the adequate interaction with the world: control of cognitive frames or, in other words, of the origin and hierarchization of the information obtained from the surroundings. Don Quixote is unable to store information with agent-specifying source tags "as told by the author of a romance" (Zunshine 75). For this reason,

---

7. Walton refers, at the beginning of chapter 5 of his *Mimesis and Make-Believe*, to a very similar situation to Quixote's where a backwoods villager called Henry bursts into a play to save the heroine. As in this example, Don Quixote's irruption reveals that "[t]he physical isolation of fictional worlds from the real world seems to have vanished" (193), showing that our hero is unable to play Walton's game of make-believe.

8. Walton denies that readers' emotions are real. He uses the example of a man who feels *quasi-fear* against the slime that appears in the movie, a "not genuine fear" (196). However, Walton accepts that "*Anna Karenina* fosters genuine sympathy for real people in unfortunate situations like Anna's" (204), an idea that Hogan develops in his *What Literature Teaches Us about Emotion*, explaining that some of our emotional responses arise from our own life experiences that narratives call to mind.

9. On the neurological underpinnings of inhibitory responses to fiction, see also pp. 55–56 and 100 in Holland, *Literature*.

fictional information wanders around his head along with the real data, corrupting his knowledge of the world and causing in our knight his inability to negotiate the paradox of fiction, to realize that the people who move him emotionally are fictional characters.[10] As a result, we may infer, he lives the fictional world of chivalry as if it were real; he is permanently transported to fiction. This failure of source-monitoring is interrupted by moments in which Don Quixote seems to acknowledge chivalry as fiction, to willingly create his disbelief. In chapter XVIII of *Don Quixote (Part II)*, Don Diego's son calls him "un entreverado loco, lleno de lúcidos intervalos" (II.18.846) ["a combination madman who has many lucid intervals" (571)]. As a discontinuous madman, he can return to an accurate perception of reality thanks to the efforts and patience of those who surround him. Hence, at the end of the chapter and in view of the disaster he caused, a remorseful Quixote acknowledges his responsibility: "vea maese Pedro lo que quiere por las figuras deshechas, que yo me ofrezco a pagárselo luego, en buena y corriente moneda castellana" (II.26.931) ["let Master Pedro decide what he wants for the damaged puppets, for I offer to pay him immediately in good, standard Castilian coin" (634)]. Even in those moments of disbelief, Don Quixote still inhabits his world of chivalry, as proved by his conviction that the enchanters are responsible for the puppet show turning from reality to a tale. Thus, instead of a madman with lucid intervals, Don Quixote is, in fact, a reader fully transported into the fictional world, with brief intervals of disbelief in which he is able to acknowledge fiction as such.

EMOTIONAL REACTION AND LACK OF INHIBITION
OF THE INGENIOUS GENTLEMAN

Before discussing what pushes Don Quixote to defend the legend's main characters, let us make a distinction between the types of emotions that reading can unleash. In relation to its origin we can distinguish between narrative emotions (or fiction emotions), "a term used to designate those affective responses directed towards characters and events (e.g., sympathy, identification)" and aesthetic emotions (or artifact emotions), which designate "emotions directed towards stylistic elements" (Koopman 185). Our gentleman, a learned man with a fine sensitivity, is susceptible to

10. As Simerka reminds us: "In many studies of the paradox of fiction, Don Quixote is alluded to as an example of a reader who devotes excessive emotional energy to his literary experiences" (202).

aesthetic emotions, as he shows with his objections to the narrator. But his outburst is caused by a sudden influx of narrative emotions: the imperative desire of defending the lovers from their persecutors.

One wonders how Maese Pedro's enactment of the legend of Don Gaiferos causes Quixote's irrepressible emotional reaction. The means to achieve this were easy: our puppeteer has presented, in a clear and Manichaean way, two opposed groups so that the audience (the reader, Don Quixote) focuses its sympathy on one of them, the group of the persecuted Christians. Patrick C. Hogan maintains that the readers' emotional response in front of a story is inseparable from their empathic response to the characters that inhabit it, their situations, actions, capacities, and so forth. The importance of this phenomenon resides in that, despite being an *aesthetic empathy* and not the practical empathy that serves us in the real world, literary works provoke in us empathic responses, just as individuals outside fiction do. In conclusion, "If nothing else, our relations to social identity groups (races, nations, classes) in stories are likely to be continuous with those relations outside stories" (Hogan 276). That is the reason why Don Quixote acts with this rage facing the story events, because it is the same rage he would use against a hypothetical persecution of a Christian knight. The knight develops a *practical* empathy that compels him to act when the rest of the audience stays at the level of an *aesthetic* empathy. He goes beyond the normal stages of transportation that would result in an inhibited emotional reaction once fiction is disbelieved as such. Hogan explains that "literary works may vary somewhat from our actual experience of emotion in contexts where action is necessary" (23) and points that unlike real-life contexts that provoke egocentric emotions and therefore demand action, literature provokes empathic emotions "parallel to the emotions we have when hearing about someone who experienced some joy or sorrow at a distance from us, someone that we can neither help nor harm" (23). Rather than remaining at a distance where he can neither help nor harm, Don Quixote—driven by egocentric emotions that demand his intervention—feels compelled to save Gaiferos and Melisendra.

Don Quixote attacks the puppets because he knows that as a knight he must (and most importantly, he *physically can*) do so: some Christians are in serious danger. In the view of Don Quixote, representation events are not fixed in an irremovable way, but subjected to a contingency of reality. For standard readers, fictional events occur somewhere in the world of the story (Holland, *Literature* 45) and they become aware that this cosmos lacks an objective existence beyond their own minds. For our knight, as we have discussed, ontological barriers between the fictional world and the real one become porous and disappear, so he feels compelled to act upon the unfolding events. As Haley noted, "In his imagination, the puppets have become not only historical beings, but living people whose lives extend forward into a future still to be lived rather than backward into an already determined past" (252). Barbara Simerka explains that Don Quixote "reacts to new and external stimuli, which normally evoke perception, via his imagination" (197). This particularity moves him to a "highly anomalous form of replotting, in which the template of chivalric adventures serves as the point of departure for new tales in which he serves as the protagonist" (Simerka 207).[11] In other words, Don Quixote's long-term state of transportation to chivalric fiction constitutes his individual experiential background, playing a fundamental role in his transportation into Maese Pedro's puppet show and subsequent lack of inhibition. Such transportation is facilitated both by the lively and empathy-eliciting performance of the legend[12] and his own familiarity with the content of the story as well as his intrinsic interest in it.[13] We see through this episode how discourse style features and experiential features are central to the experience of fiction.

We readers of Cervantes' novel don't run away when "seeing" Don Quixote draw his sword and charge against the puppet theater; our brains are inhibiting our movements. When transported into fictional worlds we actively maintain a control device that lets us know that we cannot change the story, which in turn triggers the cognitive inhibition not of our emotional reactions but of our motor actions. Knowing that we cannot act upon the narrative world nor suffer noxious effects by characters or events in the story, our brain can disconnect its reality-testing system (Holland, *Literature* 47). In other words, since nothing bad can happen to us in a fictional world, our mind doesn't spend energy testing whether what is happening is real (a defense mechanism after all). That way, the illusion of the story taking place during reading can provoke an intense sensation of truth. As Bal and Veltkamp put it, "the narrative world is distant from the world in which the reader lives, and makes it possible that the events in the story are perceived as real within the story content, even when events

11. On readers' participatory response of replotting, see Gerrig, *Experiencing* 90–96.
12. As Mancing reminds us "a live performance *is* (a mimetic) reality and the act of viewing it *is* the direct perception of that reality" ("See the Play" 197; emphasis in the original). The effects of Maese Pedro's mimetic reality on Don Quixote are even more striking to Cervantes' readers, given that such reality is created by puppets instead of real beings in a theatrical performance.
13. About the role of prior knowledge and preexisting sources of familiarity in transportation, see Green 250–1.

would not be possible in reality" (10). A narrative mode that plays with this cognitive process is metafiction, where the story stops being a fiction and becomes a fact (Holland, *Literature* 75). In all metafictional works readers have a feeling of indeterminacy toward the fiction they are reading (they can act on the physical literary work but not on its "content") that Holland relates to Freud's *uncanny*, asserting that "shifting the physicality of the story shifts systems in my brain" (*Literature* 78). From a situation where readers were not testing reality or probability, they move to a situation where they start wondering about whether what they are reading is a story or it is real. This will alter the reality-testing systems referred to before and will provoke this sensation of uncertainty that is caused by the works that challenge their readers and question the ontological-referential structure of the narrative. Readers will feel a sense of having to do something, but at the same time they know that part of what they are perceiving is a fiction, feeling uncertain about whether or not to act upon the story.[14] Through Maese Pedro's multimodal setup of the legend, Cervantes creates in this episode a metafictional environment. In this environment, Don Quixote moves from a nearly inhibited state—in which he is conscious of being in front of a representation and only acts to correct factual errors in the story—to one of complete lack of inhibition, wherein he takes action in response to events portrayed on the stage as reality. In doing this, he reacts emotionally and without restrictions to fulfill his duty as a knight-errant, coming to the rescue of the fleeing fellow Christians. He fails to resolve metafictional uncertainty. In this regard, the Maese Pedro episode also constitutes a small-scale model of the novel's reflection on the uncanny effect of metafiction, an effect that Cervantes sought to provoke in his readers through narrative strategies such as making Don Quixote and Sancho both real and fictional characters in his story.

CONCLUSIONS

Maese Pedro's puppet show helps us advance our exploration of how humans experience fiction. By adopting a cognitive psychology perspective on how Cervantes models fictional engagement in this episode, we can further reflect not only on Cervantes' project of exploring the human mind in relation to fiction as well the boundaries between fiction and

---

14. See pp. 84–86 in Holland, "Don Quixote."

reality (particularly important in *Don Quixote* part two, where metafiction is central to the novel) but also on our present interdisciplinary investigation (through the field of cognitive literary studies) of the process of transportation into fictional worlds. In Cervantes' masterpiece Don Quixote, who is *not* a madman but a transported reader unable to construct disbelief, represents both the power and effect of fiction over the human mind. Haley stated, "In proposing to discredit the chivalric novel, Cervantes does not suggest that we not read chivalric novels but only that we read them properly for what they are, outlandish and sometimes beautiful lies, fiction rather than history" (262). As we have argued in this essay, Don Quixote's transportation-gone-too-far stands precisely as an example of how our minds tend to accept these beautiful lies as reality before discrediting them, a cognitive phenomenon underlying our enjoyment of fictional stories.

BIBLIOGRAPHY

Agamben, Giorgio. *Profanations*. Trans. Jeff Fort. New York: Zone Books, 2007.
Allen, John Jay. "Melisendra's Mishap in Maese Pedro's Puppet Show." *Modern Language Notes* 88 (1973): 330–5.
Alter, Robert. *Partial Magic: The Novel as a Self-Conscious Genre*. Berkeley: U of California P, 1975.
Appel, Markus, and Tobias Richter. "Transportation and Need for Affect in Narrative Persuasion: A Mediated Moderation Model." *Media Psychology* 13.2 (2010): 101–35.
Bal, P. Matthijs, and Martijn Veltkamp. "How Does Fiction Reading Influence Empathy? An Experimental Investigation on the Role of Emotional Transportation." *PLOS ONE* 8.1 (2013): 1–12.
Bortolussi, Marisa, and Peter Dixon. "Transport: Challenges to the Metaphor." *The Oxford Handbook of Cognitive Literary Studies*. Ed. Lisa Zunshine. New York: Oxford UP, 2015, 525–40.
Cervantes, Miguel de. *Don Quijote de la Mancha*. Ed. Francisco Rico. Barcelona: Galaxia Gutenberg/Círculo de Lectores/Centro para la Edición de los Clásicos Españoles, 2004.
Cervantes, Miguel de. *Don Quixote*. Trans. Edith Grossman. New York: Ecco, 2003.
Echols, Stephanie, and Joshua Correll. "It's More than Skin Deep: Empathy and Helping Behavior across Social Groups." *Empathy: From Bench to Bedside*. Ed. Jean Decety. Cambridge: MIT P, 2012, 55–71.
Eco, Umberto. *Six Walks in the Fictional Woods*. Cambridge: Harvard UP, 1994.
Forcione, Alban K. *Cervantes, Aristotle and the "Persiles."* Princeton: Princeton UP, 1970.
Gerrig, Richard J. *Experiencing Narrative Worlds: On the Psychological Activities of Reading*. New Haven: Yale UP, 1993.
Gerrig, Richard J. "Individual Differences in Readers' Narrative Experiences." *Scientific Study of Literature* 1.1 (2011): 88–94.

Gerrig, Richard J. "Psychological Processes Underlying Literary Impact." *Poetics Today* 25.2 (2004): 265–81.

Gerrig, Richard J. "Readers' Experiences of Narrative Gaps." *Storyworlds: A Journal of Narrative Studies* 2 (2010): 19–37.

Gerrig, Richard J. "Why Literature Is Necessary, and Not Just Nice." *Cognitive Literary Studies: Current Themes and New Directions*. Ed. Isabel Jaén and Julien J. Simon. Austin: U of Texas P, 2012, 35–52.

Gibbs, Raymond W. "The Individual in the Scientific Study of Literature." *Scientific Study of Literature* 1.1 (2011): 95–103.

Goldstein, Thalia R. "The Pleasure of Unadulterated Sadness: Experiencing Sorrow in Fiction, Nonfiction and 'In Person.'" *Psychology of Aesthetics, Creativity, and the Arts* 3.4 (2009): 232–7.

Green, Melanie C. "Transportation into Narrative Worlds: The Role of Prior Knowledge and Perceived Realism." *Discourse Processes* 38.2 (2004): 247–66.

Green, Melanie C., and Timothy C. Brock. "In the Mind's Eye: Transportation-Imagery Model of Narrative Persuasion." *Narrative Impact: Social and Cognitive Foundations*. Ed. Melanie C. Green, Jeffrey J. Strange, and Timothy C. Brock. Mahwah: Erlbaum, 2002, 315–41.

Green, Melanie C., and Timothy C. Brock. "The Role of Transportation in the Persuasiveness of Public Narratives." *Journal of Personality and Social Psychology* 79 (2000): 701–21.

Green, Melanie C., and Jordan M. A. Carpenter. "Transporting into Narrative Worlds: New Directions for the Scientific Study of Literature." *Scientific Study of Literature* 1.1 (2011): 113–22.

Haley, George. "The Narrator in *Don Quijote*: Maese Pedro's Puppet Show." *Modern Language Notes* 80.2 (1965): 145–65. Rpt. in *Cervantes' Don Quixote: A Casebook*. Ed. Roberto González Echevarría. New York: Oxford UP, 2005, 241–64.

Hardy, Charlie L., and Mark Van Vugt. "Nice Guys Finish First: The Competitive Altruism Hypothesis." *Personality and Social Psychology Bulletin* 32.10 (2006): 1402–13.

Hogan, Patrick C. *What Literature Teaches Us about Emotion*. Cambridge: Cambridge UP, 2011.

Holland, Norman M. "*Don Quixote* and the Neuroscience of Metafiction." *Cognitive Literary Studies: Current Themes and New Directions*. Ed. Isabel Jaén and Julien J. Simon. Austin: U of Texas P, 2012, 73–88.

Holland, Norman M. *Literature and the Brain*. Gainesville: PsyArt Foundation, 2009.

Johnson, Dan R. "Transportation into Literary Fiction Reduces Prejudice Against and Increases Empathy for Arab-Muslims." *Scientific Study of Literature* 3.1 (2013): 77–92.

Johnson-Laird, Philip N., and Keith Oatley. "Emotions, Music, and Literature." *Handbook of Emotions*. Ed. Michael Lewis, Jeannette M. Haviland-Jones, and Lisa Feldman Barrett. 3rd ed. New York: Guildford P, 2008, 102–13.

Keen, Suzanne. "Introduction: Narrative and the Emotions." *Poetics Today* 32.1 (2011): 1–53.

Koopman, Emy M. "The Attraction of Tragic Narrative." *Scientific Study of Literature* 3.2 (2013): 178–208.

Leeuwen, Esther van, and Susanne Täuber. "The Strategic Side of Out-group Helping." *The Psychology of Prosocial Behavior: Group Processes, Intergroup Relations, and Helping*. Ed. Stefan Stürmer and Mark Snyder. Malden: Wiley-Blackwell, 2010, 81–99.

Mancing, Howard. "Against Dualisms." *Cervantes: Bulletin of the Cervantes Society of America* 19.1 (1999): 158–76.

Mancing, Howard. "Response to 'On Narration and Theory.'" *Cervantes: Bulletin of the Cervantes Society of America* 24.2 (2005): 137–56.

Mancing, Howard. "See the Play, Read the Book." *Performance and Cognition: Theatre Studies and the Cognitive Turn.* Ed. Bruce McConachie and F. Elizabeth Hart. New York: Routledge, 2006, 189–206.

Mar, Raymond A., and Keith Oatley. "The Function of Fiction is the Abstraction and Simulation of Social Experience." *Perspectives on Psychological Science* 3.3 (2008): 173–92.

Mar, Raymond A., Keith Oatley, Maja Djikic, and Justin Mullin. "Emotion and Narrative Fiction: Interactive Influences Before, During, and After Reading." *Cognition & Emotion* 25.5 (2011): 818–33.

Martin, Wallace. *Recent Theories of Narrative.* Ithaca: Cornell UP, 1994.

Miall, David S. "Emotions and the Structuring of Narrative Responses." *Poetics Today* 32.2 (2011): 323–48.

Miall, David S. "Feeling from the Perspective of the Empirical Study of Literature." *Journal of Literary Theory* 1.2 (2007): 377–93.

Moner, Michel. *Cervantès conteur: Écrits et paroles.* Madrid: Casa de Velázquez, 1989.

Nadler, Arie, Gal Harpaz-Gorodeisky, and Yael Ben-David. "Defensive Helping: Threat to Group Identity, In-group Identification, Status Stability, and Common Group Identity as Determinants of Intergroup Help-giving." *Journal of Personality and Social Psychology* 97.5 (2009): 823–34.

Oatley, Keith. "Fiction and Its Study as Gateways to the Mind." *Scientific Study of Literature* 1.1 (2011): 152–64.

Oatley, Keith. "Why Fiction May Be Twice as True as Fact: Fiction as Cognitive and Emotional Simulation." *Review of General Psychology* 3.2 (1999): 101–17.

Riley, Edward C. *La rara invención: Estudios sobre Cervantes y su posteridad literaria.* Barcelona: Crítica, 2001.

Ryan, Marie-Laure. *Possible Worlds, Artificial Intelligence and Narrative Theory.* Bloomington: Indiana UP, 1992.

Simerka, Barbara. *Knowing Subjects: Cognitive Cultural Studies and Early Modern Spanish Literature.* West Lafayette: Purdue UP, 2013.

Stürmer, Stefan, Mark Snyder, Alexandra Kropp, and Birte Siem. "Empathy-Motivated Helping: The Moderating Role of Group Membership." *Personality and Social Psychology Bulletin* 32.7 (2006): 943–56.

Walton, Kendall. *Mimesis as Make-Believe.* Cambridge: Harvard UP, 1990.

Waugh, Patricia. *Metafiction: The Theory and Practice of Self-Conscious Fiction.* London: Methuen, 1984.

Zunshine, Lisa. *Why We Read Fiction: Theory of Mind and the Novel.* Columbus: Ohio State UP, 2006.

CHAPTER 9

Theory of Mind in Early Modern Spanish Manuals of Courtly Conduct

RYAN SCHMITZ

Early modern Europe witnessed a proliferation of treatises and manuals on courtly conduct, the art of conversation, and civility. In Spain, Damasio de Frías' *Diálogo de la discreción* [Dialogue of Discretion] (1579), Lucas Gracián Dantisco's *Galateo español* [Spanish Galateo] (1593), and Baltasar Gracián's *Oráculo manual y arte de prudencia* [The Art of Worldly Wisdom] (1647) appropriated concepts from Baldassare Castiglione's seminal text *Il libro del cortegiano* [The Book of the Courtier] (1528) but also pioneered new ideas and strategies for prospering in the socially complex context of the court. The key concepts that we find in these manuals, such as dissimulation, discretion, and prudence, reflect the overarching goal of simultaneously managing the impression one made on others and accurately interpreting the observable behavior of rivals. At court, concealing one's own emotions and reactions was of the utmost importance. To obfuscate the connection between one's interior and exterior, and thus appear illegible to others, the successful courtier must first undergo rigorous self-observation with the aim of controlling one's emotions and avoid the involuntary revelation of one's thoughts, desires, and intentions. Earning widespread esteem and prestige also required the attentive observation of one's peers and the accurate interpretation of the exterior signs they displayed. In other words, survival at court required the adept application of Theory of Mind (ToM). After all, to know what elements of one's self to dissimulate and what image it would be favorable to create, the courtier must be able to quickly formulate sensible interpretations of the motives and causes of actions and to have an accurate notion of an interlocutor's interior experiences.[1]

ToM, or the effortless, automatic, and mostly unconscious mechanism of interpreting the thoughts, emotions, and intentions of another individual, has been called the most important adaptation in human evolutionary history.[2] Robin Dunbar defines ToM as "being able to understand what another individual is thinking, to ascribe beliefs, desires, fears and hopes to someone else, and to believe that they really do experience these feelings as mental states" (83). Since primatologists David Premack and Guy Woodruff put forth the concept in 1978,[3] ToM has permeated other fields of research and has become central to the study of humans in their social environment.[4] In the humanities, during the last fifteen years, scholars have examined literature and film from a ToM standpoint.[5] More recently, several studies have analyzed early modern Spanish texts from a similar perspective,[6] tracing how minds are portrayed in relation to one another and how those texts reflect and contribute to the emergence of a social and developmental psychology in Renaissance Spain. With this essay, I seek to contribute to this line of research by discussing how literature of courtly conduct from early modern Spain demonstrates a nuanced understanding of the interior and exterior dynamics of interpersonal relations, which echoes the cognitive models of the period and can be understood more clearly through the modern-day paradigm of ToM.

THE DISCREET COURTIER

Psychologist Nicholas Humphrey describes humans as *Homo psychologicus*, born psychologists "sensitive to other people's moods and passions, . . . capable of reading the signs in their faces and equally the lack of signs" (4). As cognitive literary scholar Blakey Vermeule reminds us, researchers

1. Sociologist Norbert Elias observed that the seeds of the discipline of psychology appeared in discourse on the early modern court: "This is not 'psychology' in the scientific sense, but an ability, growing out of the necessities of life at court, to understand the make-up, motives, capacities and limits of other people" (104).
2. See Tomasello; Mancing, "James."
3. See "Does the Chimpanzee Have a Theory of Mind?"
4. Representative studies include Baron-Cohen, Gopnik and Meltzoff, Goldman, Gallagher. See also Abu-Akel and Shamay Tsoory, Heyes and Frith, among others.
5. See Zunshine, *Why* and *Getting*; Leverage et al.; and Vermeule. For a discussion on ToM and its application to the study of literature, see Jaén and Simon 20–21.
6. See Jaén, "Literary;" Mancing, "Sancho;" Reed; Simerka; Simon. For a discussion on ToM in relation to Castiglione's *The Book of the Courtier* and Gracián's *Oráculo*, see Simerka's *Knowing Subjects* (pp. 105–15).

now think that "human intelligence evolved to handle the social complexity of living in groups—to outwit fellow primates, to think several moves ahead of them on a giant social chessboard, and to keep track of alliances" (30).

As evidenced by the proliferation of manuals of civil and courtly conduct, the early modern European court may have been one of the most complicated social contexts in human history. Navigating the potentially turbulent social relations required deep social intelligence since, as cultural historian John Snyder notes, "power was permanently at stake in every relationship, and flowed in sometimes unpredictable and capillary ways through the web of interrelations at court" (70).

In early modern Europe, impression management and strategies for prospering in interpersonal relations were as important in the plaza as they were in the palace, as widespread movement from the countryside to burgeoning urban centers created the need for texts that could assist the rural individual in surviving, and even prospering, in a more socially nuanced setting.[7] Juan Lorenzo Palmireno, for example, wrote a number of successful self-help manuals for the young social climber who sought to create the semblance of a liberal education and urbane sophistication despite limited means.[8] In *El estudioso cortesano* [The Studious Courtier] (1573) and *El estudioso de la aldea* [The Studious Villager] (1568), Palmireno's aim was to create "una cierta facilidad de tratar con la gente" (*Estudioso cortesano* 15) ["a certain ease in one's social exchanges"][9] by outlining precepts for civil conversation after a meal. The cultivation of ambiguity and the practice of dissimulation was a prominent and polemical characteristic of early modern Europe.[10] Montaigne famously complained: "As for this new-fangled virtue of hypocrisy and dissimulation, which is so honored at present, I mortally hate it" (491). Nevertheless, it was within the hierarchical context of the court, where power and reputation were potentially at stake in every social exchange, that the most nuanced expression of "strategic interaction" would appear.[11]

The most influential work on the ideal conduct at court was Baldassare Castiglione's *Il libro del cortegiano* [The Book of the Courtier], published in

7. For an examination of the period's best-known peasant who attempts to adapt to the socially complex milieu of the court, see Schmitz, "Sancho's."

8. On Juan Lorenzo Palmireno, see Preto-Rodas as well as Álvarez-Ossorio.

9. Unless otherwise noted, all translations are my own.

10. For an analysis of the cultivation of ambiguity in various sectors of Florentine society, see Weissman. On the important transformations in values and ethical categories in Renaissance Europe, see the work of Martin.

11. See Goffman.

1528. It was an immediate best seller, appearing in sixty-two editions in Italy in the sixteenth and seventeenth centuries and another sixty editions that were translated into at least six foreign languages between 1528 and 1619, appearing first in Spain with Juan Boscán's translation of 1534 (Burke 41, 61–66). Although many traditional, chivalric, qualities were emphasized in Castiglione's dialogue, including grace, courtesy, modesty, and urbanity, it was the new stress on prudence, discretion,[12] and dissimulation, summarized in the neologism *sprezzatura*,[13] that proved most influential in the literature of courtly conduct in early modern Spain. Snyder, who calls Castiglione's book the "fountainhead of all early modern discourse on dissimulation at court," observes that the practice of dissimulation "was a supremely self-conscious art of producing an image of oneself for others through language, gesture, and action, among other things, even if such a representation was intended to disclose little or nothing about the courtier's true intentions: *sprezzatura* was expressly designed to uncouple representation from intention" (71–75). As Barbara Simerka demonstrates, the paradox that the courtier faces, needing to fashion and perform an image of himself without appearing to employ any artifice, "also entails concealing the cognitive efforts of ToM and SI [Social Intelligence]" (112). The successful courtier, then, appears natural and transparent and thus has less need to employ ToM and SI to defend himself.

In late-sixteenth-century and early seventeenth-century Spain, treatises and manuals of courtly conduct attempted to correct the "idealistic" or utopian representation of the courtier and what was perceived as naïve humanism in Castiglione's text.[14] Damasio de Frías' understudied *Diálogo de la discreción*, for example, stressed that discretion[15] required experiential, not simply theoretical, knowledge and criticized the "bachilleres

---

12. Castiglione recommends the use of "decorous discretion" as a "very strong shield against envy" (116). His use of the term equates discretion with measured, cautious speech that avoids exaggeration and ostentation.

13. In what is likely the dialogue's most famous passage, Count Ludovico da Canossa advises, "practice in everything a certain nonchalance [*sprezzatura*] that shall conceal design and show that what is done and said is done without effort and almost without thought" (35).

14. See Gómez.

15. As I have written elsewhere, Damasio de Frías understood discretion as "an intellectual habit engaged in practical decisions; while it is similar to the Aristotelian definition of prudence, 'right reason applied to practice,' it differs in that discretion, unlike prudence, does not imply use for morally virtuous ends. Discretion encompassed such diverse qualities as mental sharpness (*agudeza*); ingenuity (*ingenio*); clear judgment (*juicio*); and good sense (*cordura*). Additionally, discretion referred to social intelligence and the art of conversation; it was often paired with forethought, caution, and dissimulation (*circunspección, recato, disimulación*); grace and affability (*gracia, donaire*); and eloquent communication appropriate for the social context" ("Sancho's" 446).

escolásticos, que jamás salen de leer en el Cortesano, envueltos siempre en preceptos decorados de estas universidades" (89–90) ["scholastic university students, who never stop reading (Castiglione's) *Courtier*, always enveloped in the decorated precepts of these universities"].[16] Lucas Gracián Dantisco's *Galateo español* (1593), a reworking of Italian author Giovanni Della Casa's *Galateo overo de' costumi* [The Rules of Polite Behavior] (1558), is similarly less focused on the ideal characteristics of the courtier than Castiglione's text and provided its reader with many examples to avoid.[17] Finally, Baltasar Gracián's *Oráculo manual y arte de prudencia* was a guidebook for surviving seventeenth-century high society. It was a widely read publication in Spain and abroad, leaving an indelible mark on French *moralistes* and German philosophers, such as Arthur Schopenhauer (Snyder 100). In it, Gracián provides advice to anyone wishing to become "the consummate person—wise in speech, prudent in deeds" ready to enter the "singular society of the discreet" (3–4).[18]

In the following pages, I discuss Spanish manuals of conduct in relation to the emphasis they place on the observation of self and others and on self-control, focusing on Damasio de Frías and Gracián. While the nearly seventy years that separate these two texts witnessed an evolution of views on the courtier, I am interested in demonstrating the strong similarities in the advice they proffer their respective audiences concerning the construction and performance of identity at court. I highlight their connections to medical and philosophical models of the period, emphasizing the importance of the body as indicator of interior experience as well as the strategies of the courtier to interpret other bodies and adapt to court life. I draw parallels between the ideas contained in these manuals— in the context of the philosophy of mind of their time—and modern-day notions of ToM, with the purpose of showing how they echo and contribute to early modern notions of social psychology.

OBSERVATION OF SELF AND OTHERS, SELF-CONTROL

Humphrey argues that it is through self-observation that the individual is capable of "doing natural psychology" or practicing a ToM. He observes:

16. For biographical details on Damasio de Frías, see Rubio González.
17. For an analysis of publications that paired picaresque narrative and conduct manuals, see Ruan.
18. Aphorism 6: "El varón consumado, sabio en dichos, cuerdo en hechos y aun deseado del singular comercio de los discretos" (104). Unless otherwise noted, I use Christopher Maurer's translations of Gracián.

"Without introspection to guide me, the task of deciphering the behaviour of my fellow men would be quite beyond my powers" (33). Early modern writers of courtly guides are similarly insistent on careful observation and awareness of self as a first step to controlling one's passions and maintaining one's composure in the fraught ambience of the court.[19] As Antonio Álvarez-Ossorio argues, writers of court guides essentially appropriate the ancient precept of *Nosce te ipsum* as their "primordial pillar" (23).[20] Damasio de Frías, for example, declares that self-awareness is the obligatory point of departure for the discreet individual—"el primer conocimiento" ["first knowledge"]—since all other success will spring forth from it:

> Porque del bien conocerse cada uno, nace juntamente el conocer para lo que es, qué cargos puede administrar y cuáles no, con qué cosas podrá salir bien y en las que no será de provecho, dónde podrá hablar, dónde le estará mejor callar. . . . (192–3)[21]

> Because with clear self-awareness comes awareness of what one is capable, what responsibilities one can or cannot administer, with what endeavors one will excel and which tasks will not be in one's interest, in what circumstances one should speak or when it would be better to stay quiet. . . .

An immediate corollary of self-analysis was self-control, particularly of one's emotions or passions. Gracián plainly states: "No ai mayor señorío que el de si mismo, de sus afectos, que llega a ser triunfo del alvedrío" (105; aphorism 8) ["No mastery is greater than mastering yourself and your own passions: it is a triumph of the will" (4–5)].

If reason's grip on the reins controlling passion were too loose, the individual's higher human faculties, such as judgment, could be impaired: "Son las passiones los humores del ánimo, y qualquier excesso en ellas causa indisposición de cordura; y si el mal saliere a la voca, peligrará la reputación" (131; aphorism 52) ["The passions are the humors of the mind and the least excess sickens our judgment. If the disease spreads to the mouth, your reputation will be in danger" (29–30)]. Isabel Jaén notes that

19. Elias has noted that from the competition at court came "the first unveiled descriptions of the human affects in modern times" (105).

20. Snyder observes that European discourse on the controversial practice of dissimulation was founded on "thorough self-analysis on the part of the dissimulator, who was to subject every word, gesture, and gaze to rigorous inner examination" (7).

21. Unless otherwise noted, all citations of Damasio de Frías' *Diálogo* come from the only modern edition of the work, published in 1929 by Justo García Soriano. This passage is from 111v of the original manuscript.

the *estimativa* faculty, or our ability to evaluate or judge, "gained particular importance in the early modern cultural period, when humanity was understood in terms of our capacity to transcend, via the faculty of judgment, our animal soul in order to embrace our rational one" ("Cervantes and the Cognitive" 72).[22] Indeed, humanist thinkers such as Giovanni Pico della Mirandola and Juan Luis Vives had argued that the particular dignity of the human position was its indeterminate quality: we could ascend the great chain of being to a more perfect, angelic form, or descend to the level of brutes.[23]

The importance that Gracián places on the passions dovetails with the work of Vives. In book three of his *De anima et vita* Vives argued that passions were skillfully placed in us by the creator to stimulate our souls; when properly managed by reason, they could help us reach truth and virtue.[24] As Foster Watson noted, Vives emphasized the "outward realized activities" of the soul (338); his descriptions of particular passions tend to center on the physiological reaction that an emotion causes—for example,

> Anger causes terrible effects in the body, effects that are unbecoming to man. When annoyance is first felt, the pericardial blood becomes hot, the heart itself begins to swell and to beat hard in the chest. But anger or annoyance is not present until the hot spirits from the heart penetrate our brain. . . . Those whose brain humors are very hot become enraged extremely fast; hence the change in their facial expression, the quivering of their voice, the difficulty in speaking, and other changes that are horrible to watch and clearly more bestial than human. (Vives, *Passions* 68)

Carlos G. Noreña notes that as an Aristotelian, Vives was "persuaded that any emotional excess was a deviation from virtue and rationality" (xiii). Similarly, Gracián advocated for moderation and avoidance of emotional excess, especially as it related to anger: "Son los ímpetus de las passiones deslizaderos de la cordura, y allí es el riesgo de perderse. Adelántase uno

22. In this regard, Gracián praises "sindéresis" (discretion, judgment, common sense) repeatedly; in particular, see aphorism 96, "Es el trono de la razón, basa de la prudencia" ["It is the throne of reason, the foundation of prudence" (53–54)]. Thomas Aquinas notes, "certain thinkers held *synderesis* to be a higher power than reason"; however, he views it as a "characteristic disposition" that nature implants into us (79).

23. See Pico della Mirandola; Vives, "A Fable." On the *scala naturae*, or great chain of being, see Tillyard. For a reading of Cervantes' *Novelas ejemplares* in relation to the great chain of being, see Schmitz, "The Great."

24. See Jaén, "Cervantes on Human" 40–41.

más en un instante de furor o contento que en muchas horas de indiferencia" (215; aphorism 207) ["The sudden movements of the passions throw prudence off balance, and here is where you can be lost. You move more in a single moment of furor or content than you do in many hours of indifference" (117)].

Emotions can cloud one's judgment, impede the use of reason, or even contaminate the sensory data that one gathers:

> *Atención al informarse.* Vívese lo más de información . . . raras vezes llega en su elemento puro, y menos quando viene de lejos; siempre trae algo mixta, de los afectos por donde passa; tiñe de colores la passión quanto toca, ya odiosa, ya favorable. Tira siempre a impresionar. (146–47; aphorism 80)

> *Be careful when you inform yourself about things.* Much of our lives is spent gathering information. . . . Seldom does it reach us unalloyed, even less so when it comes from afar. It is always blended with the emotions it has passed through. Emotion taints everything it touches, making it odious or favorable. It tries always to impress us one way or another. (45)

Ultimately, Gracián advised the courtier to observe and comprehend all of one's faculties: "Comprehensión de sí. En el Genio, en el Ingenio; en dictámenes, en afectos. No puede uno ser señor de sí si primero no se comprehende" (151; aphorism 89) ["Know yourself: your character, intellect, judgment, and emotions. You cannot master yourself if you do not understand yourself" (50–51)].

Understanding yourself and understanding others or executing ToM in early modern Spain also entailed an awareness of the temperament or humoral constitution of one's peers and rivals. In 1575, Juan Huarte de San Juan published *Examen de ingenios para las ciencias*, a controversial work that was quickly translated into French, Italian, and English and whose ostensible purpose was to identify which minds contained a natural ability for the exercise of letters and the study of science.[25] In his treatise, Huarte juxtaposes the medical studies of Galen and Hippocrates with the moral and natural philosophies of Plato and Aristotle before formulating his own theories about the physiological constitution of human wits. Following Hippocrates, Huarte stresses that the wisest and most prudent minds are those that balance the four elements in "equal weight and measure" and, in fact, all virtues depend upon the body's temperament (250).

25. See Martín-Araguz for Huarte's contribution to neuropsychology. See also Jaén's analysis of Sancho Panza in connection with Huarte's ideas ("Cervantes and the Cognitive").

Nevertheless, nature is not the only determining force: environmental conditions such as weather, geographic location, and diet help shape one's mind, as do the habits the individual forms. Huarte espouses an awareness of one's humoral constitution in order to incorporate healthy habits that could offset any existing imbalances of one's temperament; for example, by directing attention, or "imagination," via meditation and contemplation of the divine, he argued that it was possible to acquire "el temperamento que el alma racional ha menester" (274) ["the temperament that the rational soul needs"].

Many of Gracián's aphorisms similarly advise an awareness of one's own humoral orientation. In aphorism 69, he stresses that self-reflection must include "un conocer su disposición actual y prevenirla, y aun decantarse al otro extremo para hallar, entre el natural y el arte, el fiel de la sindéresis;" (140) ["knowing or foreseeing your disposition, and moving towards the other extreme in order to balance art and nature. Self-correction begins with self-knowledge" (39)]. Gracián also recommends correctly identifying other agents' temperament through attentive observation,[26] so that one can adapt accordingly:

> *Comprensión de los genios con quien trata*: para conocer los intentos. . . . El melancólico siempre agüera infelicidades, y el maldiciente culpas: todo lo peor se les ofrece, y no percibiendo el bien presente, anuncian el possible mal. El apassionado siempre habla con otro lenguaje diferente de lo que las cosas son; habla en él la pasión, no la razón. Y cada uno, según su afecto o su humor. Y todos mui lejos de la verdad. (247–8; aphorism 273)

> *Understand the characters of the people you are dealing with* in order to penetrate their intentions. . . . The melancholy person always forecasts unhappiness, and the gainsayer, faults. They think only of the worst, and, overlooking the good that is present, they announce the evil that is possible. The person swayed by passion cannot speak of things as they are: passion speaks in him, not reason. Each person speaks according to his emotions or humor, and all are far from the truth. (154)

Ultimately, executing a successful ToM in the early modern court entailed the accurate classification of one's own as well as others' temperament,

---

26. Complicating this classification was the tendency for early modern individuals to feign the melancholic temperament. Teresa Soufas notes that melancholy flourished as a "social vogue" due to its association with mental acuity and it "led would-be greats to feign the most obvious symptoms of a melancholic personality in order to be considered brilliant" (9). Damasio de Frías complains of courtiers who feigned melancholy in order to appear to possess "gravedad" [gravity] (104).

in order to counteract one's own "destemplanzas" (humoral imbalances) or take advantage of a rival's physiological disposition.

CONCEALING AND REVEALING

Control of emotion and one's humoral balance implied careful mastery of what one said, but perhaps just as important, one's bodily appearance at court, particularly with the privileged site of the face.[27] As one astute courtier observed: "un homme qui sait la cour est maître de son geste, de ses yeux, et de son visage; il est profond, impénétrable; il dissimule les mauvais offices, sourit à ses ennemis, contraint son humeur, déguise ses passions, dément son cœur, parle, agit contre ses sentiments" (La Bruyère 22) ["a man who knows the court is master of his gesture, his eyes and his face; he is deep and impenetrable; he dissimulates bad deeds done to him, smiles at his enemies, controls his temper, disguises his passions, denies his heart, and speaks and acts against his own feelings" (22)].[28]

Rival courtiers attempted to test their stone-faced interlocutors with tactics to provoke revelatory gestures and expressions that would divulge their intentions, desires, or beliefs. In many of his aphorisms, Gracián warns against such traps and he advises his reader to overcome them:

> Traza la agena astuta intención estas tentaciones de prudencia para descubrir tierra, o ánimo. Válese de semejantes torcedores de secretos, que suelen apurar el mayor caudal. Sea contraardid el reporte, y más en las prontitudes. Mucha reflexión es menester para que no desvoque una passión. (215–16; aphorism 207)

> Cunning people set these traps for prudence in order to sound matters out and fathom the minds of their opponents. Prying out secrets, they get to the bottom of the greatest talents. Your counter-strategy? Control yourself, especially your sudden impulses. (117)

Cognitive literary scholar Lisa Zunshine has coined the term "embodied transparency" to refer to "moments in fictional narratives when characters' body language involuntarily betrays their feelings, particularly if they want to conceal them from others" (23). Although her analysis is centered

27. Research on ToM and autism underlines the importance of the human face as a primary source of information for interpreting the interior experience of another agent. See Bloom, Baron-Cohen, among others.
28. Translation of La Bruyère by Jon Snyder.

on characters in works of fiction, her conclusions help us shed light on early modern treatises on courtly conduct. According to Zunshine, one of the rules for embodied transparency in prose fiction is that it must be transient lest it raise suspicions of affectation or performance on the part of the displayer or a lack of ethics in the observer. For Zunshine, this reflects real life and the human tendency to avert one's gaze or at least make such a show when another "leaks" involuntary body language and is socially vulnerable (32–33). The ethics of the early modern Spanish court, however, would seem to dictate far fewer qualms with taking full advantage of an opportunity to gather information on a rival's involuntary display.

Among the tactics that courtiers employed to gain access to the minds of others were, for instance, the use of humor, particularly via "motes" or "biting witticisms,"[29] which, at least on some occasions, were used to test a rival's self-control and to provoke an affective outburst or, in Zunshine's terminology, a moment of embodied transparency. The successful use of humor could increase one's social capital or "prestige-value,"[30] but it was a dangerous weapon to wield since one could just as easily offend a potential ally as win wide esteem as a clever wit. Castiglione outlines in great detail the types of humor common at court, such as word play, repartee, innuendo, and practical jokes.[31] In *Galateo español*, Gracián Dantisco advises the limited use of "motes" and "burlas" [practical jokes] since "el que es motejado . . . suele afrentarse y recibir enojo de ello" (86) ["he who is teased . . . often takes offense and becomes angry because of it"]. Baltasar Gracián's advice on the matter is more nuanced. While he advises against overuse of humor, noting, "Conócese la prudencia en lo serio, que está más acreditado que lo ingenioso" (144; aphorism 76) ["Prudence is known for its seriousness, which wins more respect than wit]," he also viewed insinuation ("varillas") as one of the most important tools for ferreting out the truth: "*Conocer y saber usar las varillas*. Es el punto más sutil del humano trato. Arrójanse para tentativa de los ánimos y házese con ellas las más dissimulada y penetrante tienta del coraçon" (123; aphorism 37) ["*Know what insinuation is, and how to use it*. It is the subtlest point of dealing with

---

29. Covarrubias defines "mote" as "una sentencia dicha con gracia y pocas palabras. . . . Algunas veces sinifica dicho agudo y malicioso, que en latín llamamos *dicterium*, y de aquí se formó el verbo motejar, que es poner falta en alguno" (1299) ["a maxim said with grace and few words. . . . Sometimes it signifies a sharp and biting saying, which in Latin we call *dicterium*, from which the verb 'motejar' was formed, which is to point out another's defects"].

30. The term is from Elias (111).

31. It is interesting to note that numerous examples that Castiglione cites are from his time at court in Spain or from anecdotes he heard of the Spanish royal court of King Alfonso of Aragon and Queen Isabella (118–59).

others. It can be used to test the wits and cunningly probe the heart" (21)]. Thus, the intelligent use of insinuation allowed the courtier to make external that which a rival had intended to keep from public view.

Gracián envisions impressive abilities for the courtier who, like a lynx, can use sharp vision to penetrate another's heart and see his intentions (115; aphorism 25). To avoid other adept observers one must "*Cifrar la voluntad.* . . . Compita la detención del recatado con la atención del advertido: a linces de discurso, xibias de interioridad. No se le sepa el gusto, porque no se le prevenga, unos para la contradicción, otros para lisonja" (155–56; aphorism 98) ["*Write your intentions in cipher.* . . . Let caution and reserve combat the attentiveness of others. When your opponent sees into your reasoning like a lynx, conceal your thoughts like an inky cuttlefish. Let no one discover your inclinations, no one foresee them, either to contradict or flatter them" (54–55)]. Similarly, numerous aphorisms advise the reader to construct a sort of mysterious fog around himself, to be unpredictable, and to lurk in the shadows; for example, "*Keep changing your style of doing things* . . . it's easy to kill a bird that flies straight" [32] (10) or, in a less defensive stance, ambiguity is an effective strategy for gaining and maintaining esteem: "Nunca dé lugar a que alguno le alçançe todo: mayores efectos de veneración causa la opinión y duda de adónde llega el caudal de cada uno que la evidencia dél, por grande que fuere" (154; aphorism 94) ["You can win more admiration by keeping other people guessing the extent of your talent, or even doubting it, than you can by displaying it, however great" (53)].

In arguing for the social function of intelligence, Humphrey likens the interactions of individuals in a complex society to a game of chess in which rival players, through feints and counter-feints, attempt to hide their intentions even as they try to discern those of their opponent. He notes, "the social gamesman, like the chess-player, must be capable of a special sort of *forward planning*" (21; my emphasis). Gracián's advice to his reader reflects precisely the type of gamesmanship that Humphrey outlines. With clever word play, Gracián depicts social life as a "militia against malice" and explains the complex machinations it takes to "win the attention and confidence of others":

> *Obrar de intención, ya segunda, y ya primera* . . . pelea la sagacidad con estratagemas de intención. Nunca obra lo que indica, apunta, sí, para deslumbrar; amaga al aire con destreza y executa en la impensada realidad, atenta siempre

---

32. Aphorism 17: "*Variar el tenor en el obrar.* . . . Fácil es de matar al buelo el ave que le tiene seguido, no assí la que le tuerze" (111).

a desmentir. . . . Pero la penetrante inteligencia la previene con atenciones, la azecha con reflexas, entiende siempre lo que quiere que entienda, y conoce luego qualquier intentar de falso. (107–8; aphorism 13)

Act on the intentions of others: their ulterior and superior motive . . . Cunning arms itself with strategies of intention. It never does what it indicates. It takes aim deceptively, feints nonchalantly in the air, and delivers its blow, acting upon unforeseen reality with attentive dissimulation. . . . The penetrating intelligence heads off cunning with close observation, ambushes it with caution, understands the opposite of what cunning wanted it to understand, and immediately identifies false intentions. (7–8)

Early modern models of the individual demonstrate a similar appreciation for forward planning. Both Vives and Damasio de Frías divide reason into the practical and the speculative; the former, which we share with beasts, is aimed at the good, while the latter is uniquely human and has truth as its goal.[33] It is precisely the speculative faculty that permits humans to engage in the type of forward planning outlined by both Gracián and Humphrey. Damasio de Frías points out the etymological connection between prudence and *providencia* and defines this virtue as oriented toward the future based on past experiences (41). Thomas Aquinas argued, "Only God can know future things in themselves . . . but we too can know [them] as they exist in their causes" (93–94). The prudent courtier, then, through the use of the speculative powers of his rational soul, meets the considerable interpretive demands of the socially complex, labyrinthine court to gain esteem and prosper.

CONCLUSIONS

In his seminal study *The Court Society*, Norbert Elias argues that discourse from the early modern European court understands the individual "as a *person in relation to others*" (104; emphasis in the original). Spanish manuals of courtly conduct are pulsing with advice on how to intelligently manage interactions with other human beings and how to augment one's social prestige, which, as Elias points out, was the very foundation of an individual's existence at court (95). The exceptional courtier relied on keen observation and a fine-tuned awareness of the interconnections between body and mind in order to both control his

---

33. See Jaén, "Cervantes and the Cognitive" 75; Frías 40.

own actions and interpret those of his peers. That is to say, like the prominent mind theorists of the period, such as Huarte and Vives, authors of court literature understood that the individual is an embodied agent.

The courtiers of the early modern period met the demands of a highly competitive and hierarchical social context just as theorists have suggested *Homo sapiens* did during the Pleistocene: by developing an increasingly sophisticated ToM.[34] Examining early modern court literature with a cognitive approach that brings together mind models of the period and modern-day notions of ToM can help us shed light on the astute psychological insights that court literature made in the sixteenth and seventeenth century. Moreover, such an approach encourages an appreciation of the contribution of court writers to the emergence of interpersonal psychology in early modernity, prompting us to reconsider contested notions of Renaissance individualism and selfhood.

WORKS CITED

Abu-Akel Ahmad, and Simone Shamay-Tsoory. "Neuroanatomical and Neurochemical Bases of Theory of Mind." *Neuropsychologia* 49.11 (2011): 2971–84.

Álvarez-Ossorio Alvariño, Antonio. "La discreción del cortesano." *Edad de oro* 18 (1999): 9–45.

Aquinas, Saint Thomas. *A Summary of Philosophy.* Trans. and ed. Richard J. Regan. Indianapolis: Hackett, 2003.

Baron-Cohen, Simon. *Mindblindness: An Essay on Autism and Theory of Mind.* Cambridge: MIT P, 1995.

Bloom, Paul. *Descartes' Baby: How the Science of Child Development Explains What Makes Us Human.* New York: Basic Books, 2004.

Burke, Peter. *The Fortunes of the Courtier.* University Park: Penn State UP, 1995.

Castiglione, Baldassare. *The Book of the Courtier.* Trans. Leonard Eckstein Opdycke. Mineola: Dover, 2003.

Covarrubias Horozco, Sebastián. *Tesoro de la lengua castellana o española.* Ed. Ignacio Arellano and Rafael Zafra. Madrid: Iberoamericana-Vervuert, 2006.

Dunbar, Robin. *Grooming, Gossip, and the Evolution of Language.* Cambridge: Harvard UP, 1996.

Elias, Norbert. *The Court Society.* Trans. Edmund Jephcott. New York: Pantheon, 1983.

Frías, Damasio de. *Diálogo de diferentes materias.* N.d. MS 1172. Biblioteca Nacional de España, Madrid.

Frías, Damasio de. *Diálogos de diferentes materias inéditos hasta ahora.* Ed. Justo García Soriano. Madrid: Imp. de Hernández y Sáez, 1929.

Gallagher, Shaun. *How the Body Shapes the Mind.* Oxford: Oxford UP, 2005.

Goffman, Irving. *Strategic Interaction.* Philadelphia: U of Pennsylvania P, 1969.

---

34. See Mancing, "James" 130.

Goldman, Alvin. *Simulating Minds: The Philosophy, Psychology, and Neuroscience of Mindreading*. Oxford: Oxford UP, 2006.

Gómez, Jesús. "La 'Conversación discreta' de Damasio de Frías y los estudios sobre el arte de conversar." *Hispanic Review* 75.2 (2007): 95–112.

Gopnik, Alison, and Andrew N. Meltzoff. *Words, Thoughts, and Theories*. Cambridge: MIT P, 1997.

Gracián, Baltasar. *The Art of Worldly Wisdom*. Trans. Christopher Maurer. New York: Doubleday, 1992.

Gracián, Baltasar. *Oráculo manual y arte de prudencia*. Ed. Emilio Blanco. Madrid: Cátedra, 2009.

Gracián Dantisco, Lucas. *Galateo español*. Madrid: Ediciones Atlas, 1943.

Heyes, Cecilia M., and Chris D. Frith. "The Cultural Evolution of Mind Reading." *Science* 344.6190 (June 20, 2014): 1243091-1–6.

Huarte de San Juan, Juan. *Examen de ingenios para las ciencias*. Ed. Guillermo Serés. Madrid: Cátedra, 1989.

Humphrey, Nicholas. *Consciousness Regained: Chapters in the Development of Mind*. New York: Oxford UP, 1984.

Jaén, Isabel. "Cervantes and the Cognitive Ideas of His Time: Mind and Development in *Don Quixote*." *Cognitive Cervantes*. Ed. Julien Simon, Barbara Simerka, and Howard Mancing. Spec. cluster of essays of *Cervantes: Bulletin of the Cervantes Society of America* 32.1 (2012): 71–98.

Jaén, Isabel. "Cervantes on Human Development: *Don Quixote* and Renaissance Cognitive Psychology." *Don Quixote: Interdisciplinary Connections*. Ed. Matthew D. Warshawsky and James A. Parr. Newark: Juan de la Cuesta, 2013, 35–57.

Jaén (Jaén-Portillo), Isabel. "Literary Consciousness: Fictional Minds, *Real* Implications." *Selected Papers from The 22nd International Literature and Psychology Conference, June 29—July 4, 2005*. Ed. Norman Holland. IPSA. 2005. June 15, 2015. <http://www.clas.ufl.edu/ipsa/2005/proc/portillo.pdf>.

Jaén, Isabel, and Julien Jacques Simon. "An Overview of Recent Developments in Cognitive Literary Studies." *Cognitive Literary Studies: Current Themes and New Directions*. Ed. Isabel Jaén and Julien J. Simon. Austin: U of Texas P, 2012, 13–32.

La Bruyère, Jean de. *Les caractères* (1688). Ed. Robert Garapon. Paris: Garnier, 1962.

Mancing, Howard. "James Parr's Theory of Mind." *Critical Reflections: Essays on Golden Age Spanish Literature in Honor of James A. Parr*. Ed. Barbara Simerka and Amy R. Williamsen. Lewisburg: Bucknell UP, 2006, 125–43.

Leverage, Paula, Howard Mancing, Richard Schweickert, and Jennifer Marston William, eds. *Theory of Mind and Literature*. Lafayette: Purdue UP, 2011.

Mancing, Howard. "Sancho Panza's Theory of Mind." *Theory of Mind and Literature*. Ed. Paula Leverage, Howard Mancing, Richard Schweickert, and Jennifer Marston William. Lafayette: Purdue UP, 2011, 123–32.

Martin, John J. "Inventing Sincerity, Refashioning Prudence: The Discovery of the Individual in Renaissance Europe." *The American Historical Review* 102.5 (1997): 1309–42.

Martin, John J. *Myths of Renaissance Individualism*. New York: Palgrave, 2004.

Martín-Araguz, A., and C. Bustamante-Martínez. "*Examen de ingenios* de Juan Huarte de San Juan, y los albores de la neurobiología de la inteligencia en el Renacimiento español." *Revista de Neurología* 38.12 (2004): 16–30.

Montaigne, Michel de. *Essays*. Trans. Donald M. Frame. Stanford: Stanford UP, 1957.

Noreña, Carlos G. Foreword. *The Passions of the Soul: The Third Book of* De anima et vita. By Juan Luis Vives. Intro. and trans. Carlos G. Noreña. Lewiston: Edwin Mellen P, 1990, i–xv.

Palmireno, Juan Lorenzo. *El estudioso cortesano*. Valencia: Ex Typographia Petri à Huete, 1573.

Pico della Mirandola, Giovanni. *Oration on the Dignity of Man*. Trans. E. L. Forbes. *The Renaissance Philosophy of Man*. Ed. E. Cassirer, P. O. Kristeller, and J. H. Randall, Jr. Chicago: U of Chicago P, 1948, 223–54.

Premack, David, and Guy Woodruff. "Does the Chimpanzee Have a Theory of Mind?" *Behavioral and Brain Sciences* 1.4 (1978): 515–26.

Preto-Rodas, Richard A. "The Works of Juan Lorenzo Palmireno: Popular Self-Help for the Young Social Climber in Renaissance Spain." *Hispania* 68.2 (1985): 230–5.

Reed, Cory. "'¿Qué rumor es ése?': Embodied Agency and Representational Hunger in *Don Quijote* I.20." *Cognitive Cervantes*. Ed. Julien Simon, Barbara Simerka, and Howard Mancing. Spec. cluster of essays of *Cervantes: Bulletin of the Cervantes Society of America* 32.1 (2012): 99–124.

Ruan, Felipe E. *Pícaro and Cortesano: Identity and the Forms of Capital in Early Modern Spanish Picaresque Narrative and Courtesy Literature*. Lewisburg: Bucknell UP, 2011.

Rubio González, Lorenzo. "Damasio de Frías: Un clásico para ser estudiado." *Castilla: Estudios de literatura* 13 (1988): 145–58.

Schmitz, Ryan. "The Great Chain of Being and Cervantes' *Novelas ejemplares*." *eHumanista* 20 (2012): 511–24. Web. June 30, 2015.

Schmitz, Ryan. "Sancho's Courtly Performance: *Discreción* and the Art of Conversation in the Ducal Palace Episodes of *Don Quijote II*." *Modern Language Notes* 128.2 (2013): 445–55.

Simerka, Barbara. *Knowing Subjects: Cognitive Cultural Theory and Early Modern Spanish Literature*. West Lafayette: Purdue UP, 2013.

Simon, Julien J. "Celestina, Heteroglossia, and Theory of Mind: The Rise of the Early-Modern Discourse." *Proceedings of the 2008 International Conference in Literature and Psychology*. Lisbon: Instituto Superior de Psicologia Aplicada, 2009, 119–26.

Snyder, Jon R. *Dissimulation and the Culture of Secrecy in Early Modern Europe*. Los Angeles: U of California P, 2009.

Soufas, Teresa Scott. *Melancholy and the Secular Mind in Spanish Golden Age Literature*. Columbia: U of Missouri P, 1990.

Tillyard, E. M. W. *The Elizabethan World Picture*. London: Hatton & Windus, 1956.

Tomasello, Michael. *The Cultural Origins of Human Cognition*. Cambridge: Harvard UP, 1999.

Vermeule, Blakey. *Why Do We Care about Literary Characters?* Baltimore: Johns Hopkins UP, 2010.

Vives, Juan Luis. *A Fable about Man*. Trans. Nancy Lenkeith. *The Renaissance Philosophy of Man*. Ed. E. Cassirer, P. O. Kristeller, and J. H. Randall, Jr. Chicago: U of Chicago P, 1948, 387–93.

Vives, Juan Luis. *The Passions of the Soul: The Third Book of* De anima et vita. Trans. Carlos G. Noreña. Lewiston: Edwin Mellen, 1990.

Watson, Foster. "The Father of Modern Psychology." *Psychological Review* 22.5 (1915): 333–56.

Weissman, Ronald F. E. "The Importance of Being Ambiguous: Social Relations, Individualism, and Identity in Renaissance Florence." *Urban Life in the Renaissance*. Ed. Susan Zimmerman and Ronald F. E. Weissman. London: Associated UP, 1989.

Zunshine, Lisa. *Getting Inside Your Head: What Cognitive Science Can Tell Us about Popular Culture*. Baltimore: Johns Hopkins UP, 2012.

Zunshine, Lisa. *Why We Read Fiction: Theory of Mind and the Novel*. Columbus: Ohio State UP, 2006.

SECTION V

Feeling and Ethics

Embodiment and Empathy in Early Modern Drama: The Case of Cervantes' *El trato de Argel*

CORY A. REED

The rising interest in cognitive approaches to literature and drama has prompted academics in multiple disciplines to investigate the dynamics between readers and texts and between audiences and performances, drawing on supportive research in the fields of neuroscience. This area of study, including the ideas of cognitive embodiment and empathetic observation, holds promise for the analysis of theater in the early modern period, and sheds light on an essential aspect of drama: how spectators respond to what they perceive on stage. Such an approach may indeed allow us to make further sense of early modern performances—what actually happened in the *corrales* during the staging of a play—by examining certain aspects of audience–performer interactions. In these contexts, I will discuss Miguel de Cervantes' early play, *El trato de Argel* [The Trade of Algiers], performed (successfully, if Cervantes' own words are to be believed) during the decade of the 1580s, when theatrical conventions in Spain were still fluid, and when political and economic crises called for relevant theatrical performances that actively engaged the audience in some of the most pressing issues confronting the Spanish people at the time.

I begin by identifying a problem, one that theater scholars recognize but literary-cultural theory has been only partially successful in solving. The problem, in essence, is that discursive-based theory produces readings of dramatic texts that can be far removed from what actually happens in a theater during live performance. Discursive ways of understanding a dramatic text tend to focus on aspects such as aesthetic and political abstractions and localizing meaning in a play's linguistic expression. Theater practitioners, however, are more interested in how a play's meaning manifests itself through the dynamic interaction of bodies in a physical space and the exchanges of action, movement, voice, and emotions that occur among actors and between actors and audience. This difference in how we approach drama can affect our ability to agree on even the most basic meaning of a play. Indeed, a live audience's embodied understanding of what a play is "about" can be quite different from what academics theorize the meaning to be in their analytical *readings* of play texts.

Cognitive approaches to drama might begin to reconcile the "two cultures" of theater scholars and practitioners by providing literary criticism with the means for discussing dramatic texts in the context of human interaction in the shared space of theatrical performance. Bruce McConachie and F. Elizabeth Hart contend that recent studies in neuroscience of human perception, emotions, and empathy have significant implications for the theory and practice of performance (23). Cognitive studies of performance do not negate, but instead complement and build upon, previous performance studies and discursive analyses to help us understand how audiences perceive and process meaning. If criticism has generally focused on describing *what* happens, either in a text or during the "gathering, performing, and dispersing" moments that Richard Schechner identifies in the "space apart" of the theater (176), cognitive approaches to performance are well positioned to describe *how* and *why* theatrical performance affects audiences, completing the picture with explanations of the interactive dynamics of the theatrical performance space based on studies about how the embodied human mind works. As Catherine Connor has written:

> because these cognitive studies deal with the concerns of several interrelated disciplines, they extend bridges among theories that otherwise may not appear to correspond with each other. . . . The embodied approach to cognitive theory shows us that the mind in the body and the body in the mind are overlapping operations. By understanding the interdependence of the two, scholars can bridge gaps among the supposedly distinct processes of playwriting, reading, performing, and spectating in specific socio-cultural contexts. (12)

Thus, the emerging field of cognitive studies not only helps us better understand the dramatic texts we study but can also provide a way to talk to others whose work is grounded in the practical realities of live performance.

Cognitive assessments of performance show that discursive-based performance theory is limited by an overreliance on a Saussurean semiotic framework in which communication is reduced to linguistic signs and theatrical spectators are considered "readers." Hart proposes a reconciliation of phenomenological and semiotic approaches to performance that acknowledges cognitive embodiment in the theatrical performance space (31). Following the basic cognitive premise that all knowledge is mediated by the body, Hart maintains that a theatrical performance begins in the actor's brain and that embodied knowledge enables "a focused intentionality that participates along with the body in creating a performance" (33). Embodiment, in the cognitive sense, includes body and mind and views the body as both a lived, experiential structure and the site of cognitive activity (Varela, Thompson, and Rosch xv–xvi). As Lawrence Barsalou has written, cognitive embodiment consists of "interactions between perception, action, the body, the environment, and other agents" and therefore is a useful concept for understanding not only the interaction of mind and body in an individual actor or spectator, but also the give-and-take among multiple minds and bodies engaging in physical, affective, and intellectual activity in a common space (619). A cognitive approach to the complex dynamics of live performance acknowledges integrated relationships among activities traditionally rendered separate by post-Cartesian theoretical and analytical traditions that differentiate mind and body. In fact, according to Barsalou, embodied or "grounded" cognition may be "the dominant view of cognition for most of recorded history," interrupted by Cartesian binarism and only reemerging in mainstream models of cognition in the late twentieth century (619).[1] The idea of cognitive embodiment, then, may allow us a twenty-first-century glimpse into pre-Cartesian thinking about how cognition works, putting us a bit more in touch with the possibilities that early modern writers, like Cervantes, may have envisioned for theatrical performance.

Our understanding of what happens when we observe a performing body originates with the theories of German philosophers Robert Vischer, who coined the term *Einfühlung* (aesthetic empathy) to characterize how people respond to works of art, and Theodor Lipps, who applied the term

---

1. Barsalou proposes the term "grounded cognition" to avoid the mistaken assumption that "embodied cognition" refers only to bodily states and to emphasize that cognition is grounded in multiple ways, including simulations, situated action, as well as bodily states (619).

to social interaction. Lipps theorized that an "instinct of empathy" explains how humans reproduce the gestures of expression we see in others, and how doing so evokes the feelings associated with those expressions (Zahavi and Overgaard 5). Cognitive notions of embodiment and empathy describe how audiences relate to and feel for the characters they see performed on stage, and how they respond, both emotionally and intellectually. Barsalou has written:

> Simulation plays increasingly important roles in theories of social cognition. Of particular interest is explaining how we represent the mental states of other people. Simulation theories propose that we represent other people's minds using simulations of our own minds. To feel someone else's pain, we simulate our own pain. (623)

According to Barsalou, simulation is the general mechanism that establishes empathy (623). Recent studies involving brain imaging technology have identified a system of mirror neuron circuits as the source of simulation and the bodily basis for our engagement with performance (Iacoboni, *Mirroring*; Barsalou 623). Ros King has applied these concepts to analyze audience responses to early modern theatrical performance (specifically Shakespeare), proposing both an unconscious mirroring of observed performers on the neural and muscular levels and a conscious, physical awareness of being located in a theater, observing a work of fiction (37).

How bodies engage with a performance can be understood by looking into human neurophysiology, particularly the mirror neuron system (MNS). Studies in neuroscience tell us that mirror neurons are activated when we observe other bodies in motion, seem to respond to intentionality, and may also be responsible for emotional mirroring.[2] Recent theories about this human mirroring system, such as the associative hypothesis, hold particular promise for our understanding of the role of mirror neurons in social interaction.[3] Although the MNS is the subject of controversy among neuroscientists—studies show disagreement on how this system works as well as how it might be applied to explain cultural phenomena[4]—the field of cognitive literary and cultural studies is interested in how our mirror mechanism might help to explain why and how we identify and

2. Representative studies on the MNS include Gallese and Goldman; Gallese; Rizzolatti and Craighero; Iacoboni et al., "Grasping"; Iacoboni, *Mirroring*; and Rizzolatti and Sinigaglia.

3. See De la Rosa and Bülhoff.

4. On the controversy surrounding the MNS, see Hickok; Gallese et al., "Forum"; and Glenberg.

feel with characters we see on the stage or screen (or read about in books).[5] In the theater, mirror neurons may indeed be the bodily basis for the audience's understanding of the actor's intonation, emotions, and actions, allowing the audience to perceive fear and pity, dramatic conflict, irony, or possibly even humor. A cognitive approach helps us understand why performance works, how it affects an audience emotionally and psychologically, and why humans are so drawn to the arts of imitation—explaining a biological basis for what Aristotle identified as our histrionic "instinct" (Aristotle 56).

As the reality of performed emotions is mirrored in the engaged observer, the theatrical audience participates in a cognitive process of spectating that involves both what C. Daniel Batson calls "empathetic understanding," or the ability to recognize and identify with another's experience, and "empathetic concern," an emotional response to another's suffering. The idea that empathetic concern might produce altruistic motivation is what Batson has termed the *empathy-altruism hypothesis* ("Empathy-Altruism" 41). Although this hypothesis remains controversial,[6] I believe that the relationship among empathetic understanding, empathetic concern, and altruism is an important aspect of the spectator's engagement with live theatrical performance and is crucial to any kind of socially committed theater, whether in the sixteenth or the twenty-first century. It is particularly relevant to the plays of Cervantes that I am discussing here. As Batson reminds us, studies in neuroscience reveal that humans rely on empathy to interpret the emotions and behaviors of other human beings, although the extent to which this process is altruistic or egoistic is still widely debated (Batson, "Empathy-Altruism" 45).[7] Empathy is a complex and multifaceted notion that has been studied from diverse perspectives within both the sciences and the humanities.[8] Jean Decety defines these aspects of empathy more concisely as "the natural capacity to share, understand, and respond with care to the affective

5. See Wojciehowski and Gallese.
6. On the controversy surrounding this hypothesis, see Keen, among others.
7. See Batson, Lishner, Cook, and Sawyer; and Vescio, Sechrist, and Paolucci. Batson (*Altruism*) provides a review of more than thirty experiments manipulating or measuring empathy for a person in need.
8. The eight psychological states identified by Batson are (1) knowing another person's internal state, including his/her thoughts and feelings, (2) adopting the posture or matching the neural responses of an observed other, (3) coming to feel as another person feels, (4) intuiting or projecting one's self into another's situation, (5) imagining how another is thinking and feeling, (6) imagining how one would think and feel in the other's place, (7) feeling distress at witnessing another person's suffering, and (8) feeling for another person who is suffering ("These" 4–8).

states of others" (vii). In this essay I will draw on Decety's definition to propose that a progression from sharing, through understanding, to responding informs an audience's response to watching a live theatrical performance.

Any analysis of audience response must take into account the diverse composition of a theatrical public. Here, Suzanne Keen's notion of empathic inaccuracy is useful in order to consider how empathy might work differently in each member of the audience. Keen reminds us that there is a variability in audience responses to empathetic fiction: sometimes empathy with characters does not occur, different cultural and temporal contexts may change the work of fiction's capacity to invoke empathy, and empathy for a fictional character may not correspond to the author's desired response (136). While talking primarily about narrative empathy, Keen's ideas can be modified to apply to theatrical audiences as active observers of a performed work of fiction. Theatrical performances can sometimes evoke empathy unintentionally, and certain productions might deliberately subvert authorial intentions (if and where they might be identifiable). Without trying to essentialize audience members, we can reasonably conclude that a given audience includes individuals with varying tastes and artistic sensibilities, with different educational backgrounds and experiences in the world, and who come to the theater after having been affected by the immediate emotional demands of the day (Keen 137–8). This represents a challenge for the director of any theatrical performance who seeks to create a unified empathetic response in the audience, or to deliver any kind of "message" to the public.

Relevant to this discussion is the distinction between cognitive and affective empathy. Simone G. Shamay-Tsoory defines cognitive empathy as a process that involves perspective taking (understanding another's point of view), while affective empathy refers to the more emotional reactions and sharing of feelings, which may include unconscious simulation of emotions observed in others (215–6).[9] If theatrical spectators, as King has claimed, can simultaneously simulate the emotions of the characters portrayed onstage while being mindfully aware of the fictionality of the performance and the physical presence of the theater, then both kinds of empathy must be at work. Audiences, in short, may react "automatically" to the emotional performances they witness, but this is only part of the story. Audiences also think about what they see and contextualize performances intellectually at every turn.

9. For more about the distinctions between cognitive and affective empathy, see Strayer.

How, then, do audiences understand dramatic conflict and relate to the characters and actions they see onstage during live performance? Cognitive science points to the role of embodiment, empathy, and emotional responses in the spectator's experience rather than semiotic decoding (McConachie and Hart 5). Howard Mancing argues that theatrical performance cannot be reduced to signs, or its audience to mere readers. He writes: "there is a fundamental difference between reading a text such as a novel and watching any sort of collaborative, multi-media display such as the performance of a play. . . . Seeing and knowing is not the same thing as reading and knowing" (189). Mancing is correct in pointing out that we do not, in fact, *read* films or theatrical performances: we perceive them visually and aurally and employ cognitive processes to interpret, assess, or understand what we see and hear. In his approach, Mancing builds on Allan Paivio's "dual coding theory," which maintains that cognition involves a combination of sensory perception and symbolization, drawing simultaneously on visual and auditory perception as well as symbolic or linguistic cognition. Certainly, the way we perceive what we see and hear in theatrical performance is not the same cognitive activity as gaining meaning from a system of coded linguistic signs when we read a literary text. Cervantes himself perceived this difference when he justified redirecting his plays to a reading public "para que se vea de espacio lo que pasa apriesa" (*Poesías* 183) ["so that one may observe carefully that which passes quickly (on the stage)"].[10] Cervantes was aware that reading a play takes time, whereas dramatic conflict must be perceived and understood immediately during live performance. Other forms of perception, in addition to sustained intellectual focus, must be at work during live performance in order for the audience to understand what is happening as it is happening, and Cervantes' comments demonstrate an appreciation of this difference.

As Amy Cook reminds us, "theatre audiences process extraordinarily complex information without getting lost" ("Interplay" 587). Complex plays and their intricate plots require work on the part of an audience for whom this complexity is more rewarding than, say, watching a situation comedy on television. Many Spanish *comedias* are this kind of play, whose complexity challenges the audience visually, aurally, and emotionally, as well as intellectually. Recalling Mancing's assertion that "seeing and knowing is not the same thing as reading and knowing," we might compare the process of reading complex, plot-driven plays with that of watching them performed in the theater. I cite as an example a recent production of Tirso de Molina's *Don Gil de las calzas verdes* [Don Gil of the Green

10. Unless otherwise noted, all English translations are mine.

Breeches] performed at the Theatre Royal in Bath, England. As many discover on a first reading of this play, the convoluted plot, in which multiple characters take on the form and personality of the imaginary eponymous character, culminating in four Don Giles onstage, is just too complicated for a reader to keep straight in the memory without rereading the text. Discursive explanations, in the classroom or in print, often fail to clear up the confusion; in fact, the more we try to explain complex plots with words, the more confusing they become. Yet our brains somehow manage to follow complex action when we watch it onstage. Complex plays are actually more difficult to understand by reading them than by seeing them. This is because our knowledge of the dramatic action is embodied, involving multiple kinds of perception in an engaged spectator, relying on cues that are more effectively communicated aurally and visually than through linguistic decoding.

Similar kinds of audience-challenging (and audience-rewarding) complexity characterize Cervantes' drama, both the later plays redirected to a reading public (*Pedro de Urdemalas* [Peter the Trickster] and *La Gran Sultana* [The Great Sultana] come to mind) and his earlier performed works (such as *El trato de Argel* and *Numancia*). Nearly all of Cervantes' plays are episodic, with large casts of characters and metatheatrical role playing, deceit, and disguise that can be difficult to follow on the page but that somehow work well on the stage. In commenting on his own dramatic success in the 1580s, Cervantes emphasizes the audience's approval and enjoyment of his plays, which he says were received with "general y gustoso aplauso de los oyentes" (*Entremeses* 92–93) ["general, delighted applause of the spectators"]. In this, he echoes Lope de Vega, who famously identifies a favorable audience response ("el vulgar aplauso") ["mass appeal"] as his primary goal in his *Arte nuevo de hacer comedias* [The New Art of Writing Plays] (285; line 46). Both Cervantes and Lope express an understanding that audiences first identify emotionally with the dramatic conflict in order to later contemplate the play's message intellectually. Lope famously wrote that important themes such as "casos de honra" ["problems of honor"] worked best on the stage "porque mueven con fuerza a toda gente" ["because they move everyone forcefully"] (298; lines 327–8). Likewise, Cervantes claimed to be the first dramatist in Spain "que representase las imaginaciones y los pensamientos escondidos del alma" ["to represent the hidden thoughts and imaginings of the soul"], indicating the importance of the audience's psychological and emotional identification with the internal conflicts developed in his characters (*Entremeses* 92). As a practicing dramatist, Cervantes was very aware of the appeal of live performance, and he knew how to inspire audiences to respond both emotionally and intellectually to his plays. As we shall see, cognitive approaches to the act of spectating in the theater can help us understand the relationship between cognitive and affective empathy in an audience, and how this process might evolve during a theatrical performance.

EMPATHY AND ALTRUISM IN *EL TRATO DE ARGEL*

One of the first works Cervantes composed for the stage, *El trato de Argel* predates Lope's innovations to the *comedia nueva* but nonetheless apparently enjoyed popularity on the Madrid stage. One reason for this, proposed by María Antonia Garcés, is that the play's theme of captivity was the early modern equivalent of a media sensation. According to Garcés, the Algerian slave trade was so extensive during the sixteenth and seventeenth centuries that some 600,000 Christian captives may have been bought and sold in the slave markets during this time (144–5). Garcés estimates that during the 1580s, some 10 percent of the Castilian population may have been former captives; an even greater number had family members or friends who had endured captivity in North Africa. This translates into a very large percentage of Cervantes' potential audience having some direct experience of, or personal interest in, the plight of Spanish captives (171–2).[11] The debut performance of *El trato de Argel*, whose author had himself recently returned from captivity, was surely a topical event that guaranteed a successful run (Garcés 136). One might compare this atmosphere of audience interest to our present decade, in which films depicting recent military campaigns in Iraq and Afghanistan (such as *The Hurt Locker* or *Zero Dark Thirty*) reflect an audience interest in the theme of war as entertainment and have earned critical acclaim. Of further interest is the possible role Cervantes' drama may have played in public-awareness campaigns dedicated to raising funds for ransoming Algerian captives (Fernández 14–15). If this is true, then we may conclude that some, and perhaps many, members of the audience attending *El trato de Argel* were likely to experience both affective and cognitive empathetic responses to the theatrical depiction of the horrors and trauma of captivity in the shared space of the *corral*. Given that the audience was not a monolithic entity with a unison response, each spectator would have an

11. Garcés further estimates that captives represented between 20 and 25 percent of the population of Algiers at any historical moment (144). Cervantes himself refers to some 15,000 Christian captives in Algiers, through the words of his character Sayavedra (I.436–8).

individual response depending on his or her own personal experiences, social group, age, and other factors.

Garcés persuasively argues that Cervantes, in composing *El trato de Argel*, was writing through his own captivity experience in order to resolve emotionally and psychologically his own persistent trauma. Indeed, the traumatic repetition suffered by victims may have informed the structure of *El trato* (172). The episodic framework of this play, in which numerous independent vignettes provide multiple perspectives on the experience of captivity as a backdrop to a complicated main plot involving an ethically problematized love quadrangle, is a fragmented testimony that reenacts traumatic events and the inadequacy of language to express them. The psychological complexity of this drama, along with its fragmented, episodic structure that iterates and reiterates the experience of traumatic suffering, lends itself well to a cognitive analysis of how an audience engages emotionally with a theatrical performance.

Some of the more poignant and emotionally evocative episodes in *El trato de Argel* include the brutal, physical punishment of a recaptured slave, detailed descriptions of corsair attacks on Christian ships, an extended recounting of the horrific and bloody revenge killing of a Valencian priest, and the internal crisis of faith experienced by an escaped slave wandering lost through the wilderness, all of which reiterate the intensity of suffering emphasized in Aurelio's speech that opens the play:

> ¡Triste y miserable estado!
> ¡Triste esclavitud amarga,
> donde es la pena tan larga
> cuan corto el bien y abreviado!
> ¡Oh purgatorio en la vida,
> infierno puesto en el mundo,
> mal que no tiene segundo,
> estrecho do no hay salida! (I.1–8)[12]

> Wretched and miserable condition!
> Dismal, bitter slavery,
> where suffering is as long
> as good is brief and fleeting!
> Oh living purgatory,
> hell on Earth,
> evil which has no peer,
> strait from which there is no escape!

12. All citations from *El trato de Argel* refer to act and line numbers.

Throughout the play, this "hell on Earth" is literalized through the live representation of torment, suffering, anxiety, and both physical and emotional violence. Repeatedly, the concept of the liminal space of purgatory emerges as a metaphor for expressing the unifying theme of the relentless temptation of apostasy and the daily choice faced by oppressed captives whether to convert to Islam in order to alleviate the physical suffering of the body and the psychological torment of the mind, even if such apostasy entails the permanent, spiritual loss of the soul.

Perhaps the most emotionally devastating of the scenes in this play involves the destruction of a Sardinian family, whose members are sold individually in the Algerian slave market. Cervantes' stage directions indicate the importance of the visual impact of this scene and his desire to produce an emotional, empathetic response, describing the family as "el padre y la madre y dos muchachos, y un niño de teta a los pechos" (II; after line 870) ["a father, a mother, two children, and a nursing infant at the mother's breast"]. He then proceeds to dramatize not only the debasement and dehumanization of these people, who are treated as chattel and examined like animals, but also the cries of children as they are pulled away from the arms of their mother, whom they will presumably never see again:

PREGONERO: ¿Hay quien a comprar acierte
el niño y la madre junto?

MADRE: ¡Oh amargo y terrible punto,
más terrible que la muerte!

PADRE: ¡Sosegad, señora, el pecho;
que si mi Dios ha ordenado
ponernos en este estado,
él sabe por qué lo ha hecho!

MADRE: Destos hijos tengo pena,
que no sé por dónde han de ir. (II.883–92)

. . .

MERCADER 1:   Comprad, compañero, esotro.
Ven, niño, vente a holgar.

JUAN: No, señor, no he de dejar
mi madre por ir con otro.

MADRE: Ve, hijo, que ya no eres
sino del que te ha comprado,

JUAN: ¡Ay, madre! ¿Habéisme dejado?

MADRE: ¡Ay, cielo, cuán crudo eres! (II.919–26)

AUCTIONEER: Is there anyone here who wants to buy
the mother and child together?

MOTHER:	Oh what a bitter and terrible end,
	much more terrible than death!
FATHER:	Calm, dear wife, your breast;
	if God has ordained
	to put us in this state,
	he knows the reasons why!
MOTHER:	I suffer for these two children,
	not knowing where they are to go.
MERCHANT 1:	Buy this other one, friend.
	Come, child, come to rest.
JUAN:	No, sir, I will not leave
	my mother to go with another.
MOTHER:	Go, child, as you now belong
	to the one who has bought you.
JUAN:	Oh, mother! Have you abandoned me?
MOTHER:	Oh, heaven, how cruel you are!

During this demanding scene, the actors must draw the spectators into an intense emotional conflict as it unfolds in the dramatic moment. If we consider that many members of the 1580s audience had endured captivity firsthand or had family members so affected, the empathetic response would likely be especially acute. There may have been a particularly strong effect on former captives who themselves were still working through their own traumatic experiences, still reliving them in the present moment. Dori Laub has written, "Trauma survivors live not with memories of the past, but with an event that could not and did not proceed through to its completion, has no ending, attained no closure, and therefore, as far as its survivors are concerned, continues into the present and is current in every respect" (69). Perhaps as a trauma survivor himself, Cervantes was familiar with the kind of traumatic repetition experienced frequently upon observing emotional turmoil in others. In structuring his play as a series of fragmented, repetitive episodes, each expressing an emotional aspect of captivity, he succeeds in conveying an emotional and psychological experience difficult to express through words. His audience, simply put, would have experienced vicariously some of the trauma of captivity by observing the emotional performances onstage.

But while Cervantes wants his spectators to feel emotion, he also wants them to think. This brings us to the idea of whether empathy happens immediately or takes time, and the interaction of both affective and cognitive empathy. During live performance we perceive the essence of dramatic conflict in extra-linguistic ways that actively involve emotion and affective empathy. Our affective identification with the characters observed onstage appears to be immediate. But what does an audience do with that emotion? What other factors might be at work in cognitive empathy, which also involves focused intellectual engagement? As McConachie proposes, "This empathetic process is mostly automatic, but the kind of awareness it produces lodges in memory and is easily brought into consciousness" (27). While some embodied cognition occurs instantaneously, audiences still need to pay attention, which is a conscious process in which spectators use both short-term and long-term memory in order to understand more completely (*Engaging* 29). Citing Gerald Edelman's concept of "constructive recategorization," McConachie explains that "human consciousness depends foundationally upon memory: we construct images (combining sound, sight, smell, etc.) in our mind's eye (and its ears and muscles, etc., too) primarily by integrating immediate stimuli with past categories in the mind/brain" (*Engaging* 35). It appears, then, that while affective empathy is immediate, cognitive empathy, in fact, must be a process that takes time and mindful reflection on what the mind and body are experiencing during performance.

John H. Muse convincingly argues that "discussions of empathy by psychologists, philosophers, and performance theorists largely ignore the issue of time. Just how quickly can a performance get under the skin?" (173). Muse contends that "genuine empathy—as opposed to automatic or sympathetic reactions—requires time to develop in audiences" (174) and proposes that focusing on the immediacy of an automatic empathetic response oversimplifies the emotional experience of spectatorship and downplays "the complex and gradual experience of engagement with a virtual world and the emotional lives of its figures" (176). According to Muse, how quickly our minds come to empathize may depend on how familiar we are with the story represented onstage. He cites what Susan Feagin has called "conditioners" that "lay the foundation for empathetic bridges and speed their construction" (179). In the case of *El trato de Argel*, as we have seen, these cognitive bridges would already have been formed in many of the spectators attending performances in the 1580s. Former captives and their families would have been prepared ("conditioned") to engage in more sophisticated kinds of cognition that build on emotional empathy to include intellectual evaluation and contemplation.

Rhonda Blair proposes that while an audience initially grasps what happens on stage by feeling, other mechanisms work partly at the conscious level (128, 130). Likewise, Cook sees two important dimensions of empathy: an automatic response that links an audience emotionally to the actors and a simultaneous recognition of the separation between self and other. This establishes empathy as a relationship that allows audience members to assess and evaluate the causes and "story" of the emotions they automatically feel when watching a play ("Hecuba" 79–80). Muse likewise sees empathy as a process "that does not preclude intellectual development, but is a distinct kind of intellectual involvement, and a precondition for altruistic feelings and actions" (178). For audience members to enjoy a play, they need to care. And if they care, they might, in fact, be prompted to act.

Both Blair and Cook, then, see a utopian potential in live theatrical performance (Blair 84). In this, they build upon the foundation of Batson's empathy-altruism hypothesis—envisioning a better society, and perhaps even acting on that vision, exemplifying the altruistic motivation that emerges from empathetic concern. Here, the collectivity of the theatrical experience is important to consider in light of empathy's role in motivating pro-social behavior. Stephanie Echols and Joshua Correll have studied how group dynamics influence the empathetic process, concluding that perceived membership in a group helps us to understand the affective state of others in our group:

> Human beings are a social species. We form social connections, share resources, work together to protect ourselves from threats, experience social pain when separated from the group, and even depend on others to raise viable offspring. (55)

Echols and Correll call this *obligatory interdependence*, which evolved because understanding and cooperating with others in the same group was necessary for survival (55). In *El trato de Argel*, Cervantes appeals to this obligatory interdependence by creating a strong sense of group identity in his audience that encourages empathy and action. According to theater scholar Jill Dolan, theatrical performance is best understood as a participatory forum in which an engaged audience can share, contemplate, and begin to enact change or pursue justice. This "utopian performative" is characteristic of socially committed drama and speaks to the mutual agency of performers and spectators (Dolan 456, 468). We might consider *El trato de Argel* in this light, as a socially relevant drama possibly associated with a fundraising campaign to ransom captives. Fernández finds in this play an explicit call to action (14), in the words of Aurelio near the end of the third act:

> ¡Oh, cuán bien la limosna es empleada
> en rescatar muchachos, que en sus pechos
> no está la santa fe bien arraigada!
> ⁣   ¡Oh, si de hoy más, en caridad deshechos
> se viesen los cristianos corazones,
> y fuesen en el dar no tan estrechos,
> ⁣   para sacar de grillos y prisiones
> al cristiano cativo, especialmente
> a los niños de flacas intenciones! (III.1865–73)

> Oh, how well alms are employed
> in rescuing youths, for in their hearts
> the holy faith is not well-rooted!
> ⁣   Oh, if from now on, Christian hearts
> would exhaust themselves through charity,
> and were not so restrained in giving,
> ⁣   in order to free from shackles and prisons
> captive Christians, especially
> children of weak resolve!

Muse argues that such direct appeals to the theatrical public are, in cognitive terms, "a frequent shortcut to empathy" and that plays grounded in verifiable experiences, such as *El trato de Argel*, literally ask spectators "to examine their emotional reactions to current events" (184). Direct appeals to audiences encourage them to act on what they feel, to build on the emotional foundation activated by simulation in order to effect some kind of change.[13] As Keen has written, "concord in authors' empathy and readers' empathy can be a motivating force to push beyond literary response to prosocial action" (141). If the original production was successful in expressing Cervantes' ideas and feelings about the personal toll of the captivity problem, then the empathetic response and the desire to act, in at least some members of the audience, may have been profound indeed.

Empathetic observation in a theatrical audience, then, may begin with the automatic and immediate simulation of emotion, but socially engaged playwrights like Cervantes also want us to think about the emotions portrayed on the stage, which we feel as spectators. And if *El trato de Argel* did

13. For a discussion of the relationship between empathy and activism with regard to novelistic literature in early modern Spain, see Jaén.

play a role in a campaign for raising public awareness or to solicit funds for ransoming captives, he wants us to think for the purpose of translating our thoughts into action. If we accept the cognitive understanding of empathy (expressed by Batson and Decety, as well as the cognitive literary scholars Blair, Cook, and Muse) as a process that evolves and deepens over time through increasingly complex cognitive activities involving memory and focused attention, then Cervantes' early drama demonstrates three steps in this progression. Recalling Decety's tripartite definition of empathy as "the natural capacity to share, understand, and respond with care to the affective states of others" (vii), Cervantes seeks to move his audience first to feel, then to think, and finally perhaps to act. In doing so, he utilizes the interactive nature of live performance as a collaboration between knowing bodies in a shared space dedicated to emotional and intellectual exchange.

CONCLUSIONS

A cognitive approach grounded in embodiment and empathy allows us to explore *how* Cervantes' ideas affect his audience, both emotionally and intellectually, and why they may have resonated with his early modern spectators. Certainly, an empathetic approach to drama cannot address all aspects of theatrical performance, but it may be particularly useful for examining the strategies employed by an author creating the performance text, the directorial choices involved in staging a play, and the reactions of a diverse audience. If we accept that human neurology remains similar across time periods (despite cultural differences), cognitive studies may allow us a glimpse into the dynamics of how people internalize, react to, and ultimately think about changing culture. These cognitive approaches to the analysis of fiction help us understand the very basic premises of the relationship between a work of fiction and its audience: why storytelling has such a visceral allure for us, why we crave good stories, and which cognitive dynamics actually are at work between actors and an audience sharing a performance space before returning, perhaps changed, to the wider world.

WORKS CITED

Aristotle. *Aristotle's* Poetics. Ed. Francis Fergusson. Trans. S. H. Butcher. New York: Hill and Wang, 1961.

Barsalou, Lawrence W. "Grounded Cognition." *Annual Review of Psychology* 59 (2008): 617–45.

Batson, C. Daniel. *Altruism in Humans.* New York: Oxford UP, 2011.

Batson, C. Daniel. "The Empathy-Altruism Hypothesis: Issues and Implications." *Empathy: From Bench to Bedside.* Ed. Jean Decety. Cambridge: MIT P, 2012, 41–54.

Batson, C. Daniel. "These Things Called Empathy: Eight Related but Distinct Phenomena." *The Social Neuroscience of Empathy.* Ed. Jean Decety and William Ickes. Cambridge: MIT P, 2009, 3–15.

Batson, C. Daniel, David A. Lishner, Jennifer Cook, and Stacey Sawyer. "Similarity and Nurturance: Two Possible Sources of Empathy for Strangers." *Basic and Applied Social Psychology* 27.1 (2005): 15–25.

Blair, Rhonda. "(Refuting) Arguments for the End of Theatre: Possible Implications of Cognitive Neuroscience for Performance." *Journal of Dramatic Theory and Criticism* 21.2 (2007): 125–32.

Cervantes, Miguel de. *El trato de Argel.* Ed. Florencio Sevilla Arroyo and Antonio Rey Hazas. Vol. 2 of *Obras completas de Miguel de Cervantes.* 18 vols. Madrid: Alianza, 1996.

Cervantes, Miguel de. *Entremeses.* Ed. Nicholas Spadaccini. Madrid: Cátedra, 1985.

Cervantes, Miguel de. *Poesías completas.* Ed. Vicente Gaos. Vol. 1. Madrid: Castalia, 1973.

Connor (Connor-Swietlicki), Catherine. "Bridging the Performance Gap: The Body, Cognitive Theory, and *Comedia* Studies." *Bulletin of the Comediantes* 55.2 (2003): 11–53.

Cook, Amy. "For Hecuba or for Hamlet: Rethinking Emotion and Empathy in the Theatre." *Journal of Dramatic Theory and Criticism* 25.2 (2011): 71–87.

Cook, Amy. "Interplay: The Method and Potential of a Cognitive Scientific Approach to Theatre." *Theatre Journal* 59.4 (2007): 579–94.

Decety, Jean. "Introduction: Why Is Empathy So Important?" *Empathy: From Bench to Bedside.* Ed. Jean Decety. Cambridge: MIT P, 2012, vii–ix.

De la Rosa, Stephan, and Heinrich H. Bülhoff. "Motor-Visual Neurons and Action Recognition in Social Interactions." *Behavioral and Brain Sciences* 37.2 (2014): 197–8.

Dolan, Jill. "Performance, Utopia, and the 'Utopian Performative.'" *Theatre Journal* 53 (2001): 455–79.

Don Gil of the Green Breeches. By Tirso de Molina. Trans. Sean O'Brien. Dir. Mehmet Ergen. Theatre Royal, Bath, England. Nov. 27, 2013. Performance.

Echols, Stephanie, and Joshua Correll. "It's More than Skin Deep: Empathy and Helping Behavior across Social Groups." *Empathy: From Bench to Bedside.* Ed. Jean Decety. Cambridge: MIT P, 2012, 55–71.

Edelman, Gerald M., and Giulio Tononi. *A Universe of Consciousness: How Matter Becomes Imagination.* New York: Basic Books, 2000.

Fernández, Enrique. "*Los tratos de Argel*: Obra testimonial, denuncia política y literatura terapéutica." *Cervantes: Bulletin of the Cervantes Society of America* 20.1 (2000): 7–26.

Gallese, Vittorio. "The Shared Manifold Hypothesis: From Mirror Neurons to Empathy." *Journal of Consciousness Studies* 8.5–7 (2001): 33–50.

Gallese, Vittorio, and Alvin Goldman. "Mirror Neurons and the Simulation Theory of Mind-reading." *Trends in Cognitive Sciences* 2.12 (1998): 493–501.

Gallese, Vittorio, Morton Ann Gernsbacher, Cecilia Heyes, Gregory Hickok, and Marco Iacoboni. "Mirror Neuron Forum." *Perspectives on Psychological Science* 6.4 (2011): 369–407.

Garcés, María Antonia. *Cervantes in Algiers: A Captive's Tale*. Nashville: Vanderbilt UP, 2002.

Glenberg, Arthur M. "Introduction to the Mirror Neuron Forum." *Perspectives on Psychological Science* 6.4 (2011): 363–8.

Hart, F. Elizabeth. "Performance, Phenomenology, and the Cognitive Turn." *Performance and Cognition: Theatre Studies and the Cognitive Turn*. Ed. Bruce McConachie and F. Elizabeth Hart. New York: Routledge, 2006, 29–51.

Hickok, Gregory. "Eight Problems with the Mirror Neuron Theory of Action Understanding in Monkeys and Humans." *Journal of Cognitive Neuroscience* 21.7 (2009): 1229–43.

Iacoboni, Marco. *Mirroring People: The Science of Empathy and How We Connect with Others*. New York: Picador, 2008.

Iacoboni, Marco, Istvan Molnar-Szakacs, Vittorio Gallese, Giovanni Buccino, John C. Mazziotta, and Giacomo Rizzolatti. "Grasping the Intentions of Others with One's Own Mirror Neuron System." *PLOS Biology* 3.3 (2005). Web. January 5, 2015. <http://www.plosbiology.org/>.

Jaén, Isabel. "Empathy and Gender Activism in Early Modern Spain: María de Zayas' *Amorous and Exemplary Novels*." *Rethinking Empathy through Literature*. Ed. Meghan M. Hammond and Sue J. Kim. New York: Routledge, 2014, 189–201.

Keen, Suzanne. *Empathy and the Novel*. Oxford: Oxford UP, 2007.

King, Ros. "Plays, Playing, and Make-Believe: Thinking and Feeling in Shakespearean Drama." *Embodied Cognition and Shakespeare's Theatre: The Early Modern Body-Mind*. New York: Routledge, 2014, 27–45.

Laub, Dori. "Bearing Witness or the Vicissitudes of Listening." *Testimony: Crises of Witnessing in Literature, Psychoanalysis and History*. Ed. Shoshana Felman and Dori Laub. New York: Routledge, 1992, 57–74.

Mancing, Howard. "See the Play, Read the Book." *Performance and Cognition: Theatre Studies and the Cognitive Turn*. Ed. Bruce McConachie and F. Elizabeth Hart. New York: Routledge, 2006, 189–206.

McConachie, Bruce. *Engaging Audiences: A Cognitive Approach to Spectating in the Theatre*. New York: Palgrave Macmillan, 2008.

McConachie, Bruce, and F. Elizabeth Hart. Introduction. *Performance and Cognition: Theatre Studies and the Cognitive Turn*. Ed. Bruce McConachie and F. Elizabeth Hart. New York: Routledge, 2006, 1–25.

Muse, John H. "Performance and the Pace of Empathy." *Journal of Dramatic Theory and Criticism* 26.2 (2012): 173–88.

Paivio, Allan. *Mental Representations: A Dual Coding Approach*. New York: Oxford, 1986.

Rizzolatti, Giacomo, and Laila Craighero. "The Mirror-Neuron System." *Annual Review of Neuroscience* 27.1 (2004): 169–92.

Rizzolatti, Giacomo, and Corrado Sinigaglia. *Mirrors in the Brain: How Our Minds Share Actions, Emotions, and Experience*. Oxford: Oxford UP, 2008.

Schechner, Richard. *Performance Theory*. New York: Routledge, 2003.

Shamay-Tsoory, Simone. "Empathetic Processing: Its Cognitive and Affective Dimensions and Neuroanatomical Basis." *The Social Neuroscience of Empathy*. Ed. Jean Decety and William Ickes. Cambridge: MIT P, 2009, 215–32.

Strayer, Janet. "Affective and Cognitive Perspectives on Empathy." *Empathy and Its Development*. Ed. Nancy Eisenberg and Janet Strayer. Cambridge: Cambridge UP, 1987, 218–44.

Varela, Francisco J., Evan Thompson, and Eleanor Rosch. *The Embodied Mind: Cognitive Science and Human Experience.* Cambridge: MIT P, 1993.

Vega Carpio, Lope de. "El arte nuevo de hacer comedias." *Significado y doctrina del Arte nuevo de Lope de Vega.* By Juan Manuel Rozas. Madrid: SGEL, 1976.

Vescio, Theresa K., Gretchen B. Sechrist, and Matthew P. Paolucci. "Perspective Taking and Prejudice Reduction: The Mediational Role of Empathy Arousal and Situational Attributions." *European Journal of Social Psychology* 33 (2003): 455–72.

Wojciehowski, Hannah Chapelle, and Vittorio Gallese. "How Stories Make Us Feel: Toward an Embodied Narratology." *California Italian Studies* 2.1 (2011): n.p.

Zahavi, Dan, and Søren Overgaard. "Empathy without Isomorphism: A Phenomenological Account." *Empathy: From Bench to Bedside.* Ed. Jean Decety. Cambridge: MIT P, 2012, 3–20.

CHAPTER 11

The Role of Empathy in Reading, Interpreting, and Teaching Las Casas' *Brevísima relación de la destrucción de las Indias*

BARBARA SIMERKA

The Dominican friar Bartolomé de las Casas was designated by the Spanish monarchy as "protector of the Indians" because of his writings and the advocacy he engaged in to reform the *encomienda* system of forced indigenous labor. Over the past four-and-a-half centuries, his writings about the conquest have served as a sort of palimpsest for a wide and contradictory variety of political discourses about Spanish imperialism (Clayton 33). Recent research on empathy can help us to assess the original impact and subsequent legacy of Las Casas at three levels: discursive, critical, and pedagogical. Although there is substantial debate among scholars from several fields about the exact nature of empathy, I will use the term "empathy" to denote a strong reaction to the perceived suffering of others that may entail placing oneself in their shoes, identifying with or feeling their pain, and even a desire or plan for personal or institutional action to alleviate that suffering. This essay will begin by exploring how Las Casas sought to manipulate his audience, using empathy-eliciting tactics so that his readers would care about the suffering of an idolatrous alien culture. Second, I will discuss the ways that contemporary scholarship judges the empathetic responses to Las Casas' writings, and how scholars employ those judgments to create hierarchies of merit among the missionaries, historians, and theologians of the colonial era. Finally, I will argue that we can use the knowledge about how readers respond to descriptions of suffering among social outgroups, such as those who belong to stigmatized races or religious groups, in order to evaluate and shape the ways that empathy informs our teaching goals and practices. This alternative perspective on the role of emotion and empathy in the literature classroom can inform new approaches to presenting the Las Casas corpus.

STRATEGIC EVOCATION OF EMPATHY IN LAS CASAS' RHETORIC

In *Brevísima relación de la destrucción de las Indias* [translated by Nigel Griffin as *A Short Account of the Destruction of the Indies*], Bartolomé de las Casas depicts in stark terms the mistreatment that Spanish colonizers perpetrated on the indigenous inhabitants of Hispaniola, Cuba, and the coastal regions of Central and South America. The preface employs a large number of superlative adjectives in order to establish the natives as fully human, sympathetic actors:

> los más simples, sin maldades ni dobleces, obedientísimas y fidelísimas a sus señores naturales y a los cristianos a quien sirven; más humildes, más pacientes, más pacíficas y quietas, sin rencillas ni bullicios, no rijosos, no querulosos, sin rencores, sin odios, sin desear venganzas. (11)

> The simplest people in the world—unassuming, long-suffering, unassertive, and submissive—they are without malice or guile, and are utterly faithful and obedient both to their own native lords and to the Spaniards in whose service they now find themselves. Never quarrelsome or belligerent or boisterous, they harbour no grudges and do not seek to settle old scores. (9–10)[1]

This profusion of praise sets the stage for Las Casas' construction of the history of the conquest as a tragedy for the Amerindian population, who are thus worthy recipients of pity according to the Aristotelian precepts of the era (Camacho 38–40). Las Casas follows this tribute to peaceful indigenous character with accolades about their virtuous poverty:

> Son también gentes paupérrimas y que menos poseen ni quieren poseer de bienes temporales; e por esto no soberbias, no ambiciosas, no codiciosas. Su comida es tal, que la de los sanctos padres en el desierto no parece haber sido más estrecha ni menos deleitosa ni pobre. (10)

1. All translations of Las Casas' *Brevísima relación* are from Griffin, citing page only.

They are also among the poorest people on the face of the earth; they own next to nothing and have no urge to acquire material possessions. As a result they are neither ambitious nor greedy, and are totally uninterested in worldly power. Their diet is every bit as poor and as monotonous, in quantity and in kind, as that enjoyed by the Desert Fathers. (10)

This initial portrayal of the indigenous lifestyle as a noble form of voluntary poverty includes an explicit parallel with the earliest followers of Jesus Christ. Las Casas refutes in the strongest of terms the claims of other colonial authors, who had characterized the simple life of the native inhabitants as a barbaric failure to exercise proper dominion, in order to justify conquest. The disciples are routinely used as role models for ideal Christian behavior, so his readers would be predisposed to identification with peoples depicted in similar terms.

Las Casas then develops this parallel as evidence of their natural affinity for conversion:

muy capaces e dóciles para toda buena doctrina; aptísimos para recebir nuestra sancta fee católica e ser dotados de virtuosas costumbres, e las que menos impedimientos tienen para esto, que Dios crió en el mundo. Y son tan importunas desque una vez comienzan a tener noticia de las cosas de la fee, para saberlas, y en ejercitar los sacramentos de la Iglesia y el culto divino. (10–11)

[they are] particularly receptive to learning and understanding the truths of our Catholic faith and to being instructed in virtue; indeed, God has invested them with fewer impediments in this regard than any other people on earth. Once they begin to learn of the Christian faith they become so keen to know more, to receive the Sacraments, and to worship God. (10)

In the initial paragraphs of the preface, Las Casas emphasizes (or exaggerates) all of the attributes of indigenous culture that mirror the ideals of European Christian civilization in order to move his court readers to the empathy that he saw as a necessary precondition to the legal actions he sought. His idealized portraits were intended to serve as a counterweight to the images of dehumanizing savagery that military leaders and colonists had provided in order to block European identification and empathy, in their pursuit of very different aims.

In the debates waged concerning imposed conversion and the *encomienda* system, those who opposed reforms highlighted the most stigmatized aspects of indigenous culture in order to obstruct empathy. Dating back at the least to Aristotle's model of "natural slaves," dehumanization is a time-tested tactic for justifying forced labor (Delgado 93–95). In the case of early modern Spain, empathy for the unfortunate is part of the code of Christian noble generosity, but as my work on the picaresque has shown, cultural discourses of the era were keenly interested in delineating which groups merited empathy (and charitable donations) and which groups caused their own misfortunes and hence were to blame for their own misery (*Knowing Subjects* 94–97). On a related note, Rolena Adorno asserts that Bernal Díaz also sought to manipulate reader empathy in his writings. To refute Las Casas and defend the *encomenderos*, he depicted them as a benevolent group that saved their workers from the predations of bellicose indigenous enemies who would have used them for human sacrifices ("Discourses" 250–3, *Polemics* 188–90). Adorno observes that Díaz also seeks to elicit empathy for his own plight as a falsely maligned military hero, and freely admits that she lays bare his tactics in order to disrupt reader identification with his misleading self-portrayal, which downplays his personal economic stakes in the policy debates ("Discourses" 257, *Polemics* 5–6). Kalina Christoff cites evidence that acts of dehumanization cause guilt and shame on the part of the perpetrators, who then engage in further acts and discourses of aggression in order to justify past acts—resulting in a vicious cycle of escalating abuse (1). When exploring the web of early modern and contemporary discourses surrounding the *encomienda* system and the debates about the rights of colonizers and vanquished, it is clear that all the major colonial authors—and many modern scholars—shape their discourses with an eye toward impacting the empathy of targeted readers, both early modern courtiers and current students.

Viviana Díaz Balsera (159–62) and Tzvetan Todorov (163–7) have pointed out that, to contradict the Aristotelian-based model of the indigenous as natural slaves, Las Casas exaggerates the parallels between Mesoamerican cultures and pre-Christian Greece and Rome in order to increase reader identification with the Amerindians. As Todorov, Pagden, and others have noted, early modern explorers often deployed Roman mythology and history as the lens through which they interpreted American encounters (MacCormack 5–12; Simerka, *Discourses* 27–30). In this cultural frame of reference that permitted empathetic responses to "classical" Mediterranean pagan cultures, he foregrounds those similarities to facilitate such empathetic response to this new group of converts. Ironically, one strand of postcolonial critique singles out as particularly marginalizing those European discourses that can accept cultural others as socially equal only when acknowledging sameness (Arias and Merediz 1; Adorno, "The Intellectual" 27; Clayton 36; Castro 5). Immigration policies that promote linguistic and cultural assimilation in order to foster tolerance are a modern-day variant on this discourse.

Las Casas continues the preface with an inflammatory condemnation of Spanish colonial actions. He recounts the conquest of each area with a formulaic narrative; the indigenous people greet the newly arrived Spaniards as peaceful hosts, willing converts, accommodating servants, and "mansas ovejas" or "corderos" [gentle sheep/lambs] (11, 44, 53, 87, 92, 111, 114). By contrast, the Spaniards who overwork, torture, and kill these gentle natives are depicted as "leones" [lions] (11, 87, 111), "tigres" [tigers] (11, 87, 111), and "lobos" [wolves] (11, 87). In the signifying systems of both Christian biblical narrative and Indo-European fairy tales, cultural norms direct empathy toward herbivores rather than predators. The metaphor system Las Casas employs is clearly designed to trigger a strong reader identification with the native inhabitants, despite the fact that they belong to a marginalized racial group. The identification of the slaughtered peoples with the Christian iconography of self-sacrifice surely serves as an attempt to mitigate the stigma of idolatry and to shift the empathic response from the European to the indigenous peoples.

By contrast, Las Casas describes the conquest in highly unfavorable terms in order to disrupt the automatic empathetic responses that favor one's own racial, ethnic, and national identity groups. Las Casas introduces the Spanish conquest as a needlessly barbaric attack on an undeserving population, depicted through a series of harsh infinitives: "despedazarlas, matarlas, angustiarlas, afligirlas, atormentarlas y destruirlas por las extrañas y nuevas y varias y nunca otras tales vistas ni leídas ni oídas maneras de crueldad" (11) ["tear the natives to shreds, murder them and inflict upon them untold misery, suffering and distress, tormenting, harrying and persecuting them mercilessly" (11)].

As the preface progresses, Las Casas sets up the binary framework that he will pursue throughout his history. The conquering Spaniards are not heroes but rather "despotic" and "diabolical" villains who only pretend to be Christians as they wage "injustas, crueles, sangrientas y tiránicas guerras" (13) ["unjust, cruel, bloody and tyrannical war" (12)]. This series of condemnatory adjectives is accompanied by a litany of nouns and verbs that also depict unsympathetic acts. He lists both violent acts (oppression, torment, murder, and annihilation) and acts of greed: "tener por su fin último el oro y henchirse de riquezas en muy pocos días" (13) ["They have set out to line their pockets with gold and to amass private fortunes as quickly as possible" (13)].

Las Casas equates Spanish military activity with torture rather than legitimate combat. His descriptions of combat confrontations also contribute to the metaphorical system, as the native peoples are repeatedly characterized as passive victims rather than instigators; the adjective "innocent" appears in nineteen references, while the verb "murder" or "kill" is attached to the Spaniards in an equal number; in addition the labels cruel, evil, or wicked appear in fifty instances. The anaphoric hyperbole this narrative incorporates is central both to empathic responses to his text and to the controversy that surrounds his legacy, as studied below.

At the end of most chapters, Las Casas evokes a new world Eden needlessly converted into a pitiful, depopulated wasteland. The combination of violence and pillage results in a devastation that is the antithesis of civilized colonization, as the Spaniards have not developed but rather "han despoblado y asolado" (12) ["uninhabited and left to go to rack and ruin" (12)] newly encountered lands. In later chapters, he also emphasizes acts of brutality against what today are termed noncombatants—women and children. All of these tactics serve as an attempt to disrupt the "natural" empathy readers would grant toward their own countrymen and encourage them to view the military adventurers rather than the Americans as the "other."

In the conclusion, addressed directly to King Charles, Las Casas summarizes both the repulsive Spanish aggression and the pathetic indigenous situation: "están en su colmo actualmente todas las violencias, opresiones, tiranías, matanzas, robos y destrucciones, estragos, despoblaciones, angustias y calamidades susodichas, en todas las partes donde hay cristianos de las Indias" (116) ["the violence, the oppression, the despotism, the killing, the plunder, the depopulation, the outrages, the agonies and the calamities we have described were at their height throughout the New World wherever Christians have set foot" (127)]. He asserts that he wrote the *Brevísima relación* in response to requests from courtiers, who wanted him to notify the monarch about the obstacles to implementation of the *Leyes Nuevas* [New Laws] "por algunas personas notables, celosas de la honra de Dios e compasivas de las aflictiones y calamidades ajenas que residen en esta corte" (116) ["persuaded by a number of people here at the Spanish court, their concern for the Christian faith and their compassion towards the afflictions and calamities that befall their fellow-men" (127)]. Here, Las Casas provides Charles with two triggers for an empathic response: empathy could result either as a reaction to reading the suffering of his distant indigenous subjects or as a response to the sentiments of his own courtiers. His earlier skilled manipulation of his readers and audiences had contributed to the creation of the *Leyes Nuevas* of 1542, which put an end to the worst abuses of the *encomienda* system. However, there was little actual change in the conditions of indigenous life because the most significant reforms were repealed three short years later, due to vociferous complaints from colonists (Pagden xvii). Thus, although Las Casas succeeded initially in awakening the conscience of the king and court, the empathetic reaction he elicited toward a foreign and idolatrous populace proved ephemeral and insufficient against the subsequent claims upon royal empathy from his fellow countrymen who bemoaned lost income and security.

EVALUATIONS OF LASCASIAN EMPATHY IN LITERARY SCHOLARSHIP

Strong reactions to and disagreements concerning the authenticity of the empathy that Las Casas expresses are highlighted in contemporary scholarly analysis, as voiced for instance by Daniel Castro. According to this critic's reading, the friar's advocacy for the indigenous was a mere show of empathy that he performed in order to enhance his own standing at court (5). Castro asserts that authentic empathy is based on extended sojourns in native communities and requires the ability to communicate in the language of the other (97–99). By using these standards to evaluate the empathy level of colonial missionaries, Las Casas is found lacking. Furthermore, while Castro concedes that Las Casas empathized with the physical suffering that native peoples endured at the hands of the Spaniards, he demonizes the missionary for failing to empathize with the even more acute trauma that they suffered as a consequence of forced conversion to alien spiritual and cultural practices (6–11). He uses terms like "ecclesiastical imperialism" and "cultural genocide" to disrupt the discourse of identification between the friar and contemporary social activists (6, 11). Castro proposes later missionaries like Fray Domingo de Santo Tomás, who lived among the indigenous for many years and learned their languages, as having gained the knowledge necessary for true empathy (157–8). Castro's definition of authentic empathy implies the ability to identify with forms of psychological suffering that Europeans had never experienced for themselves, which could be mirrored only after long exposure to and a deep understanding of Amerindian society. He asserts that their "contact with the immediate reality of everyday existence in the Americas, and their empirical, as opposed to theoretical, experience lent particular poignancy to their struggle in favor or reforms" (158). Castro credits a "nuanced knowledge" and genuine empathy only to missionaries like Santo Tomás who advocated for a complete withdrawal from some indigenous territories (158). Castro's enflamed rhetoric seeks to discredit the empathy attributed to one iconic figure and replace him with a more valid empathizer. Castro seeks to redirect the empathetic identification of the modern academic readers who determine historical status within the pantheon of revered rebels. The many sharply disparaging reviews of this book indicate that Castro's tactics do indeed provoke a forceful reaction, albeit not the one he intended.

Gustavo Gutiérrez offers a completely different perspective in his study of Las Casas, based on establishing a line of empathetic Catholic heroes from Jesus Christ to early modern reformers to modern-day liberation theologians (4–5). Gutiérrez emphasizes that Las Casas was operating within a Dominican discourse that routinely employed extreme language and metaphors to elicit empathy for the poor and downtrodden. Gutiérrez seeks to establish that Las Casas views empathy toward the unfortunate as the moral center of all of Christ's teachings, so that any reader who interprets the New Testament in this light must then fully support his reform agenda (45–56). Gutiérrez notes that new world missionaries asserted that because military men were incapable of true empathy, the crown needed to send preachers, not soldiers, to accomplish conversion. They also asserted that *encomenderos* willfully mislabeled their workers as bestial in order to be able to work them like farm animals; in other words, the friars accused the landowners of willfully blocking an empathic response that might have interfered with profit making.

Just as Castro exaggerates the deficit in empathy on the part of Las Casas in order to vilify him as a self-aggrandizing courtier, Gutiérrez's work comes close to sanctifying Las Casas as Christian empathy and charity incarnate. But both agree that a sincere and properly enacted empathy is the primary characteristic for any historical figure who would deserve the label "Defender of the Indians." Classroom study of empathy in Las Casas may use this vehement disagreement as a point of departure.

RESEARCH ON READING, EMPATHY, AND BIAS REDUCTION

The study of empathetic reactions in relation to early modern Spanish writings is in a nascent phase; Amy Williamsen, Catherine Connor-Swietlicki, and I have recently explored this topic in relation to *Don Quixote* (Williamsen; Connor-Swietlicki; Simerka, "Afterword" and "Mirror"). Isabel Jaén recently published an essay that scrutinizes the empathy-generating tactics in the *Novelas amorosas* of María de Zayas; her essay also provides a valuable overview of medieval and early modern notions of *misericordia* [compassion] as a precursor to the modern conception of empathy (191–3). The most significant works to date on literature and empathy are the anthology *Rethinking Empathy* (2014), edited by Meghan Hammond and Sue

Kim, and Suzanne Keen's *Empathy and the Novel* (2007), in which she compiles and analyzes a corpus of studies of empathy and actual readers.

According to Suzanne Keen, contemporary readers generally accept the idea that reading narratives that elicit empathy about social injustice can lead to drastic reforms (38, 54). The empathy stirred by the Dickens novel *Oliver Twist* is seen as having played a crucial role in the passage of child labor laws in Victorian England, just as the horrors depicted in *Uncle Tom's Cabin* spurred mass empathetic outrage and played an important role in the eradication of slavery (186). However, Keen's review of research with actual readers indicates that these widely cited examples are the exceptions rather than the rule; although many subjects agree that literature can produce the fellow feeling that leads to social change, they cannot recall examples from their own lives where reading led to socio-political engagement (66, 140). Keen notes that while some studies have shown that reading "positive depictions about members of outgroups" can increase empathy and reduce social bias, such positive feelings do not generally spur even minimally altruistic acts such as charitable donations (106, 116–7). Based on this research, Keen ultimately rejects the belief that the activity of reading about the oppression of marginalized groups is uniquely effective for inducing empathy and prompting social activism. However, I will argue that the lack of a connection among reading, empathy, and action may be due more to how literature classes traditionally engage bias than to the relationship among texts and commitment.

Research from the field of social psychology provides insights into how literature pedagogy may lead to bias reduction or progressive social action. C. Daniel Batson is one of the leading voices in the "empathy altruism controversy." He dedicated a thirty-year career to investigating what he terms "empathetic concern," the form of response that goes beyond "tender feelings" to spur altruistic action (41). He notes that skeptics of the existence of true altruism characterize pro-social action as a selfish response designed to alleviate the observer's own discomfort at witnessing the suffering of others (aversive-arousal). Batson and his associates devised a large number of test situations to gather data about when and why subjects take action to help a person in need. Although his goal was to test for the existence of true altruism—empathetic concern—by comparing scenarios in which it was easier to help or to escape the empathic response, the results indicated that when subjects expressed a high level of empathy for the people they encountered, they were more likely to render aid even when escape was easy (44–45). In relating these findings to those that Keen cites, my hypothesis is that conventional modes for teaching literature, grounded in the emotion-suppressing norms of New Criticism, may not be effective at spurring the high level of empathy necessary for altruistic action to emerge.

In their classic 1974 essay, "The Just World Revisited," David Aderman, Sharon Brehm, and Lawrence Katz describe a scenario in which a subject watches an "innocent victim" experience pain or suffering. Their study was designed to measure what type of pre-observation activity is most likely to lead to increased empathy. The options included giving no instruction at all, or instructions to observe the victim closely, imagine feeling the same pain as the victim, or imagine how the victim is feeling. The instructions that encouraged subjects to pay attention to their emotional responses did lead to an increase in empathy, but there was no empathy response at all among those who were engaged intellectually rather than emotionally. Similarly, organizational psychologists Krystina Finlay and Walter Stephan have identified a procedure for fostering empathy and reducing racial tension among coworkers through specific tasks assigned while a subject reads about oppression. The reading prompts that were shown to be the most effective for fostering empathy, and hence more congenial interracial work relationships, entail *imaginative* acts related to *emotional* mirroring (1732). They conclude that empathy-inducing activities are an effective supplement to information-based approaches to prejudice reduction (1734). Similarly, in 2000, Frank Hakemulder reported on a series of experiments seeking to identify the mechanism through which reading about a minority group might affect college student readers' beliefs about that outgroup.[2] Hakemulder and Eva Maria Koopman have just published a literature review of recent studies on this topic; their essay suggests that literary empathy should be conceptualized in conjunction with "reflection" as an additional mode of ethical reaction ("Effects" 92–94). The pre-reading activities or discussion prompts that elicit empathy are very different from the type of intellectual analysis that is standard in the university classroom, where the focus is on aesthetic and theoretical analysis rather than on emotional reactions.

Psychologist Keith Oatley has been conducting research about emotional responses to fiction for over two decades. His recent work with Raymond Mar has focused on reading as a form of cognitive simulation:

> Understanding stories as simulations can help explain why they provide a special kind of experience. The abstraction performed by fictional stories demands that readers and others project themselves into the represented events. . . . Narrative fiction models life, comments on life, and helps us to understand life in terms of how human intentions bear upon it. (Mar and Oatley 173)

2. See also Keen 85–94, 105–6.

Mar and Oatley note that the simulations readers perform have two primary foci: to understand the inner motivations of characters and to analyze and project the outcomes of complex social situations (175). Both of these simulations are thought to improve social intelligence in real-world interaction, which leads to enhanced empathy. In a previous study their team had found that people who read substantial amounts of fiction (the study included several genres of popular fiction) perform better on tests of empathy and social perception (Mar et al., "Bookworms"). In a follow-up study with Jordan Peterson they ruled out the possibility that the tests revealed basic personality traits of people who like to read, rather than the results of reading (Mar, Oatley, and Peterson, "Ruling Out"). Additional work is needed to establish more precisely the connections among expressions of empathy in abstract tests, expressions of prejudice reduction in tests of attitude, and the possibilities of increased pro-social action.

The field of critical pedagogy, mostly ignored in humanities departments, highlights both the promises and the risks of incorporating empathy in the classroom. To cite just one example, Megan Boler chastises Martha Nussbaum's *Poetic Justice*, which in her view posits "modes of empathy that permit the reader's exoneration from privilege and complicities through the 'ah-hah' experience" (255). Boler advocates a teaching praxis that encourages but also interrogates empathy and encourages students to ask themselves:

> Who benefits from the production of empathy in what circumstances? Who should feel empathy for whom? If no change can be measured as a result of the production of empathy, what has been gained other than a "good brotherly feeling" on the part on the universal reader? (261)

In place of a potentially complacent or even self-congratulatory form of identification with the suffering other, Boler proposes:

> a "semiotics of empathy," which emphasizes the power and social hierarchies which complicate the relationship between reader/listener and text/speaker. I argue that educators need to encourage what I shall define as "testimonial reading." . . . Ideally, testimonial reading inspires an empathetic response that motivates action: a "historicized ethics" engaged across genres, that radically shifts our self-reflective understanding of power relations. (256)

New studies on the relationship between literature and empathy are being published on a regular basis. David Comer Kidd and Emanuele Castano report that, after reading *literary* fiction as opposed to popular fiction or serious nonfiction, people performed better on tests measuring empathy, social perception, and emotional intelligence (Kidd and Castano 377). Kidd and Castano assert that "fiction affects ToM [Theory of Mind] processes because it forces us to engage in mind-reading and character construction" and that it is the enhancement of the ToM capacity that fosters empathy by "reduc[ing] the strangeness of others" (377). Another factor they cite is that literary fiction leaves more to the imagination, encouraging readers to make inferences about characters and be sensitive to emotional complexity (377). This study provides an additional level of nuance to the research cited earlier. All three studies measured empathy based on the rather abstract Reading the Mind in the Eyes Test, in which subjects were asked to identify facially expressed emotions. (None sought to measure whether or not such empathy produces changes in social attitudes or acts.) In an even more recent article, Loris Vezzali and others report that a team of researchers in the United Kingdom and Italy used Voldemort's racial purity project[3] in the Harry Potter series as the point of departure for discussions about bias with elementary and high school students. The report indicates that participants who identified with Harry Potter's tolerant stance during the discussions of bias were later found to have reduced prejudice concerning immigrants and homosexuals, while students who did not identify with him or who participated in control groups that did not discuss prejudice showed no change in perspective (Vezzali et al.).

EMPATHY AND APPROACHES TO TEACHING LAS CASAS: A PROPOSAL

These studies of reading, empathy, and social attitudes or altruistic actions have profound implications for literary pedagogy. Poststructuralist and identity-based literary theories have altered teaching praxis in many ways but have not challenged the reason/emotion dichotomy. Emotional responses to texts, and the use of feelings as the basis for analysis, are still denigrated as naïve or invalid. Thus, current standard methodologies for addressing literary texts actually undercut progressive goals such as prejudice reduction. The recent Modern Language Association anthology *Approaches to Teaching the Writings of Bartolomé de Las Casas* provides an illuminating case study; several of the essays in the volume emphasize pedagogical practices that are implemented with the explicitly stated goal

---

3. He sought to stop wizards from mixing bloodlines and sharing power with "inferior" populations: human, goblin, elf, giant, and so forth.

of *interrupting* students' emotional responses to the historical situation Las Casas delineates or to the author himself as a historical figure. A common thread in such essays is the idea that because this work prompts such strong emotional reactions, it is the perfect tool for teaching students how to suppress their empathetic responses in order to read objectively.

Lawrence Clayton writes that he uses the text as a case study, teaching students the norms of historiography, such as taking note of—but not being taken in by—the empathy that a chronicler expresses toward a subject when his writing incorporates "advocacy" (34). Laura Lewis also describes Las Casas as a perfect pedagogical case study for anthropological ethnography. She uses him as a point of departure for students to reflect on, both as an ethnographer whose methods they should scrutinize and as an ethnographic subject to whom they respond. In particular, Lewis sees Las Casas' writings as a good tool for students to scrutinize their initial "outrage" at the mistreatment of the indigenous people and to think about the elusive goal of objectivity in ethnographic study (43). Literary scholar Ruth Hill also depicts the passages where Las Casas evokes empathy as an opening for studying disciplinary norms; here, in the field of rhetoric. She explicitly shifts classroom discussion from how students feel to how the text creates their emotions. She specifies having students analyze tactics in the epilogue, which presents "a pathetic and fawning appeal" to reader emotions (61). The research cited earlier indicates that such an approach may indeed succeed in blocking the empathy-altruism response. For scholars who present Las Casas' text with a different primary goal, or for those who seek to guide students in weighing multiple perspectives, additional teaching tactics are needed, such as the pre-reading prompts, discussion activities that incorporate and scrutinize emotional responses, and testimonial reading practices described earlier.

As the contributors to the Modern Language Association teaching volume correctly noted, Las Casas' *Brevísima relación* offers a unique opportunity to engage students in a wide array of activities concerning the relationship between rhetorical and narrative strategies and reader empathy. However, unlike the three authors cited earlier, I encourage a multipronged approach grounded in the cognitive and critical pedagogy findings presented here. Pre-reading activities may combine early chapters of the text with excerpts from Castro and Gutiérrez, to stimulate consideration of Las Casas' own empathetic response. Initial classroom discussion may then combine rhetorical and affective analysis, with questions that allow students to consider their own emotional responses and to compare Lascasian discourses. The academic study of empathy may be introduced via classroom presentation or the assignment of additional readings such as Batson, Boler, and so forth to accompany the later chapters of the text. Subsequent classroom discussion or writing assignments can allow the opportunity to link the colonial text with current social controversies that involve race, dehumanization, and empathy. For example, in current media coverage of interracial violence and the resultant judicial processes, supporters for each side emphasize the justifiable fear of either the police force or the minority community as the springboard to empathy. As Megan Boler observes, responses of empathy are not an end goal, as they may lead no further than ephemeral pity or even self-congratulation. The connections among the reading of minority literatures, empathetic reactions to dehumanization, and bias reduction or positive social action remain controversial, with much additional research needed in the laboratory and in the classroom. However, I do believe that literary teaching strategies that elicit student empathy and help them to conceptualize the relations among text, emotion, and (re)action can form the basis for a powerful new pedagogy. The studies cited here offer insights and tactical support. The empathic response is common to all human beings, but how a culture, or an individual reader, reacts empathetically depends on a wide variety of social circumstances. What are the conditions under which we suppress, evade, ignore, or avert attention from the suffering we read about? What are the conditions that cause us to instead become vociferous advocates for a group of victims that we have read about? What kinds of synergy are needed between a particular novel or eyewitness testimony and the wider discourses that a society circulates about empathy and categories of legitimate victims? These are the kinds of questions that studies on reading and empathy could help us answer, thus enhancing the ability to shape teaching practices toward empathy and bias reduction.

BIBLIOGRAPHY

Aderman, David, Sharon S. Brehm, and Lawrence B. Katz. "Empathic Observation of an Innocent Victim: The Just World Revisited." *Journal of Personality and Social Psychology* 29.3 (1974): 342–7.

Adorno, Rolena. "Discourses on Colonialism: Bernal Díaz, Las Casas, and the Twentieth-Century Reader." *MLN* 103.2 (Mar 1988): 239–58.

Adorno, Rolena. "The Intellectual Life of Bartolomé de Las Casas: Framing the Literature Classroom." *Approaches to Teaching the Writings of Bartolomé de Las Casas*. Ed. Santa Arias and Eyda M. Merediz. New York: Modern Language Association of America, 2008, 21–32.

Adorno, Rolena. *The Polemics of Possession in Spanish American Narrative*. New Haven: Yale UP, 2007.

Arias, Santa, and Eyda M. Merediz. Introduction. *Approaches to Teaching the Writings of Bartolomé de Las Casas*. Ed. Santa Arias and Eyda M. Merediz. New York: Modern Language Association of America, 2008, 1–8.

Batson, C. Daniel. "The Empathy-Altruism Hypothesis: Issues and Implications." *Empathy: From Bench to Bedside*. Ed. Jean Decety. Cambridge: MIT P, 2012, 41–54.

Batson, C. Daniel, M. P. Polycarpou, E. Harmon-Jones, H. J. Imhoff, E. C. Mitchener, L. L. Bednar, T. R. Klein, and L. Highberger. "Empathy and Attitudes: Can Feeling for a Member of a Stigmatized Group Improve Feelings Toward the Group?" *Journal of Personality and Social Psychology* 72.1 (1997): 105–18.

Boler, Megan. "The Risks of Empathy: Interrogating Multiculturalism's Gaze." *Cultural Studies* 11.2 (April 1997): 253–73.

Camacho, Jorge. "Meta-historia y ficción en la *Brevísima relación de la destrucción de las Indias* de Fray Bartolomé de las Casas." *Hispanófila* 134 (2002): 37–48.

Castro, Daniel. *Another Face of Empire: Bartolomé de las Casas, Indigenous Rights, and Ecclesiastical Imperialism*. Durham: Duke UP, 2007.

Christoff, Kalina. "Dehumanization in Organizational Settings: Some Scientific and Ethical Considerations." *Frontiers in Human Neuroscience* 8.748 (Sept. 2014): 1–5.

Cikara, Mina, Emile G. Bruneau, and Rebecca R. Saxe. "Us and Them: Intergroup Failures of Empathy." *Current Directions in Psychological Science* 20.3 (June 2011): 149–53.

Clayton, Lawrence. "Teaching Las Casas through the Lens of a Historian." *Approaches to Teaching the Writings of Bartolomé de Las Casas*. Ed. Santa Arias and Eyda M. Merediz. New York: Modern Language Association of America, 2008, 33–41.

Connor-Swietlicki, Catherine. "Beyond Cognition: Don Quijote and Other Embodied Minds." *Cognitive Cervantes*. Ed. Julien Simon, Barbara Simerka, and Howard Mancing. Spec. cluster of essays of *Cervantes: Bulletin of the Cervantes Society of America* 32.1 (2012): 231–61.

Dadlez, Eva M. *What's Hecuba to Him?: Fictional Events and Actual Emotions*. University Park: Pennsylvania State UP, 1997.

Delgado, Mariano. "Bartolomé de Las Casas y las culturas amerindias." *Anthropos* 102 (2007): 91–97.

Díaz Balsera, Viviana. "On Barbarism, Demons, and Natural Reason: Las Casas' Rhetoric of Human Sacrifices in Pre-Hispanic Mexico." *Approaches to Teaching the Writings of Bartolomé de Las Casas*. Ed. Santa Arias and Eyda M. Merediz. New York: Modern Language Association of America, 2008, 159–66.

Finlay, Krystina A., and Walter G. Stephan. "Improving Intergroup Relations: The Effects of Empathy on Racial Attitudes." *Journal of Applied Social Psychology* 30.8 (2000): 1720–37.

Gallese, Vittorio. "Mirror Neurons, Embodied Simulation, and the Neural Basis of Social Identification." *Psychoanalytic Dialogues* 19.5 (2009): 519–36.

Gallese, Vittorio, Luciano Fadiga, Leonardo Fogassi, and Giacomo Rizzolatti. "Action Recognition in the Premotor Cortex." *Brain* 119.2 (1996): 593–609.

Gutiérrez, Gustavo. *Las Casas: In Search of the Poor of Jesus Christ*. Trans. Robert R. Barr. Maryknoll: Orbis, 1993.

Hakemulder, Frank (Jèmeljan). *The Moral Laboratory: Experiments Examining the Effects of Reading Literature on Social Perception and Moral Self-Concept*. Amsterdam: John Benjamins, 2000.

Hakemulder, Frank (Jèmeljan), and Eva Maria Koopman. "Effects of Literature on Empathy and Self-Reflection: A Theoretical-Empirical Framework." *Journal of Literary Theory* 9.1 (2015): 79–111.

Hammond, Meghan M., and Sue J. Kim, eds. *Rethinking Empathy through Literature.* New York: Routledge, 2014.

Hill, Ruth. "Hearing Las Casas Write: Rhetoric and The Facade of Orality in the *Brevísima relación.*" *Approaches to Teaching the Writings of Bartolomé de Las Casas.* Ed. Santa Arias and Eyda M. Merediz. New York: Modern Language Association of America, 2008, 57–64.

Jaén, Isabel. "Empathy and Gender Activism in Early Modern Spain: María de Zayas's *Amorous and Exemplary Novels.*" *Rethinking Empathy through Literature.* Ed. Meghan M. Hammond and Sue J. Kim. New York: Routledge, 2014, 189–201.

Keen, Suzanne. *Empathy and the Novel.* New York: Oxford UP, 2007.

Kidd, David Comer, and Emanuele Castano. "Reading Literary Fiction Improves Theory of Mind." *Science* 342.6156 (Oct. 18, 2013): 377–80.

Las Casas, Bartolomé de. *A Short Account of the Destruction of the Indies.* Ed. and trans. Nigel Griffin. London: Penguin, 1992. *Columbia University Libraries Virtual Reading Room,* 2002. Web. May 15, 2015.

Las Casas, Bartolomé de. *Brevísima relación de la destruición de las Indias.* Ed. and intro. José Miguel Martínez Torrejón. Barcelona: Galaxia Gutenberg, 2009.

Lewis, Laura A. "Pedagogical Uses of Las Casas' Texts for Anthropologists." *Approaches to Teaching the Writings of Bartolomé de Las Casas.* Ed. Santa Arias and Eyda M. Merediz. New York: Modern Language Association of America, 2008, 42–47.

MacCormack, Sabine. *On the Wings of Time: Rome, the Incas, Spain, and Peru.* Princeton: Princeton UP, 2007.

Mar, Raymond A., and Keith Oatley. "The Function of Fiction is the Abstraction and Simulation of Social Experience." *Perspectives on Psychological Science* 3.3 (2008): 173–92.

Mar, Raymond A., Keith Oatley, Jacob Hirsh, Jennifer dela Paz, and Jordan B. Peterson. "Bookworms versus Nerds: The Social Abilities of Fiction and Non-Fiction Readers." *Journal of Research in Personality* 40.5 (2006): 694–712.

Mar, Raymond A., Keith Oatley, and Jordan B. Peterson. "Exploring the Link between Reading Fiction and Empathy: Ruling Out Individual Differences and Examining Outcomes." *Communications: The European Journal of Communication* 34.4 (2009): 407–28.

Pagden, Anthony. Introduction. *A Short Account of the Destruction of the Indies.* By Bartolomé de Las Casas. Ed. and trans. Nigel Griffin. London: Penguin, 1992. xiii–xli. *Columbia University Libraries Virtual Reading Room,* 2002. Web. May 15, 2015.

Rabasa, José. *Tell Me the Story of How I Conquered You: Elsewheres and Ethnosuicide in the Colonial Mesoamerican World.* Reprint. Austin: U of Texas P, 2012.

Simerka, Barbara. "Afterword: The Future of Cognitive Literary Studies." *Cognitive Cervantes.* Ed. Julien Simon, Barbara Simerka, and Howard Mancing. Spec. cluster of essays *Cervantes: Bulletin of the Cervantes Society of America* 32.1 (2012): 263–75.

Simerka, Barbara. *Discourses of Empire: Counter-Epic Literature in Early Modern Spain.* University Park: Pennsylvania State UP, 2003.

Simerka, Barbara. *Knowing Subjects: Cognitive Cultural Studies and Early Modern Spanish Literature.* West Lafayette: Purdue UP, 2013.

Simerka, Barbara. "Mirror Neurons, Subjectivity, and Social Cognition in *Don Quixote*." *Don Quixote: Interdisciplinary Connections*. Ed. Matthew D. Warshawsky and James A. Parr. Newark: Juan de la Cuesta, 2013, 59–82.

Speer, Jeremy Reynolds, Khena Swallow, and Jeffrey Zacks. "Reading Stories Activates Neural Representations of Visual and Motor Experience." *Psychological Science* 20.8 (2009): 989–99.

Stone, Cynthia. "Confronting Stereotypes: The *Brevísima relación* as Homily, Not History." *Approaches to Teaching the Writings of Bartolomé de Las Casas*. Ed. Santa Arias and Eyda M. Merediz. New York: Modern Language Association of America, 2008, 65–72.

Todorov, Tzvetan. *The Conquest of America: The Question of the Other*. Norman: U of Oklahoma P, 1999.

Vezzali, Loris, Sofia Stathi, Dino Giovannini, Dora Capozza, and Elena Trifiletti. "The Greatest Magic of Harry Potter: Reducing Prejudice." *Journal of Applied Social Psychology* 45.2 (2015): 105–21.

Williamsen, Amy. "Quantum Quixote: Embodying Empathy in the Borderlands." *Cervantes: Bulletin of the Cervantes Society of America* 31.1 (Spring 2011): 171–87.

Xu, Xiaojing, Xiangyu Zuo, Xiaoying Wang, and Shihui Han. "Do You Feel My Pain? Racial Group Membership Modulates Empathic Neural Responses." *The Journal of Neuroscience* 29.26 (July 2009): 8525–9.

Afterword

Teaching Early Modern Spanish Literature with a Cognitive Approach

ISABEL JAÉN

COGNITIVE LITERARY STUDIES AND OUR CLASSROOM

Thanks to cognitive literary studies, we have at our disposal new avenues, concepts, and tools to explore literature in our classes.[1] One of the most important tenets of this field is that storytelling not simply constitutes a cultural phenomenon but is also central to the human mind. Stories are populated with minds and they are, in this sense, a representation of our consciousness. They are also an essential part of our lives, coming to us through a variety of vehicles: oral narratives, texts, performances, movies, and so forth.

Cognitive approaches also prompt us to examine literature in relation to other disciplines (such as psychology, neurology, philosophy, sociology, linguistics, and anthropology, to name a few) that have much to contribute to our understanding of how humans engage in fictional worlds. In this regard, cognitive approaches, which are not a critical theory as we might be tempted to view them but a knowledge interface, help us recognize that the study of human culture is in fact part of the wider investigation on human nature and, thus, must be undertaken from several vantage

---

1. For a recent and thorough discussion of cognition in the literature classroom, see Easterlin's special issue of *Interdisciplinary Literary Studies* (2014).

points within the sciences and the humanities. Scientists need to understand culture as much as cultural scholars need to understand human biology, the embodied mind that creates and experiences culture.

The study of human biology and the study of human culture are indeed inseparable, although they have been artificially decoupled by the humanities and sciences divide.[2] Cognitive literary studies seek to cross this epistemological border that exists in current university curricula.[3] In many higher education institutions, interdisciplinary studies are still viewed as experimental or supplemental, when they should be considered foundational. Interestingly, although literary studies have a long tradition of looking into other disciplines (e.g., psychology and sociology) thanks to critical approaches such as psychoanalytical theory and cultural studies, some literary scholars are still skeptical about reaching out to fields that are considered part of the "hard sciences" (e.g., biology and neuropsychology), a circumstance that significantly limits our ability to understand fiction coherently. This limitation becomes particularly unfavorable when we are dealing with early modernity, a period in which such boundaries did not yet exist.

BUILDING A COURSE ON COGNITIVE APPROACHES TO EARLY MODERN SPANISH LITERATURE

The purpose of this brief afterword is to provide teachers of early modern Spanish literature and their students with strategies and suggestions (in methodology, organization, and content) to embark together on an interdisciplinary course on fiction and the mind. To explore this connection efficiently, we must include both the ideas that circulate in the scientific and literary discourses of the early modernity (cognitive historicist approach) and contemporary notions deriving from current cognitive studies research. Such double focus is paramount to obtaining a cohesive perspective of how early modern culture viewed and portrayed consciousness. It is also very useful in considering the European pre-Scientific Revolution seeds of some of the aspects of human cognition and human nature that we today continue to explore, such as memory, imagination, and feeling.[4]

2. See Jaén and Simon.
3. On higher education curricula and interdisciplinary initiatives, see Casey, Miller, and Newell, among others.
4. See also the volume's introduction.

I offer here a prototype for a course based on the themes covered in the present volume.[5] The course is directed not only to Spanish teachers and students but also to those in other fields and literary traditions (e.g., comparative literature, English) who may be interested in including Spanish works as part of their early modern literature and culture curriculum. Although my prototype includes readings in Spanish, most of these readings are available in translation and, thus, the course can be adjusted to be carried out entirely in English. Early modern scholars and students outside Spanish studies will greatly benefit from a window to the culture of a country that gave birth to pioneer minds in humanist thought (e.g., Juan Luis Vives), helped create laws against human slavery,[6] produced a great amount of fictional works[7] that were extremely popular (e.g., chivalric romances), published books that became bestsellers in Europe (such as Cervantes' *Don Quixote*[8]—considered the second most read book of all times after the Bible—and Huarte de San Juan's *Examination of Men's Wits*), and promoted theatrical innovation,[9] among many other developments in a period that has come to be known as the Spanish Golden Age.

Pedagogy and Methodology

This course is constructed following a collaborative and process-centered pedagogy. Within this pedagogy, the course methodology includes a combination of three main elements: collaborative research, class discussions of reading materials, and short reflective narratives.

Students research in pairs—an arrangement that fosters negotiation and constant readjustment—and meet with the teacher on a regular basis beginning early on in the course, to discuss the status of their work and shape its direction. I suggest carrying out these discussions as a group instead of conducting the traditional teacher–student one-on-one interview because I believe it leads to a more interactive atmosphere and higher

5. This prototype derives from a class that I taught most recently with a focus on Cervantes' *Don Quixote* and I described in "Teaching Cervantes' *Don Quixote* from a Cognitive Historicist Perspective."
6. See Simerka's chapter in this volume.
7. In the words of Lucien Febvre and Henri-Jean Martin, authors of *The Coming of the Book*, "the two countries in which, in the 16th century, fictional works were most often written were without doubt Spain and Italy" (286).
8. On the reception of *Don Quixote* in early modern Europe, see chapter 7 of Mancing's *Cervantes' Don Quixote: A Reference Guide*.
9. Lope de Vega, known as "The Phoenix of Wits," is regarded as the catalyzer of this innovation. In addition to writing *Arte nuevo de hacer comedias* [The New Art of Writing Plays], he is believed to have penned as many as 1,800 plays.

student engagement. During the group discussions, students take turns talking about their progress, thus allowing teachers to evaluate their level of involvement in the project. This component of the methodology is not intended as a traditional assessment tool but, rather, as an opportunity for teachers to make adjustments that would further motivate and guide the student groups.

As they become ready to draft their collaborative papers, students in each pair are encouraged to write together instead of dividing the work and writing different sections of their essay separately. This aspect is particularly important because it allows students to continue to negotiate their ideas and jointly shape them in their co-narrative, training them, as I have stated elsewhere, "to be part of a community of knowledge that values diversity and exchange" ("Teaching" 115), and it is in this way consistent with an interdisciplinary and collaborative philosophy of teaching.

The collaborative research component, which takes place through frequent student–student and student–teacher close interactions as described earlier, also includes an oral presentation and discussion of each group's research work. Students find this aspect particularly useful, since it functions as a micro-scale model of a conference talk. As part of this assignment, and instead of the traditional model of reading their papers, they "summarize" in a conversational style for their peers their thesis, most important arguments, and conclusions in approximately 10 minutes with the help of a PowerPoint presentation. The synthesizing and performative nature of this talk prompts students to further look for efficient ways to communicate their ideas, adding yet another layer of reflection to their academic development. Each mini-talk is followed by class discussion in which presenters can gather feedback from their peers. Students point to this opportunity as particularly useful in helping them reconsider and revise the content presented.

The class discussion component of the course begins with conversations about the readings that are conducted in pairs with the help of a discussion guide. This strategy will facilitate interaction in a nonintimidating environment, where students will find numerous opportunities to participate. Next, teachers can open the discussion to the whole class and moderate it in a manner that promotes exchange between the groups. As this wider discussion comes to an end, the class gathers some conclusions, which teachers may then incorporate into a PowerPoint presentation to use as a follow-up for the next class.

Finally, the third component of the course consists of short narratives (approximately two pages) at the end of each module (see course organization below) in which students further reflect on the readings and the ideas discussed in class. For maximum benefit, if time allows, these narratives can be reviewed face to face via student–teacher conversation (instead of being traditionally graded and handed back to the students) and rewritten in light of the discussion.

Ultimately, this tripartite methodology is aimed at creating a series of opportunities for students to negotiate and revisit their ideas. In their leading role, teachers may use this multilayered, process-centered, collaborative structure as a template where they insert their methodological preferences and adjustments to fit the particular context of their course.

Course Content, Organization, and Objectives

My suggestion to articulate this course on cognitive approaches to early modern Spanish literature is to divide it in four modules, corresponding to the four following sections of this book: (1) The Creation of Self, (2) Embodied Cognition and Performance, (3) Perceiving and Understanding Others, and (4) Feeling and Ethics. These four themes not only represent four of the current main areas of investigation in the field of cognitive approaches to early modern Spanish literature but also comprise some of the most important concepts and lines of inquiry on human cognition—both contemporaneous (as viewed in early modernity) and contemporary (as viewed today)—such as memory, imagination, emotion, autopoiesis, Theory of Mind, and empathy. In the prototype that I am presenting, each module includes early modern texts (both "literary" and "scientific") as well as contemporary sources, consisting of the critical essays contained in the book plus complementary readings that help students grasp the concepts discussed in the course. Teachers may, again, introduce their own variations over this template by adding more readings, selecting among those suggested, and/or substituting with others that they may consider more relevant.

The first module (weeks 1 to 5) is devoted to Cervantes' portrayal of the embodied mind in the context of how humans develop and adapt cognitively to their environment. The primary readings for this module include *Don Quixote (Part I)* and excerpts from Juan Huarte de San Juan's *Examen de ingenios* [The Examination of Men's Wits],[10] along with essays by Mancing, Connor, Domínguez (from this book), and A. Martín-Araguz and

10. For courses taught in English, I recommend the recent edition by Rocío Sumillera of the early modern translation by Richard Carew.

C. Bustamante-Martínez, as well as excerpts from Gibbs; Varela, Thompson, and Rosch; and Maturana and Varela.[11] The essay by Spanish neurologists and science historians Martín-Araguz and Bustamante-Martínez may be used as an introductory reading to provide students with a glimpse at some of the most relevant topics in contemporary scientific conversations on Cervantes, Huarte, and the human mind. The excerpts from Gibbs; Varela, Thompson, and Rosch; and Maturana and Varela will be useful to explore the idea of embodiment and autopoiesis as presented by both Mancing and Connor in connection to *Don Quixote*. Chapters 4 and 5 from Huarte discuss the relationship between bodily temperament and the human faculties of memory and imagination and, when paired with the essay by Domínguez, become instrumental in exploring how the human faculties are understood during the early modern period. The main objective of this first module is to help students obtain a clearer sense of (1) how the embodied mind is viewed and portrayed in early modernity, (2) what are the links and analogies between what we often consider to be unrelated discourses: literature and science, (3) what is the contribution of these discourses to the understanding of mind and fiction, (4) how cognitive literary studies may help us explore mind and fiction by providing us with an interface based on establishing connections between disciplines and between different periods in the history of ideas, and (5) how Cervantes contributes to our understanding of human cognition through a novel that focuses on the human mind and human development. Sub-objectives one to four are common to all the course modules. In this regard, the first module, which is also the longest one, acts as the grand organizer or frame that will guide our students in their exploration of mind and literature throughout the course. The specific expected learning outcome for this module includes the students' understanding of (1) the intrinsic relationship between literature and biology, (2) how humans self-realize and develop in relation to their environment and the arts, and (3) the centrality of memory in our cognitive processes, from the point of view of both early modernity and contemporary cognitive science. Students will arrive at their conclusions on these important aspects through a combination of all the different discourses and perspectives included in the module: early modern literature (*Don Quixote*), early modern "science" (Huarte), and contemporary science (Martín-Araguz and Bustamante-Martínez; Gibbs; Varela, Thompson, and Rosch; Maturana and Varela). The blend of these diverse perspectives will allow them to reflect on the complexity of Cervantes' masterpiece and of the culture in which it was created.

11. See calendar of readings at the end of this afterword.

The second module of the course (weeks 6 and 7) recovers the theme of embodiment, placing it in the context of early modern Spanish theater. This module moves away from the textual approaches traditionally employed in literary criticism, in order to emphasize the performative facet of drama. To explore this fundamental aspect while approaching the Spanish theatrical innovation promoted by Lope de Vega, students read his treatise *Arte nuevo de hacer comedias* [The New Art of Writing Plays] alongside the essays by Burningham and Cruz Petersen, which will help them understand the essence of theater as an embodied phenomenon of storytelling that is connected to our social contexts and everyday practices. Additional readings for this module include excerpts from the work of cognitive literary scholars Bruce McConachie and Elizabeth Hart and philosopher Richard Shusterman. Through Burningham's essay, students are exposed to the limitations of approaching the study of theater as a stable artifact and learn about how performance scholars have challenged the Thespis myth of theater emerging out of ritual (a view that leaves out and marginalizes a whole variety of performance traditions). In this module, students also learn about performative contexts and how the concept of embodiment facilitates the discussion on early modern audiences' active engagement in the performances. This module is particularly useful to explore in class the idea that spectatorship, as understood and practiced in early modern Spain, is far from being the mere contemplation of a *mise-en-scène* of a text on a stage, but it encompasses instead all the different elements of being and acting in the theatrical space, including the reenacting of the performances in and out of that space.

In module three (weeks 8 to 10) students continue to explore performative subjectivity, this time in relation to categories such as gender and perception. The importance of perceiving and "reading" or understanding others during the early modern period becomes evident as students approach the essays by Caballero, Ródenas and Valenzuela, and Schmitz. The central literary readings for this module are Ángela de Azevedo's *El muerto disimulado* [The Feign Death] and Baltasar Gracián's *Oráculo manual y arte de prudencia* [The Art of Worldly Wisdom]. Readings include, in addition to Huarte, the work of contemporary cognitive psychologist Richard Gerrig. We begin the module with chapter 13 of Huarte's *Examen*, as it allows students to become familiar with early modern medical views of gender and prepares them for Caballero's essay, which will help them reflect on the cognitive processes that, along with sociocultural factors, mediate the perception of maleness and femaleness. Since literary criticism has traditionally considered cross-dressing as a mere theatrical convention that the audience accepts as such, the work of Caballero adds for our students a new dimension to the study of gender on stage by proposing that the characters' inability to recognize another character when she or he is cross-dressed reflects, in fact, human perceptual limitations within a cultural context that defines gender through sartorial conventions. This discussion on perception acts as a bridge to the ideas presented by Ródenas and Valenzuela. We take our students back to *Don Quixote*, this time to the episode of Maese Pedro's puppet show, which takes place in chapters 25 and 26 of the second part. Through this episode in conjunction with Ródenas and Valenzuela's essay, students challenge mainstream accounts of Don Quixote's psychology, discussing what are probably two of the most explored questions in relation to Cervantes' work: Is he really mad? And if so, what is the source of his madness? Moreover, by pairing the ideas of Ródenas and Valenzuela with excerpts from the classic work of Gerrig, *Experiencing Narrative Worlds*, they can reflect on the boundaries between reality and fiction. In the context of today's psychology of fiction, the theme of Don Quixote's madness is revisited in this module through the metaphor of transportation that Gerrig employs. Students ponder the power of fictional narratives as portrayed in the novel both at a micro (through Don Quixote, the spectator of Maese Pedro's puppet show) and a macro (through Don Quixote, the reader of chivalric novels) scale, as well as in relation to their own experience as contemporary readers of *Don Quixote*. Finally, as part of the reflection on how humans perceive others and on the boundaries between the genders and between fiction and reality, this module also introduces students to the contemporary psychology notion of Theory of Mind (the human ability to understand the beliefs, desires, and intentions of others), instrumental in grasping the importance that early modern subjects placed on courtly manuals and behavioral advice within the socially complex environment of the court. As part of this module, students read essays by psychologist Nicholas Humphrey and cognitive literary scholar Lisa Zunshine.[12] These readings will provide students with the terminology and the context they need to understand both the centrality of Theory of Mind in human cognition and its relevance to approach the manuals of courtly conduct, a genre that is often excluded from the curriculum of early modern Spanish literature courses.

Module four (weeks 11 to 13) provides us with an opportunity to explore feeling and ethics in our classroom, by delving into concepts such as emotion, empathy, and pro-social behavior. These concepts are fundamental to discuss the work of authors who wrote in a context of war and possession, such as Las Casas (denouncer of the Spanish occupation of

12. Other suitable readings include Premack and Woodruff, Oatley.

America and active participant in the debate on the abuse and slavery of the Americans) and Cervantes (whose plays centering on the Spanish-Ottoman war resonated with a Christian audience's fear of abduction and captivity—a fairly common occurrence at the time, in the context of maritime travel). Before the class delves into this module, we may, as a follow-up exercise, bring our students back to the content of module two, where we discussed spectatorship and the permeability between the embodied mind and the contexts of performance. Reed's essay helps explore theater as a vehicle of activism and social awareness. Through the analysis of Cervantes' plays of captivity, students reflect once more on the importance of the concept of embodiment to understand the power of enacted narratives. They are reminded of the fact that spectators experience drama through their bodies and, with their bodies, respond emotionally both to the stories presented to them and to other audience members' reactions. Reed elucidates for students how the vividness that Cervantes exhibits in portraying the tragedy of captivity not only leads to a powerful embodied and emotional experience over an audience that was familiar with this theme, but also promotes reflection and social change. In discussing this progression from feeling to thinking to acting, it is crucial to introduce our students to the empathy-altruism hypothesis and its controversy. Thus, along with present-day psychological accounts of empathy such as Daniel C. Batson's and Jean Decety's, recommended readings for this module include voices in favor as well as skeptical of the idea that literature leads to pro-social behavior and change.[13] In today's context of wondering what are the effects of fiction on our minds—which includes the conviction of many scholars that literature is central to our social and moral development—this module on feelings and ethics offers us teachers an opportunity to invite our students to the debate and to ponder important issues such as how to protect literary education (and the humanities) in the face of ideologies that fail to see its developmental value. Another important question is whether educators are failing to engage themselves and their students socially and emotionally with the world. The work of scholar Barbara Simerka on Las Casas gives us an opportunity to explore this last question. She examines the relationship between literature and empathy at two different levels by looking into Las Casas' agenda and impact in presenting the Spanish conquest and the slavery of Americans as cruel and inhuman both from the point of view of the sixteenth century and

---

13. In addition to Keen, teachers might want to include as additional reading Oatley, Mar, and Djikic as well as excerpts from Nussbaum (I recommend chapter 3) and Hakemulder.

today. Through her discussion of how we tend to approach Las Casas in the classroom from an "objective" perspective—trying to suppress students' emotional reactions—Simerka helps us ponder the value of discussing texts from an affect perspective as well as the relationship between emotion and ethics for early modern subjects and for us today.

Suggested Schedule of Themes and Readings

The following schedule corresponds to a fourteen-week-long course, but it can be easily adapted to the particular time needs of each institution by having teachers select the modules and articles they would like to cover. It includes the main readings (primary early modern works and critical articles from this book) as well as suggested additional readings (average reading is 120 pages per week).[14] Teachers can modify this skeleton by adding or replacing readings as they see fit.

Module 1

Week 1　Introduction to the course
　　　　Martín-Araguz and Bustamante-Martínez
Week 2　*Don Quixote (Part I)*: chaps. 1–12
　　　　Huarte[15]: Proemios [Proems]; chaps. 1, 4
Week 3　*Don Quixote (Part I)*: chaps. 13–25
　　　　Mancing, this volume
　　　　Gibbs: Introduction
　　　　Varela, Thompson, and Rosch: Introduction, chap. 8
Week 4　*Don Quixote (Part I)*: chaps. 26–39
　　　　Connor, this volume
　　　　Maturana and Varela: chaps. 1, 2, 4
Week 5　*Don Quixote (Part I)*: chaps. 40–52
　　　　Domínguez, this volume
　　　　Huarte: chap. 5

14. All readings are available in English translations except for Martín-Araguz and Bustamante-Martínez; Azevedo.
15. Optionally teachers may ask students to read the introduction to the *Examen* by Guillermo Serés (pp. 19–42) or, for courses in English, Rocío Sumillera's Introduction, which also covers the reception of Huarte's work in England.

Module 2

Week 6   Burningham, this volume
         McConachie, "Evolutionary"
         McConachie and Hart: Introduction (pp. 1–8)[16]
Week 7   Lope de Vega, *Arte nuevo de hacer comedias* [The New Art of
         Writing Plays]
         Cruz Petersen, this volume
         Shusterman

Module 3

Week 8   Huarte: chap. 13
         Azevedo, *El muerto disimulado* [The Feign Death]
         Caballero, this volume
Week 9   *Don Quixote (Part II)*: chaps. 25, 26
         Ródenas and Valenzuela, this volume
         Gerrig: chap. 1[17]
Week 10   Gracián, *Oráculo manual y arte de prudencia* [The Art of Worldly
         Wisdom]
         Schmitz, this volume
         Humphrey
         Zunshine

Module 4

Week 11   Batson
         Decety
         Keen
Week 12   Cervantes, *El trato de Argel* [The Trade of Algiers]
         Reed, this volume
Week 13   Las Casas, *Brevísima relación de la destrucción de las Indias* [A
         Short Account of the Destruction of the Indies]
         Simerka, this volume

Week 14   Research Presentations

16. Additional recommended readings for this section include Tribble and Sutton;
McConachie, "Introduction"; and Cook.
17. I recommend Holland to pair with Gerrig as additional reading.

WORKS CITED

Azevedo, Ángela de. *El muerto disimulado. Women's Acts: Plays by Women Dramatists of Spain's Golden Age.* Ed. Teresa Scott Soufas. Lexington: UP of Kentucky, 1997, 91–132.

Batson, C. Daniel. "The Empathy-Altruism Hypothesis: Issues and Implications." *Empathy: From Bench to Bedside.* Ed. Jean Decety. Cambridge: MIT P, 2012, 41–54.

Casey, Beth A. "Administering Interdisciplinary Programs." *The Oxford Handbook of Interdisciplinarity.* Ed. Robert Frodeman, Julie Thompson Klein, and Carl Mitcham. Oxford: Oxford UP, 2010, 345–59.

Cervantes, Miguel de. *Don Quijote de la Mancha.* Ed. Francisco Rico. Madrid: Real Academia Española, 2004.

Cervantes, Miguel de. *Don Quixote.* Trans. Edith Grossman. New York: Ecco-HarperCollins, 2004.

Cervantes, Miguel. *Trade of Algiers.* Trans. Pamela A. Peek. *The Trade of Algiers: A Translation of Cervantes'* El trato de Argel. Diss. U of South Carolina, 1994. Ann Arbor: UMI. *ProQuest Dissertations & Theses Global.* Web. June 15, 2015.

Cervantes, Miguel de. *El trato de Argel.* Ed. Florencio Sevilla Arroyo and Antonio Rey Hazas. Vol. 2 of *Obras completas de Miguel de Cervantes.* 18 vols. Madrid: Alianza, 1996.

Cook, Amy. "Introduction: Texts and Embodied Performance." *Affective Performance and Cognitive Science.* Ed. Nicola Shaughnessy. London: Bloomsbury, 2013, 83–90.

Decety, Jean. "Introduction: Why Is Empathy So Important?" *Empathy: From Bench to Bedside.* Ed. Jean Decety. Cambridge: MIT P, 2012, vii–ix.

Easterlin, Nancy, ed. *Cognition in the Classroom.* Spec. issue of *Interdisciplinary Literary Studies* 16.1 (2014): 1–205.

Febvre, Lucien, and Henri-Jean Martin. *The Coming of the Book: The Impact of Printing 1450–1800.* Trans. David Gerard. New York: Verso, 1997.

Gerrig, Richard J. *Experiencing Narrative Worlds: On the Psychological Activities of Reading.* New Haven: Yale UP, 1993.

Gibbs, Raymond W., Jr. *Embodiment and Cognitive Science.* Cambridge: Cambridge UP, 2006.

Gracián, Baltasar. *The Art of Worldly Wisdom.* Trans. Christopher Maurer. New York: Doubleday, 1992.

Gracián, Baltasar. *Oráculo manual y arte de prudencia.* Ed. Emilio Blanco. Madrid: Cátedra, 2009.

Hakemulder, Frank (Jèmeljan). *The Moral Laboratory: Experiments Examining the Effects of Reading Literature on Social Perception and Moral Self-Concept.* Amsterdam: John Benjamins, 2000.

Holland, Norman N. "*Don Quixote* and the Neuroscience of Metafiction." *Cognitive Literary Studies: Current Themes and New Directions.* Ed. Isabel Jaén and Julien J. Simon. Austin: U of Texas P, 2012, 73–88.

Huarte de San Juan, Juan. *Examen de ingenios para las ciencias.* Ed. Guillermo Serés. Madrid: Cátedra, 1989.

Huarte de San Juan, Juan. *The Examination of Men's Wits.* Trans. Richard Carew. Ed. Rocío G. Sumillera. London: Modern Humanities Research Association, 2014.

Humphrey, Nicholas K. "The Social Function of Intellect." *Machiavellian Intelligence: Social Expertise and the Evolution of Intellect in Monkeys, Apes, and Humans*. Ed. Richard W. Byrne and Andrew Whiten. New York: Oxford UP, 1988, 13–26.

Jaén, Isabel. "Teaching Cervantes' *Don Quixote* from a Cognitive Historicist Perspective." *Cognition in the Classroom*. Ed. Nancy Easterlin. Spec. issue of *Interdisciplinary Literary Studies* 16.1 (2014): 110–26.

Jaén, Isabel, and Julien J. Simon. Introduction. *Cognitive Literary Studies: Current Themes and New Directions*. Ed. Isabel Jaén and Julien J. Simon. Austin: U of Texas P, 2012, 1–9.

Keen, Suzanne. "A Theory of Narrative Empathy." *Narrative* 14.3 (2006): 207–36.

Las Casas, Bartolomé de. *Brevísima relación de la destrucción de las Indias*. Ed. and intro. José Miguel Martínez Torrejón. Barcelona: Galaxia Gutenberg, 2009.

Las Casas, Bartolomé de. *A Short Account of the Destruction of the Indies*. Ed. and trans. Nigel Griffin. London: Penguin, 1992. *Columbia University Libraries Virtual Reading Room*, 2002. Web. May 15, 2015.

Mancing, Howard. *Cervantes' Don Quixote: A Reference Guide*. Westport: Greenwood P, 2006.

Martín-Araguz A., and C. Bustamante-Martínez. "*Examen de ingenios*, de Juan Huarte de San Juan, y los albores de la neurobiología de la inteligencia en el Renacimiento español." *Revista de Neurología* 38.12 (2004): 16–30.

Maturana Romesín, Humberto, and Francisco J. Varela. *El árbol del conocimiento: Las bases biológicas del conocimiento humano*. Madrid: Editorial Debate, 1990 [1984].

Maturana Romesín, Humberto, and Francisco J. Varela. *The Tree of Knowledge: The Biological Roots of Human Understanding*. Trans. Robert Paolucci. Rev. ed. Foreword by J. Z. Young. Boston: Shambhala, 1992 [1984].

McConachie, Bruce. "An Evolutionary Perspective on Play, Performance, and Ritual." *TDR: The Drama Review: A Journal of Performance Studies* 55.4 [T212] (2011): 33–50.

McConachie, Bruce. "Introduction: Spectating as Sandbox Play." *Affective Performance and Cognitive Science*. Ed. Nicola Shaughnessy. London: Bloomsbury, 2013, 183–97.

McConachie, Bruce, and F. Elizabeth Hart. Introduction. *Performance and Cognition: Theatre Studies and the Cognitive Turn*. Ed. Bruce McConachie and F. Elizabeth Hart. London: Routledge, 2006, 1–26.

Miller, Clark A. "Policy Challenges and University Reform." *The Oxford Handbook of Interdisciplinarity*. Ed. Robert Frodeman, Julie Thompson Klein, and Carl Mitcham. Oxford: Oxford UP, 2010, 333–44.

Newell, William H. "Undergraduate General Education." *The Oxford Handbook of Interdisciplinarity*. Ed. Robert Frodeman, Julie Thompson Klein, and Carl Mitcham. Oxford: Oxford UP, 2010, 360–71.

Nussbaum, Martha C. *Cultivating Humanity: A Classical Defense of Reform in Liberal Education*. Cambridge: Harvard UP, 1997.

Oatley, Keith. "Theory of Mind and Theory of Minds in Literature." *Theory of Mind and Literature*. Ed. Paula Leverage, Howard Mancing, Richard Schweickert, and Jennifer Marston William. West Lafayette: Purdue UP, 2011, 13–26.

Oatley, Keith, Raymond A. Mar, and Maja Djikic. "The Psychology of Fiction: Present and Future." *Cognitive Literary Studies: Current Themes and New Directions*. Ed. Isabel Jaén and Julien J. Simon. Austin: U of Texas P, 2012, 235–49.

Premack, David, and Guy Woodruff. "Does the Chimpanzee Have a Theory of Mind?" *Behavioral and Brain Sciences* 1.4 (1978): 515–26.

Serés, Guillermo. Introducción. *Examen de ingenios para las ciencias*. By Juan Huarte de San Juan. Ed. Guillermo Serés. Madrid: Cátedra, 1989, 11–122.

Shusterman, Richard. "Somaesthetics: A Disciplinary Proposal." *The Journal of Aesthetics and Art Criticism* 57.3 (1999): 299–313.

Sumillera, Rocío G. Introduction. *The Examination of Men's Wits*. By Juan Huarte de San Juan. Trans. Richard Carew. Ed. Rocío G. Sumillera. London: Modern Humanities Research Association, 2014, 1–70.

Tribble, Evelyn B., and John Sutton. "Introduction: Interdisciplinary and Cognitive Approaches to Performance." *Affective Performance and Cognitive Science*. Ed. Nicola Shaughnessy. London: Bloomsbury, 2013, 27–37.

Varela, Francisco J., Evan Thompson, and Eleanor Rosch. *The Embodied Mind: Cognitive Science and Human Experience*. Cambridge: MIT P, 1993.

Vega Carpio, Lope de. *El arte nuevo de hacer comedias en este tiempo*. Ed. Eric W. Vogt and Vern Williamsen. *Comedias.org*. The Association for Hispanic Classical Theater, June 30, 2002. Web. June 15, 2015.

Vega Carpio, Lope de. *The New Art of Writing Plays*. Trans. William T. Brewster. Ed. Brander Matthews. New York: Dramatic Museum of Columbia U, 1914. *Archive.org*. Web. Sept. 24, 2009.

Zunshine, Lisa. "Theory of Mind and Fictions of Embodied Transparency." *Theory of Mind and Literature*. Ed. Paula Leverage, Howard Mancing, Richard Schweickert, and Jennifer Marston William. West Lafayette: Purdue UP, 2011, 63–91.

INDEX

Note: Locators followed by the letter 'n' refer to notes

dissimulation, 7, 118n15, 164, 166–67, 167n15, 169n20, 176. *See also* discretion; prudence

Dixon, Peter, 38, 150n3, 154

Domínguez, Julia, 6, 26n37, 61n12, 223–24

Don Gil de las calzas verdes [Don Gil of the Green Breeches] (Molina), 189

Don Quixote (Cervantes), 157, 209
    and arms and letters, 63–68
    and autopoiesis, 5–6, 42–44, 49–50, 53–55, 58–59, 61–66, 68–69, 224
    and embodied cognition, 103, 223–24
    and individual development, 27, 71
    and literary characters, 38, 42
    Maese Pedro episode of, 149–54, 159n12, 160, 226
    memory and imagination in, 75, 79–89
    and metafiction, 161
    and readership, 221, 221n8, 226
    Ricote episode of, 21
    and teaching, 27, 221n5
    and Theory of Mind, 16, 20, 20n20

Don Quixote (character), 47, 63, 65, 68, 80, 148–49, 152–54, 156n7, 159n12
    and arms and letters, 43–44, 46
    and embodied cognition, 39–42, 50
    and emotions, 157–60
    and humoral theory, 75, 83
    and madness, 7, 149–50, 156–57, 161, 226
    and memory and imagination, 6, 81–89
    and perception, 61, 83–85
    as reader, 80–84, 87–88, 156, 158, 226
    and structural coupling, 47–49
    and transportation, 7, 150–51, 155–59, 161, 226

Dudai, Yadin, 75–76, 78

early modern Spanish theater. *See* comedias

Edelman, Gerald, 57, 59n9, 61n10, 195

Egido, Aurora, 83–85

Elias, Norbert, 165n1, 174n30, 176

Elis, Pedro, 6, 96, 98–100

embodied cognition, 13–14, 14nn2–4, 38, 46n3, 183, 185, 224. *See also* enaction
    and autopoiesis, 42, 50, 53–54, 70, 224
    and cognitive approaches to early modern Spanish literature, 14–16
    and *comedias*, 16–17, 123–24
    definition of, 37
    and *Don Quixote*, 103, 223–24
    and Don Quixote, 39–42, 50
    and genres, 17–18
    vs. grounded cognition, 185n1
    and performance, 6, 94–96, 99, 103, 105, 112, 114, 184–86, 189–90, 195, 198, 223, 225, 227

embodied transparency (Zunshine), 173–74

embodiment. *See* embodied cognition

emotional contagion, 21n22, 103
    definition of, 103n16

empathy, 14, 27, 56–57, 61, 64–65, 67, 70–71, 223
    aesthetic (Einfühlung), 21n22, 185–86
    aesthetic vs. practical, 157–58
    affective vs. cognitive, 21n22, 188n9, 191, 194–95
    and bias reduction, 210, 212–13, 215
    and Cervantes, 21–23
    definition of, 198, 202
    kinesthetic, 99, 103
    and Las Casas' rhetoric, 203–8, 214
    and Las Casas scholarship, 23, 208–9
    and literary research, 209–10
    and mirror neurons, 56n5, 57–58, 57n6, 100n11, 186
    and performance, 17, 123–24, 183–84, 186, 188–89, 191, 193–98
    and prosocial behavior, 8, 23n27, 27, 187, 187n7, 196–98, 197n13, 210–12, 215, 226–27
    (*see also* empathy-altruism hypothesis)